POLITICAL PHILOSOPHY NOW

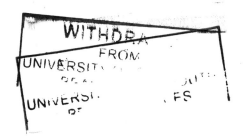

POLITICAL PHILOSOPHY NOW

Adorno and Critical Theory

Hauke Brunkhorst

UNIVERSITY OF WALES PRESS • CARDIFF • 1999

©Hauke Brunkhorst, 1999

British Library Cataloguing-in-Publication Data
A catalogue record for this book is available from the British Library

ISBN 0–7083–1528–3 paperback
0–7083–1529–1 cased

The right of Hauke Brunkhorst to be identified as author of this work has been asserted by him in accordance with the Copyright, Designs and Patents Act 1988.

Typeset at Wyvern 21
Printed in Great Britain by Gwasg Dinefwr, Llandybïe

Contents

Acknowledgements

The Kulturwissenschaftliches Institut in Essen, which is part of the Wissenschaftszentrum Nordrhein-Westfalen, has given me a lot of support in producing this book. I have been a fellow at the institute since spring 1995, with the enjoyable task of completing projects such as this. In particular, I have to thank Gertrud Koch, who was at that time the head of the research group on 'Democracy, Media and Political Culture', of which I was a member.

In writing a book on Adorno, the Frankfurt School version of critical theory and experimental ideas of freedom, I have learned a lot from the discussions in Albrecht Wellmer's colloquium during my time in Berlin, when I was a visiting professor at the Otto Suhr Institut from 1991 to 1993. The disputes with my friend Christoph Menke were particularly important for my reconsideration of Adorno's philosophy. So in the end, encouraged by Wolfgang Kersting and Howard Williams, I decided to write another book on Adorno after my first book was published in German in 1990. In particular, I have to thank Howard Williams for fine-tuning my sometimes unclear English. Peter Tamm and Wolf Dallmeyer from Flensburg University helped me with the bibliography and the index. I thank Ulla Sanders from the Kulturwissenschaftliches Institut for typing most of the manuscript. The support from the library of the institute was also important. I thank Brigitte Blockhaus and Gesine Worm. Last, but not least, I thank Jeremy Gaines for a lot of translation from German to English which I worked into the text.

An earlier version of Chapter 3, section 4, appeared in David Rasmussen's *Philosophy and Social Criticism* (vol. 22, no. 5, 1996) under the title 'Rorty, Putnam and the Frankfurt School' (London: Sage Publications). I have also incorporated in Chapter 1 some materials from *The Handbook of Critical Theory* (edited by David M. Rasmussen, Oxford: Blackwell Publishers, 1996), to which I contributed 'Theodor W. Adorno: aesthetic constructivism and a negative ethic of the non-forfeited life'.

Introduction

The work of Theodor W. Adorno is an important mile-stone in the post-Hegelian philosophical search for non-reified forms of life and existence. Adorno, as a member of the Frankfurt School and its most important and original thinker, presents an alternative to Heidegger's longing for a *Dasein*, which is not caught by the categories of a philosophy of consciousness, technical rationality and onto-theology. Adorno's attempt goes in the *same* direction as that of Heidegger, yet it is a more radical critique of metaphysical a prioris than Heidegger's question for Being. Early romanticism and modern aesthetical experience are at the core of Adorno's negative thinking of the 'non-identical'. The concept of 'non-identical' is connected with an experimental understanding of freedom – anywhere in between John Stuart Mill's *On Liberty* and Nietzsche's radical freedom from autonomy.

The main concept for Adorno as a philosopher is the concept of 'non-identical'. He is often called the 'thinker of the non-identical'. What does Adorno mean in referring to the 'non-identical' in opposition to 'identifying thinking'? 'Identifying thinking' or 'identity thinking' for Adorno *first* means the subsuming of single events or objects under general concepts. These concepts never can grasp the whole thing, the object or event in its concrete totality. They can only represent some aspects and have to neglect others. Adorno interprets this as a very fundamental form of injustice which subjective thinking perpetrates against real objects, be it social or natural objects. If we acknowledge one side of the object we have to disregard the other sides. The first meaning of 'non-identical' is by implication the blind spot of all identifying thinking: the shadowed aspect of an object or event, whose other aspects are lit up by thought and discussion. As we never can reach a full or comprehensive understanding of all sides of a single event in its totality, we always have to do some 'injustice' to an event or object. Identifying thinking is unjust insofar as Adorno (along with the romantic tradition) claims that the object might have a moral right to be identified equally by all its aspects. This basic form of 'injustice' is unavoidable as long as we are beings who think and discuss. If we talk or think *about* something we have to use identifications. We cannot describe propositional contents without some predicative or identifying operations. Therefore the possibility always remains that we may neglect important aspects of the object or slight it in some way. The only thing we can do is to be aware that there might be important aspects of an object or event which we have overlooked or forgotten. This 'forgetfulness' can be part-remedied by a *second reflection*, or 'Eingedenken'. What Adorno calls a 'second reflection' and sometimes 'open thinking' is his version of Heidegger's 'forgetfulness of being'.[1]

Yet the best, and for Adorno himself the most adequate, examples of the achievements of 'open thinking' or 'second reflection' do not stem from philosophy but from modern art. This can be illustrated nicely by the inventions of cubism whose paintings Adorno appreciated so much. Traditional paintings – to put it in brief – usually rely on an illusionary perspective. They represent a three-dimensional object on a two-dimensional canvas *as if* it were three-dimensional. Cubism breaks this illusion asunder. Cubist paintings present a variety of views of the same thing at once – be it a face or a viola or whatever. The point here is that these different aspects are *incompatible* from the point of view of perception in reality as well as in illusionary and representational painting. Cubist paintings, which present front-views, back-views or side-views of the same thing at the same time, are 'paradoxical' or 'dialectical' insofar as they *present* something for a single view that can never be *re*presented as the perspective of a single view. They present aspects of the thing or object that may *exist* at once in *reality*, but never can be perceived, described or represented from the ever-limited and particular point of view of the spectator. The method of the cubists therefore could be interpreted as the attempt to do 'justice' to those aspects of the object which are shadowed by the necessarily one-sided point of view of common perception, conceptual description or artistic representation. Cubist paintings therefore are a good analogy for Adorno's negative dialectics. They present a way of access to the thing itself (*die Sache selbst*) in its totality. But this totality of the thing itself can never be represented as an identity object, because the latter has to be broken asunder to present all or many of its non-identical aspects. The totality of the thing itself only can appear – in Adorno's words – as a 'shattered' and 'fragmented' totality. The *second* meaning of 'identifying thinking' is *metaphysics* or *idealism*. A broad definition of Adorno's view of metaphysics and idealism is that he believes that we must not overlook what could be their weaknesses. Referring to the 'non-identical' in this respect means to refer to the possibility that philosophical thinking could be wrong in its presupposition of making a clear distinction between essence and surface, and to grasp the essence through philosophical concepts. Against metaphysics Adorno claims for 'justice' the 'non-identical' and the excluded 'surface' of things, events, forms of life, bodies, emotions, passions, drives, etc. Adorno's critique of metaphysics is fallibilistic, because there is no ultimate knowledge of the essence of all things. If Adorno charges metaphysics for repressing or excluding the 'non-identical', he asserts that there is no justifiable comprehensive doctrine which allows us to identify the real essence of our mortal bodies, contingent emotions and transient projects. Any form of 'identifying thinking' could be wrong, for we can never grasp the totality of the world. There could be an aspect which we did not identify in our vocabulary and that would falsify the philosophical theories formulated in the terms of this vocabulary. The vocabulary that we hold to be true at a point of time t1 can emerge to be the monoglossic vocabulary of a ruling class at a later point of time t2. Here Adorno, the Marxist, goes along with post-metaphysical thinkers such as Peirce, Dewey or Popper, who all have made a strong case against the claim of metaphysics to reach some form of eternal and undestroyable knowledge. Even more radical than Peirce and Popper, Adorno rejects the idea that there could be *any* a priori knowledge. For Adorno (and here he comes close to Quine's critique of the two dogmas of empiricism), there exists no pure logical or analytical truth which can be separated totally from the linguistical, social and material context of a historical world. The function of *second reflection* on what metaphysics neglects and excludes, is to keep in mind the fallible and contingent status of human knowledge and all human affairs.

The *third* meaning of 'identifying thinking' is *instrumental reason*. Even if we are aware of the fallible and revisable status of all knowledge, this knowledge can be connected with the technical interest of knowledge and the knowledgeable subject to *dominate* the object and the world. This, for example, is the idea of Popper or Quine. 'Identifying thinking' in the meaning of 'instrumental reason' is the abstraction from the perspective of the Other or the Otherness of objects or people, who themselves are objects of thinking of philosophy, science, political or social theory. What is identified is every possible perspective and interest with the *single* view of the knowledgeable subject or the agency of that knowledge. By means of this identification the subject of instrumental reason becomes the subject of domination. This idea is strange to analytical philosophers like Popper or Quine, but it comes very close to the basic ideas of French poststructuralists and deconstructionists like Derrida or Foucault, and it has predecessors in the young Karl Marx, in sociologists like Max Weber (and his theory of rationalization) and in Neo-Marxists like the young Georg Lukács who was deeply influenced by people like Max Weber. Referring to the excluded perspectives and interests of 'the Other', the notion of 'non-identical' here means a political critique of all forms of one-sided and repressive domination. As far as domination is connected with instrumental reason, the critique of identifying thinking is a critique of all forms of domination, not only domination of men over men or women, but also domination of *nature*, be it the external or the inner nature of the subject itself. This is worked out and connected with the critique of metaphysics in the book written by Adorno and Max Horkheimer at the end of the war, the *Dialectic of Enlightenment*. The thesis of this book is this: the more rational the instrumental reason of the subject is, the more irrational the object of subjective or instrumental reason becomes as a whole.

It is important to make a clear distinction between these three meanings or aspects of meaning of 'identifying thinking' versus 'non-identical', even if Adorno himself never did this. The distinctions are important for *political reasons*. Whereas identifying thinking in the first sense is *unavoidable*, it is *avoidable* in its second and third senses. To cancel identifying thinking as such (first sense) would mean to annihilate mankind, and a critique of identifying thinking which would be more than 'Eingedenken' or second reflection (expressed in aesthetic experience and works of art) would be completely utopian, as Adorno well knew. This most radical version of a critique of identifying thinking directly leads to a negative form of theology. But metaphysics and dominating forms of instrumental reason (the second and third senses of identifying thinking) *are* avoidable and therefore could be objects of political and social change, be it revolutionary or reformatory.

The importance of the distinction between the second and the third meaning of 'identifying thinking' was clear in the famous 'positivity debate' of the 1960s. Adorno in his debate with Karl Popper in great part agreed with the latter's idea of a critical science. As we now can see, the reason for this agreement comes from the *second* sense of 'identifying thinking' versus 'non-identity'. But the difference deepens if it comes to the *third* sense. For Adorno, fallibility alone is not enough to avoid unconscious and uncomprehended relations of domination, repression and unjust exclusion. Therefore only a theory that keeps present the critique of instrumental reason as the reason for domination is a *critical* theory in Adorno's understanding of that term.

The first chapter of this book gives a sketch of Adorno's intellectual biography. In the course of his life, Adorno found himself in many contexts: between Horkheimer, Benjamin, and Kracauer in the 1920s; in relation to the heroes of Vienna's new music (Schönberg, Berg); in the old German university; in his fragile relations with American social scientists in the 1930s and 1940s; in his late career as a leading intellectual of postwar Germany. Adorno's life and philosophical outlook is deeply rooted in the German culture of idealism and romanticism. But – in contrast with German professors like Arnold Gehlen or Martin Heidegger – Adorno never reduces the German cultural tradition to authenticity, romanticism and Hölderlin. For Adorno this culture is co-originally rooted in Kantian enlightenment *and* Wagnerian romanticism, in Hölderlin *and* Heine.

What I will try to show is that Adorno's negative dialectic is deeply influenced by Kant's already negative idea of dialectical antinomies. Most important in his career was the early and determining influence of reading Kant's *Critique of Pure Reason* every Saturday afternoon with his much older friend Siegfried Kracauer. As a more radical critic of the European tradition of metaphysical thinking, Kant's version of dialectics is closer to Adorno than Hegel's attempt to transform the Kantian scepticism concerning the 'thing in itself' into an at least affirmative philosophy of history, governed as it is by the idea of a 'rational totality'. Adorno always rejects that idea, referring instead to the fragmented and reified reality of modern societies. The fragmentation of modern life for Adorno is deeply ambivalent. The real history of modernity disproves Hegel in two ways.

On the one hand, Adorno describes fragmentation in terms of reification and alienation. The whole of modern society in this respect is a totality, but no longer a rational one, no longer a totality of reason. For Adorno modern societies tend to be closed systems. And a system has, as the German sociologist Niklas Luhmann today says, 'no reason' (*keine Vernunft*).[2] In this respect Adorno's analysis of modern society comes close to coherence with functionalistic approaches and systems theory.[3] However, just that loss of reason which sociologists like Parsons or Luhmann would describe in a 'neutral', eventually affirmative way, becomes for Adorno the object of a critique of 'the system' as an 'administered world' (*verwaltete Welt*). As a sociologist Adorno grounds his critique of late capitalism in the distinction between (societal) *modernity* and (cultural) *modernism* (see Chap 1, s. 12 below). In this Adorno follows the young Karl Marx, and today he would find himself on the side of the communitarian critics of modern society.

On the other hand, Adorno affirms alienation as a precondition of all human forms of happiness and he views fragmentation as the great chance for potential freedom from all repressions of the ethical life, the insidious tyranny of neighbourhood opinion and the danger of totalitarianism associated with any notion of totality. In modern art fragmentation means a much more radical freedom of expression than traditional forms of artistic action were able to disclose. From this point of view Adorno would reject the for-and-against positions of the current conflict in political theory, both liberalism and communitarianism.

In order to bring it closer to Adorno's anti-Hegelian stance one could say: insofar as modernity is rational, it is no longer a totality. Adorno's ethic of damaged life is seen in his collection of aphorisms, published under the title of *Minima Moralia*. This book is the autobiographical product of the exile from Nazi Germany, which led Adorno via Cambridge, UK, to New York and Santa Barbara, California. The ethical reflections from the perspective of the 'damaged life' are reflections from a point of view, which is equidistant from the European Past and the American Future. The promises of the Past, which are the heritage of the European spiritual traditions, have all been broken by the fascist Present. Hegel stated that America is the land of the Future, but as Adorno tries to show in his famous chapter on the 'cultural industry' in the *Dialectics of Enlightenment*, it has lost its utopian energy. At the end of the war when he wrote this chapter Adorno was living at the centre of the 'cultural industry' in Southern California.

Adorno's political and social philosophy is shaped by the experience of fascism, Bolshevism, the Second World War, the Holocaust, totalitarianism and the cold war. In the 1930s Adorno, Horkheimer and their colleagues at the New York Institute of Social Research, who all started as leftist Marxists, became more and more critical of the Soviet regime under Stalin. At the end of the war the critique of the current epoch of late capitalism (which was explored in the *Dialectic of Enlightenment*) came very close to a critique of both systems: Western expertocratic and elitist democracies and Eastern bloc totalitarian socialism. In the long period of the cold war after 1945 Adorno's critique of the administered world saw little difference between the opponents of the new world order. In terms of political theory Adorno was at first a Marxist critic of *capitalism*; later, during the war, he became a critic of *totalitarianism*, who was aware of the totalitarian tendencies of the Western world too. And during the cold war Adorno came close to *convergency-theorists* like Raymond Aron. From this part of Adorno's work not much has survived after 1989. What is left from the *Dialectic of Enlightenment* today is – in political terms – the critique of *domination of nature* as a fundament of all forms of 'power discourses' (Foucault) spread over the modern society. I give a synopsis of my critical view of that book in Chapter 2. On the other hand there is Adorno's *Aesthetic Theory* with its basic idea of *experimental freedom*. This idea too has survived the breaks of 1989. That is one of the reasons why I have put it at the centre of this book. It is one major thesis of this book that Adorno's aesthetics is much less pessimistic than the philosophy of history developed in the *Dialectic of Enlightenment*.

The second chapter gives a brief account of this famous book by Horkheimer and Adorno. I try to distinguish those aspects of the book that can be defended even now in a rational discourse from those parts of book that cannot. What can be defended is the critique of the myth of instrumental rationality, the objections against the intertwining of reason and class-domination, and the reflections on the ambivalences of Western rationality to include (potentially) everybody (and even everything) and at the same time to exclude (actually) the unreasonable aspects of nature, forms of life, or non-rational or 'mad' people, thoughts, expressions. What especially can be defended in a rational discourse is the famous thesis of that book that even myth is enlightenment. But the converse is much more problematic. Internal to the thesis that enlightenment returns as myth is a conservative bias of a philosophy of the history of decay. It is true only as a critique of instrumental rationality, not of modern reason as a whole. Adorno's reflections on the 'origins of subjectivity' part ways with Heidegger's philosophy of origin. But Chapter 3 will demonstrate that Adorno later left his path quite markedly.

Chapter 3 on 'Adorno, Heidegger and Postanalytical Philosophy' gives an account of Adorno's main thesis on Heidegger's ontological difference: 'Kein Sein ohne Seiendes' ('no Being without existence'). Adorno here comes close to the post-Quinean holism of modern linguistic philosophy. He is not a linguistic philosopher, but his attempt to overcome all a priori thinking, even Heidegger's historical a priori of being, is comparable with the approach of post-empiricist philosophy. Adorno's method is more negative, close to Derrida's procedures of contradictions and paradoxes, which the latter calls 'deconstructionism'.

I have tried to position Adorno in a complex network of coalitions and oppositions within contemporary philosophical discourse. This entails a lot of simplification, but the advantage will be the drawing of clear boundaries and sometimes surprisingly new coalitions. Against Heidegger's philosophy of the origin (*Ursprungsphilosophie*) Adorno is in the boat of postmodernism. Like Rorty, Adorno is much more interested in the Judaeo-Christian heritage of practical solidarity than in the Greek-rooted, neo-pagan 'History of Being'. Yet against 'postmodernists' like Kuhn, Feyerabend or Foucault, who share with Heidegger a radical version of relativism and contextualism, Adorno should be placed on the side of Karl Popper and his critique of the 'myth of the framework'. And last but not least, fighting against parochialisms *à la* Rorty Adorno could find himself alongside his more universalistic Frankfurt School successors, Apel and Habermas, even if he would have opposed the latter's linguistic turn.

Chapter 4 considers Adorno's aesthetic theory. This is Adorno's original contribution to the broad stream of post-metaphysical philosophy. I try to reconstruct the idea of freedom which Adorno

relates closely to the aesthetic experience of modernity. Freedom
for Adorno is neither arbitrariness nor rational control and planning of one's own life. Speaking in terms of political theory,
Adorno's conception of freedom is equidistant from the negative
freedom of liberalism and the positive freedom of Aristotelianism
(or positive freedom in the sense of a Kantian moral autonomy).
Adorno's model of freedom seeks a conscious exposure of the self
to the contingencies of situations which the subject cannot dominate nor control. I would call this an experimental understanding of
freedom and autonomous modern art is the institutional location
of such freedom. The basic idea is to overcome and destroy each
old and reified language of fixed meaning in order to find some
new meaning, or to renew the original sense and force of the old
metaphors and vocabularies. Yet Adorno's work cannot be
reduced to the idea of aesthetic world disclosure (like Rorty or
Heidegger), for he tries to relate this idea to the concept of a
rational identity which no longer represses or excludes the 'non-
identical'. For Adorno – who at this point differs from more tragic
negativists like Derrida – aesthetic innovation is internally connected with enlightening the learning processes of a public.

My reading of Adorno defends the post-metaphysical aspects of
Adorno's 'Negative Dialectic' and 'Aesthetic Theory'. I try to avoid
too strong a utopian reading, centred around the idea of reconciliation. In my reading, Adorno becomes a methodological instead of
an ontological negativist, which for a long time was the accepted
interpretation of Adorno's work on music, literature, philosophy
and social science.

Adorno makes use of dialectical operations primarily to overcome fundamentalistic oppositions and metaphysical dualism, e.g.
that between mimetic (or aesthetic) reasonableness and instrumental rationality, or between identifying thinking and the 'non-
identical', or between the false progress in domination over nature
and a completely different true progress in salvation. In the 1960s
he wrote:

> The progress of the mastery over nature which, according to Benja-
> min's comparison, proceeds in an opposite sense of true progress that
> would have its *telos* in redemption, is not without all hope. It is much
> more in each current form of the easing of the suffering which remains,
> rather than in averting the final disaster, that the two concepts of pro-
> gress commune with one another.[4]

1 • Between Frankfurt and New York

On 3 February 1965, the radio station Sender Freies Berlin (Radio Free Berlin) broadcast a polemical conversation between Theodor W. Adorno, the emigrant who had returned to Germany after the war and already become the representative figure of new left intellectualism, and the intellectual on the right, Arnold Gehlen.[1] A major scholar of philosophical anthropology who had certainly not withheld his services from Hitler, Gehlen was still an influential thinker within the mandarin world of academia.[2] This was the same milieu in which Adorno had grown up, but which he had been forced to flee. Although both men initially avoided any open disagreement, the discussion between them none the less eventually came to that point. Gehlen finally put the following question to Adorno:

> Yes, the child hiding behind its mother's skirts experiences both fear and the minimum or optimum of security that the situation allows. Herr Adorno, here again you will of course recognize the problem of maturity (*Mündigkeit*). Do you really believe that we should burden all people with the task of dealing with fundamental problems, of expending their reflective energy, of making the sorts of fundamental mistakes with profound after-effects we made because we attempted to chart our own course? I would very much like to know.

Adorno answered:

> I answer you quite simply yes! I have a mental image of both objective happiness and objective despair, and I would say that, as long as people are exonerated and are not expected to exercise complete responsibility and self-determination, their happiness in this world will remain an illusion. An illusion that will some day explode. And when this happens, the consequences will be devastating.

Gehlen then responded: 'Now we have arrived at precisely the point at which you say yes and I say no.'[3]

Here we have all the essential components of an intellectual discourse that emerged first in favour of Adorno in the tendential shifts of the 1960s, and then in favour of Gehlen in the 1980s. Ultimately, the thematic difference between them is between a premodern, Aristotelian concept of reason, and one that is modern and, in spite of all negative dialectic, out-and-out enlightened. Gehlen, along with Aristotle, proceeds on the assumption that there are always only a few people who are capable of acting rationally and reflectively on their own initiative – or are even in a position to do so. The majority, however, would collapse under the burden of reflection if it were thrust upon them. It is precisely in this unfair demand that Gehlen sees the challenge posed to humanity by modern industrial culture. Any such suggestion of general maturity is truly new, the crisis and danger of modern times have led to the destruction of our institutional bridle through the power of reflection.

Adorno proceeds along with Descartes and Kant on precisely the opposite assumption, that is, that the capacity for rational action is 'the best distributed thing in the world' (Descartes) and that the potential for reflection and freedom is something that is present in equal measure in all human beings without restriction. For Gehlen, the crisis of the modern era results from an excess of reflection, while for Adorno the opposite is the case. Along with the early Kracauer, he always defended the thesis that capitalism rationalized too little rather than too much. Gehlen is interested in a therapeutic treatment of cultural crisis that draws narrow institutional parameters for transformation through freedom and reflection. In contrast, Adorno wishes to *transcend* institutional surplus-repression, the restriction of reflection by the forces of ideology, economics, and bureaucracy.

Gehlen is certainly no orthodox Aristotelian, but rather a modern conservative. He actually concurs with Adorno *vis-à-vis* the notion of the contingency, alterability, and variability of modern institutions; to him they are no longer the mirror of timeless structures, the reflection of an ideal version of existence, the expression of an inalienable truth. They fulfil socially necessary functions and exonerate our nature, which is inadequately protected by our instincts. This same function can be realized in very different ways, and the degree of its respective necessity is always a question of experience. But while Gehlen's modernism remains *functionalist*, Adorno's is *cultural*. Whereas Gehlen perceives only its anarchically dysfunctional solvent power, the destructive tendency of what he contemptuously refers to as 'avantgardist circles', Adorno's gaze is directed toward the expansion of our freedom through an autonomous aesthetic modernity.[4]

Characteristic of the divergence between the two men are the differences in their ethical positions. After yet again extolling a reluctance to learn on the part of 'many people', Gehlen resignedly admits to Adorno: 'Ah, my God, you know, what I am actually seeking in reality is something honourable that one can serve. And this is what I continue to consider ethics.' Adorno concedes that ethics is a matter of obligation, and thus to a certain extent an institutional concern; still, he wants to be able to distinguish between one sort of obligation and another. While the functionalist Gehlen remains an ethical conventionalist, Adorno brings into play a specifically modern perspective on morality by including the autonomy and self-realization of all people:

> But this sense of obligation can nonetheless take the form of adaptation and subordination, such as you seem to be emphasizing here, as well as the form that I would want to emphasize more strongly, that is, that precisely in attempting to take this sense of obligation seriously, one attempts to change whatever prevents one – as it indeed prevents all people . . . from living to one's own potential, and to realize whatever potential is hidden within one.[5]

The gap between Adorno and Gehlen is not just caused by subject-matter, but stems from life itself. When, for example, Gehlen speaks of 'the errors of life we have gone through, with their profound after-effects',[6] he may have been thinking of his own commitment to the Nazi cause in the 1930s. In this case the 'we' would be decidedly out of place since Adorno was an opponent of the fascists with whom Gehlen aligned. Objectively, as Adorno was persecuted by the Nazis, he could never have been in the position of committing a comparable 'error of life'. As well as loss of liberty, exile means being excluded from having a scope for action or a range of different opportunities to choose from. Adorno and Gehlen grew up in a comparable social setting: the German educated middle classes. They share a background in the German universities and their unique form of education in the humanities. The year 1933, however, marked a *biographical rupture*, which burdens the objective differences between them with the weight of opposing and incomparable destinies and errors of life.

1. A much loved child

In later reflections on his life Adorno noted:

> I was born in 1905 in Frankfurt. My father was a German Jew, and my mother, herself a singer, was the daughter of a French officer of Corsican – originally Genovese – origin and of a German singer. I was born and raised in an atmosphere dominated completely by theoretical (even political), artistic, and above all musical interests.[7]

The political culture of his parent's house was liberal and cosmopolitan. The close relationships with which Adorno grew up in the south of Frankfurt were secure and thoroughly bourgeois, in a cultural hothouse. He used this phrase in *Minima Moralia*, a collection of aphorisms written in America during the Second World War concerning the true life in the false. Autobiography left its mark in the text, which reflected on the socializing fate of the precocious young genius that Adorno was.

> He who matures early lives in anticipation. His experience is a-prioristic, an intuitive sensibility feeling out in images and words what things and people will realize only later. Such anticipation, saturated, as it were, with itself, withdraws from the outer world and infuses its relation to it with the colour of neurotic playfulness. . . . Only later does he live through, in their crude violence, situations, fears, passions, that had been greatly softened in imagination, and they change, in conflict with his narcissism, into a consuming sickness. . . . The infantile traits in the hand-writing of the precocious are not an empty warning. For they are an irritation to the natural order, and spiteful health feasts on the danger threatening them, just as society mistrusts them as a visible negation of the equation of success with effort.[8]

One can say without exaggeration that Adorno accepted the undeserved good fortune that befell him readily and without pretension. He was neither contorted nor disfigured by the burden of work or the sweat of his brow. Instead he experienced a lightness, a playful ephemeralness, and a fortuitous coincidence that Adorno ascribed to the actual utopia of fortune, to the utopia of a 'cloudless day'. The 'idea of the absolute', he would write later, is not the eternal, but the temporal and infinite past that is 'ephemeral . . . as the aroma of wine'.[9] The evil world, and with it philosophical labours and the struggle for *Dasein*, broke through late and abruptly into the artificial life of the 'hothouse plant'. Adorno could always justly claim to have lived a happy childhood, which helped all his dormant talents to emerge quickly.

Admittedly the family in which he grew up was not one of those 'happy families' of which Tolstoy spoke, which are so similar to each another that recounting their history is not worthwhile.[10] The relationships in Adorno's family were very different from the classical scheme of bourgeois socialization. Adorno's father was a wine wholesaler with close relatives in Rheingau and England. At the turn of the century he converted to Protestantism, as many liberal Jews of his time did. Contrary to the Freudian scheme, he was a rather peripheral figure in the family – hardly the authoritarian, awe-inspiring and respect-instilling type cut from the neurotic bourgeois mould. Even more deviant from the Oedipal type was Theodor's relationship with his mother, for whom the young boy was allowed to experience love in duplicate. In addition to his Catholic mother, whose maiden name Adorno he later took, there was also in their home her sister Agatha, herself an accomplished pianist. She was so much present that 'Teddie', as he sooner or later was known even by his friends, called both of them mother. Thus he, the only and much loved child of the Wiesengrunds, found in both women the dual confirmation of his early developing self-esteem: his emotional sensibilities and his musical sense. 'You can enjoy an authentic musical experience in your childhood', he later wrote, 'if you are lying in the bedroom, are ordered to sleep, and unauthorized listen with wide opened ears to the Beethoven sonata for piano and violin, which is played in the music-chamber'.[11]

Since the bourgeois society of the external world regulated by the principle of exchange disrupted such a happy childhood only at a very late date, Adorno was able to oppose his own well-developed ego to the surging reality principle. Adorno's deeply ambivalent relationship to the institutions of modern ethical life was nourished by the background of his childhood and of his own

family. Against the identitarian power of thinking and of the normative that trained individuals to be 'disciplinary-individuals'
(Foucault) and functioning segments of the bourgeois world order,
Adorno offered the rebellious power of the 'non-identical', the
anarchistic movement and impulse that always withdraws from
integration. The 'extremely tender and subtle layer' of the inner
subjectivity, of the spontaneous, and of the instinctive was woven
with the memory of a childhood of private happiness that was
neither organizable nor institutionalizable. But this non-identical,
as Adorno later called it, requires an institutional framework.[12]

The nature of the completely socialized individual can come into
its own only where there is institutional alienation. The *Dialectic
of Enlightenment*, which Adorno completed in 1944 during his
California exile, together with Max Horkheimer and with the help
of Leo Löwenthal and his wife Gretel, explicitly stresses that *all*
desire in human life is a product and consequence of alienation.[13]
And in *Minima Moralia* he claims:

> One realizes with horror that earlier, opposing one's parents because
> they represented the world, one was often secretly the mouth-piece,
> against a bad world, of one even worse. Unpolitical attempts to break
> out of the bourgeois family usually lead only to deeper entanglement
> in it, and it sometimes seems as if the fatal germ-cell of society, the
> family, were at the same time the nurturing germ-cell of uncomprom-
> ising pursuit of another.[14]

The family is the medium of bourgeois repression. But this medium
of repression can reproduce itself only by producing individuality
and with it a potential for emancipation, that withstands the
repression of the authoritarian and bureaucratic society. This society can totalize repression only by abolishing the family. It has
become one of the dangers of the present epoch that the end of the
family could 'paralyse' the forces of opposition: 'With the family
there passes away, while the system lasts, not only the most effective agency of the bourgeoisie, but also the resistance which, though
repressing the individual, also strengthened, perhaps even produced him.'[15] 'Individuality', he writes later in the 1960s, 'is just
as much the product of (social) pressures as it is that centre of
power that stands over against it.'[16]

Fascism expelled Adorno and his friends from Germany in 1933 and forced them into exile in Switzerland, England, France, and finally in the United States, in New York and the West Coast. Adorno's theory of fascism was different from both orthodox Marxism and revisionist Freudian-Marxism. For Adorno fascism was more than a totalitarian variant of coercive class-domination and instinct repression. He was convinced that the historical singularity of its 'encompassing collective order' was connected less with bourgeois institutions and expropriations than with the totalization of domination, profit, and repression *accomplished* by the liquidation of all the repressive institutions of the bourgeois order. If Adorno once said that the bourgeois is virtually the Nazi, it would be valid only in connection with the insight that the Nazi constitutes itself above all in the liquidation of the bourgeois. In a letter addressed to Walter Benjamin dated 1 February 1939, Adorno explained his delay in answering Benjamin's last letter:

My Dear Walter,
    This time, the delay in my answering has nothing to do with theoretical issues. The reason on this occasion was the most recent events in Germany. I do not know whether you are aware of the degree to which it has affected my parents. My father managed admittedly to get out of jail, but during the pogrom he sustained an injury to his already bad eye; his office premises were destroyed and a short time later his right to dispose over his entire income was withdrawn. My mother, who is 73 years old, was also under arrest for two days. Once the two of them had at least started to recuperate from their ordeals somewhat my father was seized by a severe bout of pneumonia; he seems to have overcome the worst, but it will keep him in Germany for weeks, perhaps even months to come, although, with the assistance of some American friends, we have succeeded in securing permission for my parents to enter Cuba. I am sure there is no need for me to say that we will continue to be extremely disquieted until they have embarked on their journey and quit the terrible country. And nor need I say that the attempt to help them has completely preoccupied me for many weeks.[17]

Adorno's parents eventually arrived in Cuba in the spring of 1939.
    From the perspective of these events, the 'grassy seat' of *Minima Moralia* expresses Adorno's sadly transformed relationship to his parents, who lost not only their strength but also their 'awesomeness'. They became far more tragic victims than their children:

One of the Nazi's symbolic outrages is the killing of the very old. Such a climate fosters a late and lucid understanding with our parents, as between the condemned, marred only by the fear that we, powerless ourselves, might now be unable to care for them as well as they cared for us when they possessed something. The violence done to them makes us forget the violence they did. . . . The rising collectivistic order is a mockery of a classless one: together with the bourgeois it liquidates the Utopia that once drew sustenance from motherly love.[18]

For Adorno, the critical sociologist, the social aspect of family life is a medium of domination. Socialization, if it is successful, is a process that ends up in a repressive society of class-domination. The socialized individual has to function as a means of reproduction of a repressive totality. Insofar as the family is a main agent of socialization, it is a medium of domination. However, as a medium of domination, the process of socialization in the family can be successful if and only if it follows its own logic. This implies motherly love and tenderness, and a realm of intimate interaction and freedom which a repressive society cannot manipulate, direct or control. As a means of repressive socialization family life can only work if it 'stands up against' the repressive totality. Fascism, in liquidating the bourgeois order, also liquidated the ambivalence, the dialectic of the medium and with it the *dialectic* of the process of enlightenment and rationalization.

Most important for Adorno is the example of art. In his *Aesthetic Theory*, Adorno argues that the autonomy of art is a function of the social structure of the bourgeois society.[19] Yet as an instrument of bourgeois class-domination, even as 'affirmative' great art, the work of art opposes all forms of repression and domination. If it is 'great' or 'avantgarde', art is the most radical critique of the repressive totality. But it can be such critique only as a means of repression.[20] Art is 'social primarily because it stands opposed to society'.[21] All opposition to the repressive society is possible only within this society: 'In the last analysis art cannot be understood when its social essence has not been understood – and that goes also for the kind of art which withdraws completely from society.'[22]

In his polemic against Husserl's epistemology from the 1930s, Adorno identifies the same dialectic of the medium in music, intimate communication ('tenderness'), and in philosophical concepts:

All music was once in the service of shortening the *longueurs* of the high-born. But the Late Quartets are hardly background music. According to psychoanalysis, tenderness is training in reaction to barbaric sadism. But it has become a model for humanity. Even the decaying concepts of epistemology point beyond themselves.[23]

Music, tenderness or epistemic concepts do not *as such* transcend and oppose the existing society, but – under certain conditions (e.g. as 'great' and 'authentic' or 'broken', 'fragile' or 'avantgarde' art) – they *can* become a 'centre of power that stands against' its own societal and historical conditions of possibility.

2. The dialectic of the medium

In their *Dialectic of the Enlightenment* Horkheimer and Adorno generalized Adorno's interpretation of the deep ambivalences of family life and socialization agencies in modern societies. They developed it towards a general theory of the media. It shows that the rationality of the instruments *mediating* subject and object is *not* reducible to mere instrumental rationality.

The paradigm case of *instrumental rationality* is a deliberately operating subject using instruments to have effects on an object or other subjects treated as objects. To *act* rationally in an instrumental or a strategic sense we have to have some purposes, some useful means, abilities, and facilities to realize them. Purposes and means are connected with a subject through practical deliberation or practical syllogisms. A person P wants x, and can reach x only if she does y, uses z, etc., and therefore P does y, z, etc. Insofar as the purposes (what a person wants) depend on the *arbitrary will* of the subject Horkheimer and Adorno also call instrumental rationality 'subjective reason' (*subjektive Vernunft*).

The much broader concept of *media* is developed from Hegel's theory of mediation (*Vermittlung*). A medium basically is some instrument mediating subject and object. But the use of media must not follow syllogisms, conclusions and plans which have an author or a subject of deliberative action. In the course of cultural and social development language, religious belief, technology, etc. become media. The broad Hegelian notion of mediation is the background of all reflections of Adorno and Horkheimer, which are concerned with the topic of tools, industry, money, art, discursive logic, reason or mass-media communication. All of them can become media of domination.

But the *ratio of domination* (*Vernunft der Herrschaft*) is not simply the same as the *domination of reason* (*Herrschaft der Vernunft*). The *ratio of domination* is rational insofar and only insofar as it preserves domination and fulfils the interests of those who are dominant in a social situation, e.g. a ruling class. Rationality here is a mere means of domination. But that does not mean that *reason* is dominating what people do. The *domination of reason* transcends mere domination and goes beyond the limits of instrumental reason to the extent that this becomes universal. As in Martin Heidegger's thought, instrumental reason is the historical a priori of modern times. But it is merely a *historical* a priori and thus not some fate that is inescapable and unchangeable.

Horkheimer and Adorno admittedly wrote with a view to the history of class struggle that the 'impotence of the workers' is neither an unfortunate coincidence nor an evil 'stratagem by the rulers, but the logical consequence of the industrial society into which the ancient Fate – in the very course of the effort to escape it – has finally changed'.[24] However, and here Horkheimer and Adorno part company with Heidegger, 'this logical necessity is not conclusive'.[25] The difference between *ratio of domination* and *domination of reason* distinguishes between the mere *affirmation* of historical a prioris (Heidegger) and the *critique* of history that is *immanent*.

The self-same Logos which by dint of the logical consequences of industrial society transforms autonomy into heteronomy, omnipotence into impotence, also *checks* the tyranny and blindness of domination. The impotence of the servant is *not unlimited* if only as a result of that inner interweaving of reason and domination. The self-same reason that ensures the domination of the master over the servant, of capital over labour, of bureaucracy over the masses, of the collective over the individual, also sets limits for such domination. Insofar as the *domination of reason* (*Herrschaft der Vernunft*) sets limits for the domination of human beings over human beings it transcends the *ratio of domination* (*Vernunft der Herrschaft*). Where domination in Max Weber's sense has become rational and for the sake of its own power is dependent on reason, it has to limit itself. Media, whether intimate communication in the family, the steam engine, money, law, or the TV set, are *qua* instruments of domination at the same time *the limitations* of such domination. 'It is the servant that the master cannot check as he wishes. Domination ... has become objectified as law and organization and must therefore restrict itself.'[26] Throughout, Horkheimer and Adorno pay attention to the fundamental difference between the tyrannical rule of Ancient Egypt and the quite different rule of law which comes to bear, as relentless as it is inconspicuous, in the rationale of domination as the domination of reason.

The subject of domination *wants* to master the rationality of its means. But it cannot control them completely, it cannot subsume them under its own subjective interests. The means of the subject are objective and almost neutral since everybody from the master to his slave may use them. Horkheimer and Adorno interpret this as the internal dialectic of instrumental or subjective reason. The notion of *subjective* reason is paradoxical or self-contradictory.

Instrumental reason itself is therefore not *purely* subjective.[27] For it claims an objectivity, which no one can possess, that holds true universally, irrespective of station and for all in equal measure. By dint of this, and this alone, instrumental reason itself contradicts the tyranny of subjective domination. By virtue of the fact that the instrument takes on an independent life *vis-à-vis* the person who created it for his/her own benefit and use, it limits that person's 'freedom' but it also overcomes the limited perspective of a social atom that only calculates its own benefit. In the objectivity of the means we find the mediation that forces egocentrism to become decentred. Horkheimer and Adorno write: 'The instrument achieves independence: the mediating instance of the spirit, independently of the will of the master, modifies the directness of economic injustice.' It is precisely this independence which always separates reason from domination.

> The instruments of domination, which would encompass all – language, weapons, and finally machines – *must allow themselves to be encompassed by all. Hence in domination the aspect of rationality prevails as one that is also different from it.* The 'objectivity' of the means, which makes it universally available, already implies the criticism of that domination as whose means thought arose.[28]

Here, as elsewhere in the *Dialectic of Enlightenment*, Horkheimer and Adorno distinguish between the *instrumental effects* and the *non-instrumental impact* of reason, between reason as a means of domination and reason as the critique of such domination. They thus always focus on the difference between the *generalized 'us'* on which any 'objectivity for all' is based, and the *particular 'us'* of universal domination. Only in light of this difference is it possible for reason, which has become irrational and non-reflective, to reflect on itself. And only in the course of such self-reflection do the authors of the *Dialectic of Enlightenment* manage to distance themselves from the indictment they themselves have passed down, namely that enlightenment is totalitarian. With the benefit of such distance, a non-destructive deconstruction of reason becomes possible, which would at the same time be its salvation. It is this which Adorno then undertook in his *Negative Dialectics*.

The origin of the idea of a negative dialectics is not Hegel's theory of *final* mediation and *final* reconciliation of all paradoxes and antagonisms of the modern society. For Hegel this final reconciliation is the achievement of a 'reflection' of all contradiction in the light of the objective spirit of the state's institutions and in the light of the philosopher's contemplative gaze on the whole as *the* truth. Adorno's notion of dialectics is linked to the theory of antinomies developed by Kant in his first *Critique*. This book is, I suggest, along with some esoteric ideas from Walter Benjamin,[29] the very origin of *Negative Dialectics* in material as well as in biographical terms.

3. Siegfried Kracauer and the Kantian sabbath

Beginning in grammar school, Adorno took private lessons in composition and piano playing. These years were stereotypical for a precocious genius. Before his *Abitur* he skipped a grade and was even exempted from his final oral exams. When he was fifteen he met Siegfried Kracauer, the editor of the *Frankfurter Zeitung*, who was fourteen years his senior.[30] Kracauer, called by his friends 'Friedel', quickly became his intellectual and philosophical mentor. Every Saturday they would read Kant's *Critique of Pure Reason* together. Later, in a famous essay on Kracauer from 1964, Adorno remembers the obstinate and profound introduction to Kant which Kracauer gave to his much younger friend:

For a very simple reason, I may be qualified to make a start on this by outlining some of the features of the figure of Kracauer: he and I have been friends since I was a young man. I was a student at the Gymnasium when I met him near the end of the First World War. A friend of my parents, Rosie Stern, had invited the two of us to her house. She was a tutor at the Philanthropin, where Kracauer's uncle, the historiographer of the Frankfurt Jews, was a member of the faculty. As was probably our hostess' intention, an intensive contact sprang up between us. . . .

For years Kracauer read the Critique of Pure Reason with me regularly on Saturday afternoons. I am not exaggerating in the slightest when I say that I owe more to this reading than to my academic teachers. Exceptionally gifted as a pedagogue, Kracauer made Kant come alive for me. Under his guidance I experienced the work from the beginning not as mere epistemology, not as an analysis of the conditions of scientifically valid judgments, but as a kind of coded text from which the historical situation of spirit could be read, with the vague expectation that in doing so one could acquire something of truth itself. If in my later reading of traditional philosophical texts I was not so much impressed by their unity and systematic consistency as I was concerned with the play of forces at work under the surface of every closed doctrine and viewed the codified philosophies as force fields in each case, it was certainly Kracauer who impelled me to do so. As he presented it to me, Kant's critical philosophy was not simply a system of transcendental idealism. Rather, he showed me how the objective-ontological and subjective-idealist moments warred within it, how the more eloquent passages in the work are the wounds this conflict has left in the theory. From a certain point of view, the fissures and flaws in a philosophy are more essential to it than the continuity of its meaning, which most philosophies emphasize of their own accord.

Without being able to account for it fully, through Kracauer I perceived for the first time the expressive moment in philosophy: putting into words the thoughts that come into one's head.[31]

This study, and the relationship with Kracauer generally, left deep philosophical traces in Adorno's work. It is no exaggeration to say that the *Critique of Pure Reason* was the key work in Adorno's intellectual development. The idea of a negative dialectic, which is Adorno's most unique philosophical contribution, owes much to it. This influence is particularly evident in Kant's antinomies, since they do not nullify contradiction, but maintain it and allow thought to move back and forth between its opposing extremes. A dialectic is a 'movement between the extremes' that penetrates 'completely through the extremes' without synthesis and middle term.[32] Such a dialectic is for Adorno not only a source of philosophical meaning, it is also the grounding assumption of his aesthetic constructivism and his ethical theory of the non-forfeited life.

Kant's antinomies of pure reason and the dichotomies and bifurcations which part the realm of freedom sharply from that of necessity and causal determination are a clear and sober expression of the real contradictions of the bourgeois epoch. Kant's theoretical expressions of these contradictions do, according to Adorno, avoid all ideological transfigurations of the 'false', repressive, and damaged forms of life. Adorno and Horkheimer always read Kant as a philosopher who profoundly rejected the ideological attempt of all metaphysics from Plato to Hegel to overcome the contradictions of freedom and necessity by means of pure reason, by constructing a higher, spiritual world, or by declaring the philosophical insight into the necessities of history already to be the highest level of realized freedom, as Hegel did.

Adorno takes only the negative side of Hegel's dialectics as a method of processing through contradictions, what Hegel himself has called 'den Ernst, den Schmerz, die Geduld und Arbeit des Negativen'.[33] Adorno's step away from Hegel's *speculative* understanding of dialectics is a step back to Kant; just a step, not a return to some sort of Neo-Kantianism. Adorno keeps an equal distance from speculative metaphysics of reconciliation and from all Kantian dualism between the transcendental and the empirical world. He overcomes Kantian dualism by a Marxian reading of Kant's dichotomies and antinomies as being real contradiction within our social life world. Dialectics for Adorno is a methodological programme used to dissolve the objectivism of 'identifying thinking'. What Adorno calls 'identifying thinking' one nowadays could call with Jean Piaget 'egocentrism'.[34] The meaning and purpose of dialectical operations is *decentring egocentrism* in all its appearing forms.

Negative Dialectics claims to 'have consistently thought through what dialectics means'.[35] Occasionally, Adorno terms dialectics a high-level reflective empiricism to the second power. To his mind, dialectics is the experience of consciousness in addressing itself. Only a reader of Hegel from an experimental stance measures Hegel against his own yardstick:

> Reading Hegel would be ... an experimental procedure: letting possible interpretations simply occur, proposing them, to contrast the text and given, reliable interpretations. ... John Dewey, a contemporary thinker who for all his positivism is closer to Hegel than their two purported viewpoints suggest, called his philosophy experimentalism. The reader of Hegel would do well to take on something of this stance.[36]

Dialectic is the reflective, conceptual permeation of the experiences we make. It is an unwavering method of rendering objective self-misunderstandings fluid, or of proving by cognitive effort that all objectivity rests on mediation.[37]

Clearly, the concept of dialectics remains underdetermined if construed as holistic empiricism. Holistic empiricism is familiar in so-called post-analytical philosophy nowadays following Quine's powerful critique of the dogmas of empiricism. And holistic empiricism comes close to the insights of Hegel's dialectics insofar as its basic assumption proposes that we can understand single words, sentences or other symbolic or meaningful events only within a broad context of symbols, language and culture. Reference and meaning cannot be isolated from the totality of that context. This basic assumption of holistic empiricism is the same in Hegel's dialectical concept of 'totality'. Words are inherently interrelated within the meaning of the whole context in the same way as what Hegel calls 'moments' are interrelated within a 'totality' of such moments. But this is not the whole story of dialectical thinking. The holism is completed with the notion of contradiction and paradox forming tensions internal to all holistic experience. The *negation* of holism, contextual totality and all past experience preserved in the totality of meaning is built into such totality as a permanent threat against its unity. Therefore we never can reach the totality we are longing for, and which we *must* presuppose to comprehend a single sentence or event. Negation always can happen, and tear asunder all affirmative totality of language games, world-views or forms of life. As Hegel put it, dialectics always entails the 'riposte' which 'tears it free' of all past experience. Dialectics is the contradiction and negation, even in the classical meaning of the word, which refers back to dialogue and thus to the role of the person who disputes something. Opposition in dialogue involves the negation of what is assumed positively, of the affirmative; this negation contradicts our experiences and conventions. In this sense, all dialectics is negative.

Adorno takes up this idea and gives it a radical edge. Here, dialectics is aimed not at the contents, the substance of being, but at the contradiction of the substance of what is and what should be; not at the richly structured concrete whole, but at its opposition to the reflective structure of abstract freedom; not at the affirmation of the final consensual agreement with the world, but at the oppositional division of the roles in dialogue; not at the diverse shape of experience, with all its contrasts, but at the separation of material experience and regulative utopia. 'The concept of utopia', Siegfried Kracauer remarked in the 1960s critically but accurately of Adorno's *Negative Dialectics*, 'is therefore logically used in a purely formal manner by him as a concept marking a border.'[38] Negative dialectics, Kracauer continues, is an 'unfettered dialectic which completely eliminates any ontology'.[39]

Following directly on from Kant and Hegel, Adorno's negative dialectics hinges on the genesis and dissolution of antinomies. 'Reflective thought only points beyond itself by virtue of reflection; contradiction, despised by logic, becomes the vehicle of thought: the truth of logos.'[40] Here, contradiction is not a mere opposition of concept and reality, but is rather innate to the concept itself. The concept corresponds to reality, and yet again it does not.[41] The contradiction between the posited and thus motionless concept and the fluid concept becomes the 'agent of philosophizing'.

> By dint of being posited – that is because its meaning is confronted with the substance construed under that concept – its identity with the matter at the same time reveals its non-identity; in other words, what emerges here is the fact that concept and matter are not one and the same. The concept which remains true to its own meaning must therefore change itself.[42]

According to Kant and Hegel, the contradiction which arises when we apply a 'rational idea of the unconditional', i.e. an unconditional claim to validity, to the world, constitutes the core of all antinomies. Unconditional claims to validity and truth are claims to a seamless concordance of thought with *the* one reality. If the unconditional is projected onto the world, then it has to be presented as the complete epitome of all its conditions; this means, as

Hegel says, presenting it as 'itself unconditional, as infinite'.[43] No presentation can however construe that which is actually infinite as being *of* this world, in other words as being part of the finite world, let alone conceive of it as a finite series of steps. Owing to their claim to unconditionality, reason and truth are therefore antinomic in structure. To the extent that we try to explore the conditions for them and make them an issue within the world, we become entangled in contradictions. Adorno writes:

> Truth of itself becomes an objective, no longer nominalistically reducible idea. This is the case because the claim to truth gives the equally unconditional claim to truth of any limited and therefore untrue judgement the status of protest, and because it negates the subjective *adaequatio* by means of self-reflection.[44]

Any claim to truth that we make is necessarily limited and conditioned by our perspective; it can be disputed, because we never control all the conditions of truth of a sentence. But however limited a judgement may be, it nevertheless lays claim to unconditional truth and thus negates the limitation of the perspective, as the latter is always only subjective. The antinomy arises from a self-referential negation of a universal claim. The subjective *adaequatio* is negated by self-reflection, as Adorno puts it. As a consequence, a contradiction arises. However, it is the untenability of contradictions which sets things in motion and compels subjectivity to transcend itself. 'Truth sheds its subjectivity: *because no subjective judgement can be true and yet each must wish to be true*, truth transcends itself and becomes "in itself".'[45] Here, dialectical movement proves to be the decentring of egocentrism.

The projections of the paranoiac are an extreme case of egocentrism. In the *Dialectic of Enlightenment*, Horkheimer and Adorno declare this to be the model of anti-Semitism: 'Anti-Semitism is based on a false projection. It is the opposite of true mimesis, and fundamentally related to the repressed form; in fact, it is probably the morbid expression of repressed mimesis. Mimesis imitates the environment, but false projection makes the environment like itself.'[46]

While true mimesis is aimed at decentring, the thinking of the anti-Semite is different; here, his false projections place only his own subject at the centre of things. In fascism, or so Horkheimer and Adorno generalized, 'this behaviour is made political' and the system is 'deemed the reasonable norm in the world'.[47] The relation here resembles that between the advanced races and the more primitive ones in the projections of the racist,

> so the sick individual is able to confront other individuals with a lust for power and persecution. In both cases, the subject is at the centre and the world is simply the occasion for his madness; the world becomes the powerless or omnipotent epitome of all that is projected onto it.[48]

Construing the world as an epitome of all that is projected onto it is a precondition for the genesis of antinomies that, were it not possible to dissolve them, would have fatal consequences.

> The naked pattern of power as such, which dominates all around it as well as its own Ego, which decomposes with it, seizes all that is offered to it and incorporates this, irrespective of the specific nature thereof, into its mythic fabric. The closed circle of eternal similarity becomes a substitute for omnipotence. It is as though the serpent which said to the first humans 'you will be as God' had redeemed its promise in the paranoiac. He makes everything in his own image.[49]

The opposite conclusion supports Adorno's assumption that the biblical 'ban on images' contained a force that decentred egocentrism and liberated identifying thought of all false projections. Paranoiacs who create a world in their own image at the same time deny and repress all contradictions between their image and the world. They idolize the image.

Contradictions and antinomies for Adorno are not only something to avoid. On the contrary, they have a productive function of finding new solutions to problems and innovative concepts in theory as well as in practical life, as in Kant's transcendental dialectics. This can also be applied to modern art, and to the process of socialization and in therapeutic communication.

The transformation 'from extreme to extreme', from expression into construction and from technical rationality into mimetic expressivity, is evident in Adorno's comments on Schönberg's music. He claims that 'after his tenth work, his compositions swing between the extremes of the totally thematic and the unthematic; he sought not a balanced systematization but rather to hold both extremes in abrupt opposition'.[50] By holding the extremes in abrupt opposition music becomes the paradigm of a decentred subjectivity.

For Adorno even the idea of a non-forfeited life, in which the ego develops where the id was, culminates in a maintenance of oppositions that threaten to destroy the ego and to shatter its stable identity. The unique achievement of a strong ego, which is meant to take the place of the free-floating impulse of the id, is for Adorno in no way the repression of its impulses or the denial of its natural 'bodily lust'. Adorno has a strong predilection for romantic metaphors of fluidity and amorphousness, of the diffuse and the impulse which overwhelms the ego: 'Only he who were able to determine utopia in the blind somatic desire that knows no intention, and stills the last, would be capable of an idea of freedom that endured.'[51] But at the same time Adorno warns of the 'horror of the amorphous' and against false immediacy. The 'non-identical' is not simply the 'unidentical': 'Dissociation is possible only against identity, falling under its concept; otherwise it would be pure, unpolemic, innocent variety.'[52] A non-forfeited life does not retreat behind that dynamic of modern times that allows us, as Hegel says, to experience more in one day than the inhabitant of the ancient world did in his entire life. This requires us to integrate spontaneous impulses and our projected freedom determined both theoretically and practically by constructive rationality. Only the rational, strong, and complex ego is in itself differentiated enough to allow impulse and nature to be what they are – or, as Adorno often says, to be what they want to be of their own accord. Our 'non-identical' drives and spontaneous impulses can come to authentic expression only before a background constellation of a rational identity.

From early on Adorno adopted a position regarding the conservative critique of rationality and enlightenment similar to his friend Siegfried Kracauer. He adopted the latter's critique of the 'action-circle' (Tat-Kreis, whose members included, among others, the brothers Ernst and Georg Jünger) of the 'conservative revolution' (people like Möller van den Bruck, Oswald Spengler, Carl Schmitt, Gottfried Benn or Martin Heidegger) developed in the 1920s, according to which capitalism rationalizes not too much, but too little. 'Ideals, which the intellect has not imbibed and tasted, are useless products of nature',[53] Kracauer wrote in the 1920s. Adorno would later not forgo any opportunity to crusade 'without a model' (this is the title of one of Adorno's books in the 1960s, *Ohne Leitbild*) against the grammar school mush of so-called 'eternal values'.[54] Despite this crusade, when studying for his *Abitur* Adorno read the *Theory of the Novel* by Georg Lukács and the *Spirit of Utopia* by Ernst Bloch. These two books fascinated him most among their works. They belong with the *Critique of Pure Reason* at the cornerstone of his thought.

> The dark brown 400-page volume, printed on thick paper, promised something of what one hoped from medieval books and what I when a child felt from the leather-bound *Heroic Treasure*: a belated magic book of the eighteenth century full of obscure references, many of which I still reflect on today. The spirit of utopia appeared as if it were written by Nostradamus' own hand. The name 'Bloch' also had this aura. Dark as a passageway and threateningly muted as a trumpet blast, the dread expectation he awakened was made quickly suspect as shallow and inferior to the concepts of philosophy, with which I was becoming familiar.[55]

For Adorno an essential function of aesthetic modernity is to generate meaning out of several sources: out of the ephemeral, out of what is 'withdrawn from the world of appearance' (Freud), out of the subsiding form of good and long stable traditions, and even out of handed-down, already existent, ageing, and 'used up' material. Though this modernity does not depart from the hermeneutic circle, which links what is present and future to what is past, it radically denies its own truth content for the sake of the possible new. It must allow everything it constructs to emerge out of a receding semantics of the historical.

This phrase is as valid for Gustav Mahler's music as for Eichendorff's lyrics. Adorno notes that everything with which Mahler dealt, 'is already there . . . His themes are dispossessed. Here nothing sounds as one is accustomed to hear: all is diverted by a magnet . . . precisely the misused position for it a second life as a variant'.[56] Just as in Hegel's philosophy a *second nature* is created out of spirit, in Adorno's negative dialectic a *second* immediacy emerges *after* the radical redemption of the 'dull oppositionlessness' (Hegel) of the original. In modern music everything depends on the construction of a *second musical language* that sublates the false opposition of uncultured and cultured art. The dissociated spheres of the music of high and low culture form the *first* language of affirmative music, be it 'classical' and 'harmonious', or the mere product of cultural industries as popular music. The *second* language of 'negative' and 'avantgarde' music overcomes the dissociation and fragmentation of the two spheres of the first language not by reconciliation but by constructing a new heterogeneous unity: both spheres now communicate but their communication is a never-ending process of contradictions and negations. Cultural music is transformed into dissonant sounds, included in experiments completely alienated from the well-known, restful sounds that affirm the ear of the bourgeois during leisure time. Elements of so-called 'low culture music' and sounds of the everyday life are invented as disruption of the artistic closeness. This in turn helps the cultural good, sunken in a false immediacy, to gain a new life. Such was Mahler's achievement:

> Jacobinean, the lower music storms into the upper . . . The self-satisfied polish of the mediate form is demolished by the disproportionate sound from the pavilions of the military band and the palm-garden orchestra . . . Symphonic music digs for the treasure, that alone the roll of the drums or the murmur of voices promises ever since music established itself domestically as art. It would seize the masses, that flee from the culture-music, yet without conforming to them.[57]

Everything new is merely the result of experimental variation of the old and of constructive reinvention of the past. When this succeeds to the extent it does in Eichendorff's poems, the 'unfettered romantic' moves 'without realizing it to the threshold of modernity'.[58] This is 'the modern element' in Eichendorff that reaches the 'most extraordinary effects with a stock of images . . . which must have been threadbare even in his day'.[59] Adorno noticed that Eichendorff's poem *Sehnsucht* contained 'almost no feature that is not demonstrably derivative, but each of these features is characteristically transformed through its contact with the others'.[60]

4. 'By the way, both are communists'

When Adorno started his study of philosophy in Frankfurt with Hans Cornelius, he was already completely outside the Neo-

Kantian mainstream of the scholastic philosophy of that time that Cornelius himself represented. He concluded his study with his dissertation on Husserl, a dutiful exercise which he quickly completed. Nevertheless, Cornelius exerted a lasting though indirect influence on Adorno, mediated by a young Max Horkheimer who had just finished his post-doctoral thesis and had become Cornelius's assistant.

The son of an undertaker from Stuttgart, Horkheimer was no scholastic philosopher either, but he did stand closer to the traditional style of German philosophy than did Adorno. During his preparations for his doctoral exam, Adorno got to know Horkheimer and his friend Friedrich Pollock, both of whom lived at that time in a hotel in Königstein, near Frankfurt. 'By the way, both are communists', he wrote to Leo Löwenthal on 16 July 1924, with whom he had already been friends for some time, 'and we have lengthy and passionate discussions about materialist conceptions of history at the end of which we concede to remain much opposed.'[61] A lifelong friendship between Horkheimer and Adorno developed, resulting in their collaboration on the *Dialectic of Enlightenment*. Later, upon their return to West Germany after their exile, they developed their role as the most notable figures of the so-called Frankfurt School in the 1950s and 1960s. The very term 'critical theory' refers to the thinking of the negative developed by both of them.

Horkheimer soon recognized Adorno's genius and, after taking the helm at the Institute in Frankfurt, rapidly made him one of his closest collaborators. Adorno had, as Horkheimer once put it, a 'keen view of the existing world sharpened by hatred' and this coalesced well with the misanthropic inclinations of the Institute's director, who understood himself as its 'dictator'. There was, however, one difference between the two men from the very outset. Adorno was not so much interested in social science and research as in music and aesthetic theory. From the point of view of an aesthetic modernism, he made a sinister and radical critique of all non-aesthetic modernity. Here he was as close to the French surrealists as was his friend Walter Benjamin. The aesthetic idea of freedom from all institutions of a repressive society was very different from a more scientific idea of freedom as controlling and planning this society and its economic anarchy, which was basically Marx's idea. Combining Marxism with aesthetic avantgardism, as

Adorno did, led towards criticism of Marxist ideas of a controlled and planned realm of freedom as being not free enough to express all our desires and wishes.[62]

Whereas Adorno considered the modern social sciences more as a necessary evil and was spell-bound by the experimental understanding of freedom championed by the modern art world that was exploding on the scene at the time, Horkheimer's notion of art remained rather more conventional throughout his life – as did his essay-writing style. Although deeply influenced by Schopenhauer's pessimism in his youth, Horkheimer in the 1920s and early 1930s took a much more positive view of the potential of technology and science. It was Horkheimer who developed in these years the idea of combining a Marxist social philosophy with modern techniques of social research. At the very beginning this was closely connected with the idea of a planned economy on the ground that the more scientific the better for overcoming capitalism. In the 1920s and 1930s his faith in science was much greater than Adorno's ever was. When Horkheimer's faith in science waned, and he started to believe that it was part and parcel of a fully irrational form of domination, Adorno at least still had the art of modernity to clutch onto as a trace of freedom in *real life*.

During the crisis years in the Institute at the end of the 1930s, when Horkheimer decided to move with a small group of conspiring colleagues from New York to California, Adorno, in his jealousy, managed to squeeze out all his competitors and to be the only person to commence work at Horkheimer's side on the dialectics project – the project that was to spawn the *Dialectic of Enlightenment*.

As a philosopher, Max Horkheimer today stands in the shadow of Theodor W. Adorno, yet he was the actual designer of the Frankfurt School. Without the intellectual figure of Horkheimer, the historical existence of the Frankfurt School would be unthinkable. Since Kuhn we have come to expect the heads and founding fathers of schools to provide something like a paradigm, an exemplary, school-forming scientific achievement; but none is to be found in Horkheimer's work. True, the works Horkheimer published between 1930 and 1940 do have a programmatic force. They give direction and orientation to the research done in the Frankfurt circle, the Institute for Social Research, and the *Zeitschrift*. But a towering paradigmatic achievement, of the kind to belabour generations of critical social scientists with puzzles, can scarcely be found concealed behind the markers set out in the 1931 inaugural lecture, 'The Present Situation of Social Philosophy and the Tasks of an Institute for Social Research', or the classic 1937 text, 'Traditional and Critical Theory'. Anyone who expects to find the fundamental philosphical concept of critical theory there will be disappointed. The exemplary work that stands out above the entire current of undogmatic Marxism in this century, from the early Frankfurt School through Habermas, had already appeared in 1923, namely Georg Lukács's collection of essays, *History and Class Consciousness*. I will come back to this in the next section.

Yet the operationalizing of the paradigm as a programme of critical social research, its coalescence into a philosophical, social-scientific school that forms a tradition of its own, remains the decisive intellectual merit of Horkheimer. He, not Lukács, was the first to lead Marxism unambiguously into conjunction with the research programmes of the social sciences, and in doing so, he was following an original philosophical impulse to transform metaphysics into a set of hypotheses to be worked out scientifically and tested by scientific methods. The best of the philosophical tradition should withstand that transformation into science. This was Horkheimer's way of spelling out the old platonic idea that reason is science. Modern science – in contradiction with the platonic view – does not end up with insights into eternal truth, yet it is from the outset fallibilistic and has accepted that we cannot escape time and history.

Horkheimer's attacks on the philosophical tradition's fundamentalism and on its subject–object dualism move within the broad currents of post-Hegelian thought. But Horkheimer gives up the search for a philosophical way out of the crisis of philosophy. Instead, his materialism seeks out contradictions and aporias and does not wish to break out of them at all. Yet Horkheimer does not stop at deconstructivism. His way out is the needle's eye of social research, through which all philosophy that wishes to survive must henceforth pass. This is the idea of a social-scientific transformation of philosophy.

Horkheimer's philosophical intuitions revolve around such projects as materialism as empirical research and scientific disenchantment. He is defending materialism as an individualistic, utilitarian ethic of happiness or, complementarily, of the solidarity of all life in the face of universal suffering. Dialectics in Horkheimer's point of view is a method of mediating and transcending contradictions. He understands dialectics from its critical function as the negation of the prevailing order, and insight of unabridged reason.

The finitude and worldliness of human life, the brute fact of the privation and misery suffered by 'far and away the greatest part of humanity', of their hopes and longings, and the claim to worldly happiness of 'individuals who are, in all seriousness, transitory': these things imprinted themselves so decisively upon Horkheimer's thinking in the 1930s that he even defended the 'finite quantities' of mathematics against the idealistic affront of 'deriving them from the infinitely small by means of the infinitesimal calculus'. Horkheimer criticizes the tendency in the mathematical natural sciences to make 'the wretched world which the scholar sets eyes on ever more expressible in the form of differential equations' and thereby to efface any trace of sensually experienceable reality, and he criticizes the foundationalism of Western metaphysics, which is in league with domination: to idealize and transfigure the empirical lifeworld, grounding it in an 'eternal logos', in 'eternal ideas' beyond this world and its 'earthly possibilities'.[63]

That is Horkheimer's (and along with him Adorno's) central argument against the idealistic metaphysics of philosophers from Plato to Hegel: they stand in 'the service of transfiguration', because they believe they must ground 'the misery of the present' and the 'material privation' of the 'earthly order' – in short, empirical reality – in an 'overarching' 'second reality'.[64] In view of the irredeemably affirmative alliance between 'optimistic metaphysics' and 'social pessimism', Horkheimer sometimes finds it difficult to hold fast to his own programme of materialistically preserving the truth content of idealism and metaphysics, of taking up the inheritance of philosophical reason in the materialistic context of a theory of society, of reconstructing traditional theory as critical theory.[65] Metaphysics stands convicted of the crime of transfiguration, which can no more be atoned and made amends for than the misery and suffering of the past.

Horkheimer here comes close to other approaches of post- or anti-metaphysical thinking of the twentieth century. Hermeneutical and existential philosophers have replaced transcendental subjectivity with the contingency of the concrete historical situation of human beings. Prior to all recognition and cognitive knowledge is our concern of 'being-in-the-world' (Heidegger). Analytical and linguistic philosophers have reminded us that the only transcendental borders of the human lifeworld are the borders of our language. As a Neo-Marxist, Max Horkheimer complements these approaches with a third version: the ideology-critical. Here the transcendental structure of the knowing subject is replaced by the structure of class-domination of a historical formation of the society. By this move the philosophical critique of metaphysics is related towards a political critique of the present society.

The systematic motive that connects (as we will see in Chap. 3, s. 4) Horkheimer's radicalized ideology critique with Heidegger, Gilbert Ryle and Wittgenstein is the critique of the dualism of philosophical thinking. Again and again, he polemicizes against the 'demotion of the known world to a mere exterior', the 'Cartesian isolation of intellectual substance from all spatial reality', 'the splitting of the world into two mutually independent realms', the 'dualism of thought and being, understanding and perception', and protests 'against the assumption of an absolute, transhistorical subject'.[66] The paradigm of traditional theory is the 'scientific method' of axiomatic-deductive reasoning, which remains 'alive throughout the pursuit of the specialized sciences':

> Traditional theory and reality belong to two distinct and separate provinces . . . Theory remains in the realm of contemplation. Philosophers have frequently made something absolute out of this aspect of theory and, under the title of 'logos' or 'spirit', have deified the subject of these intellectual activities. It appears in their systems as the creator of the world.[67]

Above all, however, Cartesian rationalism disregarded the historically mediated selectivity of our knowledge, the conditionality of 'spirit', and failed to take account of its interwovenness with an opaque background 'cast in shadows', with a 'world' that is not conscious and transparent: the primacy of 'material existence', of 'praxis', the 'lifeworld', the 'unconscious' and 'preconscious'. 'The rationalistic separation of the human being into two independent halves, body and mind, has removed the entirety of unconscious and half-conscious psychic processes from scientific theory.'[68]

Ultimately, therefore, Horkheimer can denounce Cartesian dualism – the 'notion of knowing the supposedly unconditional and thereby of being unconditional oneself' – ideology-critically as 'a narcissistic projection of one's own temporally conditioned ego onto eternity'.[69] For constructing an 'unconditional order', an eternal and absolute truth, an 'ultimate, absolutely valid knowledge', means 'intellectually eternalizing the earthly conditions underlying it'. This 'transfiguring function' 'reveals' the 'indwelling inhumanity' of philosophy.[70]

Adorno shares with Horkheimer the materialistically motivated criticism of philosophical idealism. But his own stance towards what now is called 'philosophy of consciousness' is more complex. As we have already seen, Adorno's idea of dialectic owes as much to Kant's notion of 'antinomies' as to Hegel's idea of an immanent critique, and he is much more critical towards Hegel's holism than Horkheimer, even if he does not reject it totally. Whereas Horkheimer in questions of aesthetic value is closer to the concept of the beautiful (or the ugly as the other, less affirmative side of the beautiful), Adorno prefers the sublime and the hope of inventing new or 'utopian' views of the world that might be disclosed only by a sublime type of experience. This difference is related to the other difference mentioned above: Adorno does not rely as much as the early Horkheimer does on scientific argumentation and rational discourse. Although always defending rationality against its conservative critics, Adorno's interest is in the instant when it comes to transcend the existing rational discourse from within. This is why Adorno much more than Horkheimer tries to redeem the utopian elements in the transcendental notions of subjectivity and the unconditional. His plan of materialistic criticism here is to save the best parts of idealism rather than to get rid of it completely, which is the more radical intention of Horkheimer's antiphilosophy.

5. Lukács and critical theory

In the early developmental phase of a 'critical theory' this term was not only connected with a logic of negativity, but became a code-name for 'Marxism' or – to be more precise – for the original theory of Karl Marx. If Horkheimer and Adorno talked about their own heterodox reading of Marx, they talked about 'critical theory'. Horkheimer preferred the denotation 'critical theory' to

Marxism or Neo-Marxism, especially during his exile in America, where in the 1930s and 1940s the theory and the name of Marx were closely linked with communism and Stalinism. The American mind was basically anti-communist, with the exception of a short period during the war when the United States and the Soviet Union were allies.

For Adorno the core of Marxism was the theory of the 'commodity form' and the critique of 'commodity fetishism'. In that analysis the work of early Marx, the famous 'Paris Manuscripts' with the central notion of 'alienation', were still alive in the *Capital* of the late Marx. An example of Marx's critique of the 'real abstractions' of exchange-value which is something like a 'missing link' between the early and the late Marx is the following quotation from the *Grundrisse*. Here he understands money (anticipating Weber, Adorno and the functionalist sociology of our days) as a system-integrating medium of norm-free socialization:

> Money ... is not purely a mediating form of commodity exchange. It is a form of exchange-value which has arisen out of the process of circulation, it is a social product which creates itself from the relations which individuals enter in circulation. As soon as gold and silver (or any other commodity) have developed into a measure of value and a means of circulation (whether it be in their physical form or represented by a symbol), they become money, without social will or social action. Its power appears to be fate and the consciousness of people, particularly in social circumstances which are undermined by a deeper development of exchange relations, struggles against this power that a substance, a thing, has over them; against the supremacy of cursed metal, which appears to be pure insanity. It is first in money, and indeed in the most abstract and thus most meaningless, incomprehensible form – a form in which all mediation is superseded – that there appears a transformation of reciprocal social relations into a fixed overarching social relation which subsumes individuals. And indeed the appearance is much the harsher since it arises from the presupposition of free, determined, atomistic, private persons who are related to each other only by reciprocal need in production.[71]

Marx was the author of the *Communist Manifesto* and the *18. Brumaire* on the one hand, and of the *Grundrisse* and the *Capital* on the other. In writings of the first type his own political commitment was in the foreground, in the latter the theoretical interest in scientific explanation. But Marx's works cannot be divided so clearly into works of practical and works of theoretical concern. The *integration* of both perspectives is the basic idea of his whole work that reflects the idea of the dialectical unity of theory and practice.

In *Capital* Marx integrates the *theoretical* perspective of the observer of an objective process of economic reproduction with the *practical* perspective of a virtual participant in collective struggles about material distribution and ethical and legal recognition ('class struggles'). The perspective of the observer coincides with the functionalist approach in sociology, but the perspective of the participant is correlated with the perspective of historical peoples and social classes fighting to overcome oppression and expropriation. The synthesis of these two perspectives is the 'value-theory' concerning the market value of labour as well as the commodity form in general. Marx's 'value-theory' is at once an explanation of economic growth and the circulation of constant and variable capital, and a stern critique of inequality and class-domination. The latter aspect is worked out as a general critique of *reification* that binds people to the ideology that makes social relations, the product of men's 'concrete labour' appear as natural necessities, but which are simply the objective effects of the anonymous market processes of 'abstract capital'.'Reification' (defined in general as the 'appearance of people and interpersonal relations as objects, things and as relations between objects, things'[72]) here means the transformation of *concrete* 'labour power' into *abstract* 'variable capital'. Following Alfred Sohn-Rethel, Adorno speaks of a process of 'real-abstraction'. By means of the exchange between labour and capital, 'living labour' is transformed into and subordinated to 'dead labour'.[73] One of the main aspects of this transformation and subsuming of labour in the economic process of the reproduction of capitalism is its *quantification*. Labour becomes *calculable*.

In *History and Class Consciousness*, Georg Lukács linked this theory to Max Weber's theory of the process of *disenchantment* and *rationalization* of the world (which Habermas later called the 'rationalization' and – with critical intentions, following in this respect Marx, Lukács and Adorno – the 'colonization of the lifeworld'[74]). For Lukács the connection between Marx's 'reification' and Weber's 'rationalization' is the principle of *calculability*. If, in the context of Marxian labour value-theory, reification is

connected with the quantification of labour in time/money relations, so also for Weber rationalization is 'the knowledge or the
belief that one can – in principle – master all things through calculation'. It is precisely this which Weber also calls the 'disenchantment of the world'.[75] And Lukács writes: 'We are concerned above
all with the *principle* at work here: the principle of rationalisation
based on what is and *can be calculated*.'[76]

Already for Weber money was the medium which most purely
embodied the conditions of *formal rationality*: 'From a purely technical point of view, *money* is the most "perfect" means of economic calculation. That is, it is formally the most rational means
of orienting economic activity.'[77] Precisely therein is concealed the
problem which so disturbed Marx and then, more than anyone,
the Western Marxists: the power of *real abstraction*. Weber saw
this:

> A rational economy is a functional organization oriented to *money*-
> prices which originate in the interest-struggles of men in the *market*.
> *Calculation* is not possible without estimation in money prices and
> hence without market conflicts. Money is the most abstract and 'imper-
> sonal' element that exists in human life.[78]

The rationalization of the work process makes it a functional
mechanical system via *abstraction* carried out by its human agents.
There is only room in this 'rational order' for mutually communicating human actors insofar as they are 'useable instruments for
dominating and rationally re-ordering the world';[79] otherwise they
are, according to Lukács, *'mere sources of error'*.[80]

The categorization of Weberian 'rationalization' alongside
Marxian 'reification' goes so far in Lukács that he finally talks in
one breath of 'rationally reified relations'.[81] In connection with
Marx, Lukács speaks also of the universality of the category of
commodity: 'The commodity can only be understood in its undis-
torted essence when it becomes the universal category of society as
a whole.'[82] And in connection with Weber, Lukács expresses the
same thing in these words: 'that the principle of rational mechanis-
ation and calculability must embrace every aspect of life'.[83] For
Lukács 'rationalization' (Weber) and 'reification' (Marx) are the
two sides of the one coin.

It is precisely this aspect of *History and Class Consciousness* which makes the book something like a (Kuhnian) *paradigm* for 'critical theory', not only for early Horkheimer and Adorno, but also for Jürgen Habermas, who takes it up in his *Theory of Communicative Action*.[84] Yet Adorno and Horkheimer very soon gave up Georg Lukács's theory of the revolution, which was – in their perspective – far too closely related to Lenin and the Russian Revolution of 1918. This other central aspect of *History and Class Consciousness* separates Lukács and the Frankfurt School. For Adorno and Horkheimer the integration of the working class into capitalist society was the basic problem of all *Neo*-Marxism and a refutation of Marx or Lukács's far too optimistic philosophy of history. The year that made the twentieth century for Horkheimer and Adorno was not 1918 but rather 1933 when Hitler came to power.

In February 1939 Adorno wrote to Walter Benjamin thematizing Franco's triumph in Spain: 'Nothing appears more symptomatic to me than the repetition in Barcelona of what took place in Vienna a year ago: the same masses cheered the fascist conqueror who on the previous day still cheered the opposition.'[85] For Adorno the Marxian 'value-theory' became a central instrument of cultural critique. He concerned himself with applying this theory, especially the doctrine of commodity fetishism, to new phenomena, rather than grounding and questioning the theory itself.[86]

The Weberian–Marxist reification theory was used by Adorno from the outset (above all other members of the Frankfurt Institute for Social Research) with great success in ever new applications and detailed investigations, from the early critiques of positivistic science and investigations into the fetish character of music to the countless cultural sociological studies connected with the 'culture industry' chapter of the *Dialectic of Enlightenment*. In his 1938 essay 'Über den Fetischcharakter der Musik und die Regression des Hörens' Adorno tries to demonstrate that market-oriented arrangements of fragments of classical music (the minuet from Mozart's E flat major Symphony, played in radio potpourris without the other components of this symphony, is one of Adorno's examples) lead towards a reified fetishism of the so-called 'beautiful' parts that is analogous to and stems from the universality of the commodity-form. Under the soft dictatorship of the market the listener has no chance to get a new and insightful perception of the fragmented parts, unlike – following Adorno – the case with cubist paintings or dissonant music. Psychological regression and the culturally reinforced integration of the working class, pseudoactivity instead of civic or revolutionary praxis, are some of the disastrous results of the cultural industry's fragmentation of the art-work's totality. Adorno always confronts this regressive type of 'fragmentation' with the progressive one internal to the more esoteric works of modern art. In his essay, as well as in the chapter on 'cultural industry' in the *Dialectic of Enlightenment*, Adorno argues that changes in the mode of production affect the general consciousness of listeners. He tries to reveal changes in the reception of certain characteristics like the cult of the melody, of the voice, of the first violin, and then links them with specific economic concepts like 'late capitalism', 'totalized markets', 'consumer society', 'exchange-value', 'commodity-form' and so on. On a more empirical level, closely related to the research of the Institute for Social Research on authoritarianism, these features are linked to types of psychological retrogression in listening. Adorno here tries to demonstrate that a 'musical child language' (Adorno's examples are the 'jitter-bug', the 'radio amateur' or 'the man with a knack for jazz') can be correlated with 'docile passivity, imitation of pregiven patterns, and bitter resentment of the "abnormal" ' that are certain aspects of the authoritarian character.[87]

The theory of reification is the doctrinal core of the great systematic projects of the Frankfurt School from the *Dialectic of Enlightenment* to *One-Dimensional Man*, from the *Critique of Instrumental Reason* to *The Structural Transformation of the Public Sphere* and the theories of motivation crises and that dwindling resource, 'sense' or 'meaning' (*Sinn*). It is surely no coincidence that critical theory at this stage returned repeatedly to Max Weber. So, for the authors of the *Dialectic of Enlightenment* the concept of enlightenment converges with the Weberian concept of the disenchantment of the world and the book's central thesis that enlightenment was totalitarian rests directly on its version of rationalization as calculability, as 'domination through calculation'. And it is in a particular study of Max Weber that Herbert Marcuse develops the thesis of his 'one-dimensional man' from the tendency immanent in technical rationality to assimilate itself to domination. In the way technique dominates nature, its very rationality is a means to dominate man (for the ambivalence of this analogy of technical control and social domination see s. 2 above and Chap. 2). Finally, this concept of rationalization is central to Habermas's earliest attempts to reground critical theory in a 'theory of communicative action'. Altogether the attempts to solve the 'puzzle' of reification in the frame of a critical theory of society were extraordinarily successful, both scientifically and politically/practically (from Adorno's corrective influence on the intellectual-cultural climate of the post-fascist republic of West Germany up to the European and American student movement).

For Adorno himself, Lukács, Marx and Weber were only one side of his intellectual biography. The other ones were related to ' the friendship with Walter Benjamin – the correspondence recently published by the Frankfurt Suhrkamp-Verlag[88] demonstrates the extent of their co-operation – and, most important, to the Vienna circle of new music, to Alban Berg and Arnold Schönberg.

6. Benjamin and the dialectic of progress

In 1923 Adorno met Walter Benjamin in Frankfurt. The two quickly became friends. The dark and puzzling work of Benjamin, eleven years his elder, played an important role in the development of Adorno's thought. He became indebted to Benjamin not only for his 'micrological' method, but most of all for his idea of a negative dialectic.[89] Adorno's development of an outline of his negative dialectic began in his inaugural lecture of May 1931 and continued unabated for the rest of his life. He seasoned Benjamin's 'arrested dialectic' (*Dialektik im Stillstand*) with Hegel's dynamism. Moreover, Benjamin's posthumously published historical-philosophical theses and his project of an aporetic-ambivalent 'domination of the domination of nature' were important influences on the *Dialectic of Enlightenment*. But Adorno distanced himself both from Benjamin's all too manifest theological impulses, and from his overly forceful revolutionary hope for the utopian potential of the new art of the masses. At the end of his life Adorno would leave behind not a *theological-political* fragment as Benjamin did, but an *aesthetic-theoretical* one which retained a distance from both politics and theology. Walter Benjamin, as his essay on violence clearly shows, came very close to Carl Schmitt's political theology centred on the state of emergency. Under conditions of political emergency, which Benjamin connected with a Marxian proletarian revolution and a biblical idea of absolute justice, the destiny of the whole was in the hands of a revolutionary power and a 'divine violence' to make by its own arbitrary will the decision to change and 'rescue' the world.[90] Less voluntaristic than Benjamin, Adorno remained upon the comparatively more secure path of Kantian and Hegelian dialectics, forming ideas which were not particularly modest, but far more conventional than Benjamin's. In *Negative Dialectic* he claims 'to have consistently conceived of what dialectic means'.[91] Adorno undertook a project that integrated Marx and Horkheimer's enlightenment idea of *consciousness-raising* critique with Benjamin's aesthetic theological idea of a *rescuing* critique.[92]

Illuminating here is a talk Adorno gave in 1962 at the annual meeting of German philosophers in Münster. Its title is 'Progress', and it is in some respects a late response to Benjamin's thesis on the philosophy of history from the end of the 1930s, which deeply influenced the course of critical theory during the war, and ended up in the *Dialectic of Enlightenment*.[93]

In the 1930s Walter Benjamin sharply criticized the social democratic concept of progress, for it reduced 'human progress' to the 'advancement of their skills and knowledge'.[94] This notion of the 'progress of mankind itself', in line with the infinite perfectibility of mankind and its irresistible forward momentum, could not, or so Benjamin claimed, 'be sundered from the concept of its progression through a homogeneous, empty time'.[95] For Benjamin at least *all* historical progress is bound to the concept of a 'homogeneous, empty time'. The meaning of this is that progress internal to history is empty and senseless, not *real* progress but only more of the same. Progression *in* time and *internal* to history is vulgar Marxism, a positivistic conception of social democracy. There is only one way out of the negative dialectic of progression in the domination of nature by means of social regression (and vice versa), and that is to give up the notion of progress in history and time entirely. From this perspective, which is no longer a historical (and no longer a historical-materialistic) one but theological, the very moment of revolutionary power is the moment of realizing all emancipation at once. The Benjaminian revolution *ends* all history instead of *changing* it for the better. The Revolution (with a capital 'R') is the moment to stop time and history. Benjamin's famous tiger's jump into the past of history (into its 'origin'?) is the timeless point

of time when the dead are rescued and the destroyed nature is
healed. In order to be able to *depict* the empty time of that
advancement of all progression internal to history as 'one single
catastrophe, which keeps piling wreckage, after wreckage' at our
feet, Benjamin had to resort to the vantage point of the 'angel of
history', who, without being able to intervene, is nevertheless able
to survey history *as a whole*.[96] In order to be able to imagine from
this perspective a change of direction from this catastrophic form
of progress, Benjamin has at least to assume that human practice
exhibits a '*weak* Messianic power', which in that empty and homogeneous time could 'blast out' the *hidden* 'location' of a 'time filled
by the presence of the now'. This functions for him as the 'model
of Messianic time'.[97] Throughout Benjamin makes the claim that
revolution is the only conceivable praxis that could serve as the
'historical materialist *model*' of the time of Messianic redemption.
Anything less than a total revolution is not enough, and even then
it is not quite clear whether it does not also require 'redemption'
from outside or from above – that is to say 'transcendental
intervention *per se*', as Adorno later remarked critically.[98] What
Adorno dislikes about Benjamin's Messianism is the point of view
of a divine observer outside any socio-historical reality which Benjamin had to adopt.

Unlike Benjamin, Adorno endeavours to avoid both the 'transcendental intervention' that is the Messianic revolution and resur-
rection that *concludes history*, and any position purely within that
socio-historical reality, that is the political realism of mere
adaption, that *leaves the world at least as it is*. Adorno distinguishes 'progress' just as sharply from transcendental 'redemption' as
he does from its opposite, the merely factual 'course of history'.[99]
'Progress' is neither a pure 'idea' nor pure 'facticity'.[100] 'Idea' here
stands for Benjamin's Messianism, and 'facticity' for the vulgar
Marxian reduction of progress to its technical dimension. Adorno
wishes to attain a vantage point half-way between 'idea' and 'facticity' – and to this extent, although watering down Benjamin's
Messianism, he nevertheless adopts it. To this end, he retains a
'secularized in some manner or other' and yet 'ineradicable' 'element of redemption' in his concept of progress. This *renewed
weakening* of Messianism enables Adorno to adopt a more relaxed
attitude toward the achievements of a merely 'social democratic',
profane form of progress, achievements to which no one could
object. Adorno explains this with an example:

Anyone who modestly rubs their hands with satisfied glee when remembering the Titanic – because was it not the ice-berg which first holed the notion of progress – forgets or chooses to leave out the fact that this by no means fateful accident prompted measures to be introduced which prevented unplanned natural disasters in shipping in the fifty years thereafter. It is part and parcel of the dialectics of progress that the historical set-backs which are themselves triggered by the principle of progress . . . also lay the grounds which enable humankind to find means of avoiding them in the future. It is mediated in terms of that order which would instill the category of progress with true validity, in that the devastations which progress cause can at most be repaired *by its own powers*, and never by re-establishing the older state which fell victim to it.

Here Adorno goes against Benjamin's voluntarism of disasters which is a kind of fatalism:

The progresses in the exploitation of nature, which in Benjamin's image runs counter to true progress, the telos of which is redemption, is not without all hope. The two concepts of progress communicate with each other not first by averting the final catastrophe but rather in every current instance of ongoing suffering being alleviated.[101]

We thus become aware of how true progress relies and depends on the progress in the exploitation of nature, at a point below Benjamin's 'angel's view' of history. This dependence is based on the distinction Benjamin stresses between *technological* and *ethical* progress, a distinction deriving from Kant and Rousseau. Only from the perspective of this distinction is a differentiated assessment of 'social democratic' progress possible. For it is only *blind* to the extent, as Benjamin himself notes, that it 'recognizes only the progress in the mastery of nature, not the retrogression of society'.[102] However, this blindness can be corrected by the usual learning processes and considerations, and for such a correction (in most cases) neither the '*weak* messianic power' of a 'revolution' is needed, nor even the 'transcendental intervention *per se*' which Adorno rejects.

7. Truth is set by Schönberg

Initially Adorno's study of philosophy was only a diversion for him. In the early 1920s his area of interest was musical criticism and aesthetics, and his dream was to compose. Between 1921 and 1931 he published nearly 100 works on composition, mostly critiques for radio. At the end of this period Adorno was a respected and feared music critic who relentlessly sided with the Schönberg School.

The music scene in Frankfurt at the time was in fact very open to modernist influences. Hermann Scherchen, for a time chief conductor of the museum concerts, was himself an early champion of the Vienna avantgarde. Under his direction, in the summer of 1923 the major Frankfurt Musical Festival took place, with pieces by Schönberg, Schreker, Stravinsky, Bartók, Busoni, Delius, and Hindemith, among others. Even Kurt Weill, who was not yet an established figure at the time, was, as Adorno wrote in an unpublished review, represented by a 'skilful, if still clearly incomplete quartet'. The young critic praised Scherchen for having concentrated on the music, for having forgone 'social pomp', for having 'avoided the cult of the virtuoso conductor', as well as for his refusal to make concessions to the 'coarse conception of music by the larger public, which emphasizes enjoyment' and he thanked Scherchen for not having confined the programme to one nation. In this review Adorno expressly regrets the absence of contemporary French musicians (caused by the French occupation of the Rhineland) who promised to be 'a good corrective to German music, which originates in a tragic being and deep impatience'. From the very beginning Adorno was a follower of the age of 'New Music' and its disenchanting constructionism, that echoed the then new functionalism in architecture. The late romanticism of the Wagner age, with its bathos of depth and fate, its long since hollow 'glorification of life and death' was the declared enemy of new music and the atonality which it championed. Adorno, having just gained his doctorate in philosophy, admired Hindemith's 'cruel demystification' of romanticizing obfuscation, but also warned against the dangers of irrationalism in Hindemith's music, its 'moody nature', apparently inimical to all civilization, and the way 'the soul's origins broke to the surface in it'.[103]

The closer Adorno's connections to the Schönberg School became, the more hostile he was to any abbreviations of Schönberg. Early in 1925 the young Adorno went to Vienna as the pupil of Alban Berg, to be trained as a composer and concert pianist. 'Everything Schönbergesque is sacred', he wrote on 8 March to

Kracauer, adding the ominous note, 'otherwise only Mahler is approved of these days, and whoever opposes is derided'. In the newspaper *Die Musik* he exalted Schönberg's authority in unconditional terms: 'it is not proper for any critic to oppose the contemporary works of Schönberg; truth is set by them'.[104]

Despite his emotional fascination with Schönberg, the early Adorno, who was far more successful as a critic than as a composer, remained entirely rational in his quest for an aesthetic for the new music. Schönberg's twelve-tone technique was entirely systematic and as such represented in Adorno's eyes the decisive advance from nature and immediacy to technical media-producing art in a 'rationalizing process of European music'. It was to him no less than art's demythologization: 'the material has become clearer and freer and eradicates for all time the mythical conditions of number, as they dominate high tone lines and tonal harmony'.[105]

With great enthusiasm Adorno simultaneously launched two careers after his formal education was complete: those of philosopher and musician. But in the mid-1920s both came to a halt. Adorno had to give up the dream of being a composer and put his post-doctoral thesis for starting his academic career as a 'Privatdozent' on hold. After his successful doctoral thesis on Husserl's transcendental phenomenology in 1923 Adorno worked on his post-doctoral thesis on Freud and Kant ('Der Begriff des Unbewußten in der transzendentalen Seelenlehre') in 1927. In this book he tried to make compromises with both of his academic teachers, with Cornelius and Cornelius's assistant Horkheimer. This led to a split in his thesis. The main part of it was Cornelian and entailed a more or less Neo-Kantian critique of Freud's notion of 'unconsciousness'. Yet the end of the thesis, Adorno tried to deal with Horkheimer's Marxism by adding a critical defence of Freud as a paradigm of a materialistic theory of society and its social-psychological substructure. Adorno emphasized the social preconditions of psychoanalytical therapy. Where a neurosis was primarily socially conditioned, therapy was proposed to be useless. Unfortunately this explication of his thesis for Cornelius was not Kantian enough and for Horkheimer not Marxian enough. Angrily Adorno withdrew his thesis.

After he was failed by Cornelius, he only succeeded in finishing his post-doctoral thesis in 1933 with Paul Tillich. He was also only able to teach a few semesters. In 1933 Adorno was one of the first victims of the anti-Semitic job bans which no longer allowed German Jews to become civil servants. After futile attempts to enrol as a journalist and piano teacher, he went in 1934 to England in order to continue his studies at Oxford. Once there he came to know the analytic philosopher Gilbert Ryle, whose thought admittedly had little effect on his own. After a final visit to Frankfurt in 1937 Adorno flew to New York, where he became a member of Horkheimer's Institute for Social Research. His first task in the Institute was to oversee the musical component of the Radio Research Project headed by Paul Lazarsfeld. After some initial difficulties, Adorno became a highly skilled empirical social researcher both during his subsequent years in America and after his return to postwar Germany. Benjamin's micrological method proved to be helpful in his development as a researcher. Adorno subsequently proved so successful in his social research in Germany that long after his death an entire strand of social research, termed 'objective hermeneutics', is still based on his methodology.[106]

8. Exile is not an adventure

The one-sided, controversial, but brilliant account of Adorno's multifaceted and ambiguous experiences of exile is his theory of the culture industry developed in the *Dialectic of Enlightenment* and in numerous other individual studies. His thesis is that in the age of Hollywood and television the enlightenment risks turning into mass deception. Kant's depiction of art as 'purposiveness without a purpose' had become, as it was called in a polemic formulation replete with black irony, 'purposivelessness with a purpose': the instrumental nihilation of the meaning of life. Holding to the *difference* between enlightenment and mass deception, Adorno denounced the culture industry as a betrayal of the original intentions of the enlightenment. Its consciousness-raising critique undermined Benjamin's one-sidedly favourable rescuing critique of the cinema, jazz, and of entertainment.

Where Benjamin saw a great chance for a revolutionary transformation of art by the new technical mass media, Adorno and Horkheimer were much more sceptical. They both emphasized the obvious power of the new media in fascist dictatorships, their manipulative potential to impose the will on the leaders to passive scholar and intellectual. It was not until he arrived there, in New York and in Santa Monica on the shores of the Pacific Ocean, that the gravity of lived life was instilled with negativism: 'But life does not live.' The first section of *Minima Moralia*, written in 1944 in California, starts with this motto by Ferdinand Kürnberger, an adage that exposes the tautological conservatism of the German philosophy of life as precisely that. The experience of the persecuted and expelled individual causes utopia, in the face of the largest of all oceans, to shrink to the size of a message in a bottle. It will at some point perhaps land on a distant shore in the future, should a fortunate Messianic wind be blowing, to be opened by an unknown person who cannot otherwise be reached.

It was this spirit in which the *Dialectic of Enlightenment* was written. Enlightenment was totalitarian, science a mirror of hierarchy and repression, reason entwined with domination – this is the thesis of the first chapter on the concept of enlightenment. And the first excursus of the book explained the mythological and historical origins of instrumentalism and the totalitarian one-sidedness of enlightened European thinking. The origins were to be found in the story of Odysseus's adventures. For Adorno and Horkheimer, Odysseus was the 'first bourgeois' who sacrificed his whole self and all its dreams and wishes to the myth of a self-dominating consciousness. The history of the origin of the autonomous subject shows the heteronomy behind the subject's will and freedom and depicts the illusory character of that freedom and its prize: the domination and annihilation of the subject's own inner nature. The dark side of enlightenment can be discovered, as the second chapter of the book explains, by reading Kant and De Sade together. What in Kant's moral subject is forgotten is its origin in sadistic drives. De Sade is the forgotten truth of Kant's categorial imperative. All reification, the book claims, is a form of forgetting. In this claim Adorno and Horkheimer are very close to many German philosophers of the twentieth century. Philosophy and science for Heidegger is the reification of our life by means of the suppression of Being, for Husserl reification is caused by the scientific repression of life, for Benjamin it is the repression of true experience and authenticity, for Bloch the repression of utopia, and for Adorno and Horkheimer the repression of our inner nature. And this suppression and repression come back as 'reification', as a special blindness of modern technology or modern moral

and authoritarian masses of people. And that, Adorno and H
heimer in the famous chapter of the *Dialectic of Enlightenmen*
the cultural industry argued, was true not only in fascist coun
but also in democratic regimes like the USA and in totalitaria
authoritarian socialism such as the Soviet Union under Sta
regime as well.

All in all America remained foreign to Adorno. During his
Adorno never gave up the hope of coming back to Europe
Germany. His distance from American culture was not so far
the arrogant and ignorant 'distinction' of the old European
cated classes. It was not free of the élitist or mandarin habi
the German professor. This comes immediately from the first p
of a later essay on 'Scientific Experiences in America':

> I have never denied that from the very first to the very last day
> myself to be a European. As a matter of course I wished to pro
> the continuity of my intellectual life and I became fully consci
> this only too rapidly in the America. I still remember how, durii
> early days in New York, I was shocked by an emigrant like myse
> my wife, when she, daughter of a so-called good family, declared
> used to go to a philharmonic concert; now one goes to Radio C
> did not wish to emulate her in any way.[107]

But Adorno also experienced the *other* extreme:

> According to a tradition that opposes all civilization and dates b
> before Spengler, people think they are superior to the other cor
> because it has merely produced freezers and automobiles wherea
> many has spawned the culture of the Spirit. However, because th
> becomes rigid, becomes a purpose in itself, it also tends to let ge
> real humanity and to become self-satisfied. In America, by contra
> omnipresent feeling of being-for-others, of 'keep smiling' also e
> ages people to be sympathetic and participate in the lot of the v
> The energetic wish to establish a free society – instead of only an:
> positing freedom as a mental construct and voluntarily degradir
> self in submission in one's own thought – does not forfeit its be
> qualities merely because its realization is set limits by the social :
> Arrogance toward America in Germany is unjust. Abusing a
> ideal, it serves only the stuffiest of instincts.[108]

Adorno's mood in his exile in the Far West in Californ
not only troubled by this ambivalence of the educated Eur

deliberation as well. The technique is blind with respect to the ecology of the social system, the Kantian moralist blind to the ecology of the subject's inner nature. The repression of nature is the prize of rational moral freedom of the intellectual self. Justice in a realm of intelligible freedom is injust against its own 'material' or empirical subjectivity. Yet Horkheimer and Adorno never wanted to reject enlightenment, science, reason, morality as a whole. So they explicitly wrote in the foreword of their book that the critique of enlightenment was meant dialectically as a negative preparation for grounding a *new* and *better* concept of enlightenment to rescue reason against its own tendency to destroy itself. This does not come out in the book, which is overwhelmed by the dark mode of the American exile of its authors during the time of the Holocaust.

It was only once he was in exile that, or so Herbert Marcuse maintained, Adorno's 'fear of existence became so ensconced in his mind and body' that for him 'living and thinking became one and the same'.[109] The pain at the loss of his familiar European surroundings triggered infinite sorrow in him. In exile, Adorno claimed that he always noted down his dreams immediately after waking up. He later selected a certain number of them for publication; in them, impressions of America are mixed up with European locations. Scenes from Baudelaire and Delacroix take place on the Hudson River, an Arab army marches down Frankfurt's riverside road, and President Roosevelt receives Adorno in the Oval Office, until finally crocodiles with the heads of exceptionally beautiful women emerge from the Main River and put a seductive end to the dream. 'One encouraged me. Being eaten does not hurt. To make it easier for me she promised me the nicest things first.' The high bridge over the Silent Ocean has the colour of red sandstone (with which Adorno was so familiar from Amorbach in the Odenwald in Germany), when suddenly he and his Aunt Agathe turn up among Negro huts full of life before a gateway opens up through a cave and leads them out of the settlement: 'We stepped through it and found ourselves standing, quite moved by happiness, on the square in front of the Royal Residence in Bamberg: The Miltenberger "Schnatterloch".'[110]

Exile is 'no adventure', but rather Hitler's triumph:

> Late at night in the subway a young girl sat down opposite me, the only other passenger . . . Her clothing revealed her to be an emigrant

... What made her attractive was her poor and helpless appearance coupled with her stubborn insistence on her own grace. In the observer, pity, hardness and an absorbing desire intermingled. I had to smile; and I smiled at her. She pulled herself together and her tired face became covered with the sort of rejection she believed was lady-like. In Vienna, where she might have come from, or yet again in Berlin, she would have smiled back; ... in New York she forbid herself to do so, made herself unfriendly and pulled her skirt down over her slender knees. Do you not know, said the gesture, that we are in America ... ? Do you not know that we must start a new life? You are yourself an emigrant. But if you were really someone, you would not have to have yourself trundled home by the subway, but would have at least purchased your own automobile. Without knowing it, she obeyed the compulsions of an existence that had transformed her beauty into a natural monopoly – the only thing she was able to use when talking with powerful bosses, busy aid organizations, impatient relatives. Her very last possession was what she possessed least ... We must realize that the price we have to pay for life is that we no longer live ... I looked up and she immediately brushed her skirt down again: meanwhile she had no doubt crossed her legs again. That is Hitler's triumph, I thought. He has not only taken away our country, our language, and our money, but also confiscated that last little smile. The world he has created will soon make us as evil as he is ... However, we had arrived at my stop and I swiftly got out. At the kiosk up on street level I bought a 'Times' from the sleepy newspaper vendor and searched through it for news of victory ... There was no victory to be found in it. Sad and with the much too heavy paper under my arm, I walked down Broadway.[111]

The last sequence demonstrates nicely Adorno's infinite grief. The loss of his native Germany is expressed in his disgust for the voluminous and much too heavy New York newspaper.

When he returned to America in the 1950s to renew his American citizenship, he wrote to Horkheimer with an eye on the old Europe before his departure from Paris: 'Max. The unconditional: there is nothing else!'[112] He believed that America would no longer be able to conceive of the unconditional in the European tradition of education. But that was a blindness, from which even his sense for dialectic had not been able to protect him. Adorno never recognized the similiarities between pragmatism and unorthodox Western Marxisms like that of the Frankfurt School, which – in spite of some deep differences – were very strong (see Chap. 3, s. 4.)

Adorno never really understood liberal institutions and democratic politics which were successfully established in Western societies. In this respect, Adorno did not differ much from the German mandarin point of view (like that of Heidegger or Gehlen). Yet Adorno, in spite of all his critique in the *Dialectic of Enlightenment*, never scorned enlightenment. Even Nietzsche, whom Adorno admired, was in his reading Nietzsche the enlightener, the materialist critique of artificial bourgeois ideology. After the war, back in Germany, Adorno was a negativist and revolutionary utopian in theory, yet in praxis he was a social democratic reformer.

9. Cleared ruins: from re-education to positivism debate

Although after the war 'the ruins of Europe were cleared away', in Adorno's estimation European culture was still in ruins.[113] What he found upon his return was an university milieu stamped utterly with the *Geisteswissenschaften* or human sciences and a post-war culture that was open and liberated from the pressure of the Nazi domination. But he also found a young literature 'of which anything can be said, except that it is young'. In its texts Adorno felt himself recalling 'an army boot richly and carefully filled up with purple and golden brown foliage'. This resurrected culture combined a depoliticized discourse with a universalization of the provincial and an evident lack of 'explosive force, lust for adventure, even envy'. True intellectual passion corresponded to something circular, dead, rigid.[114] 'My seminar', he wrote in 1949 to Leo Löwenthal, 'is like a Talmud school . . . It is as if the ghosts of murdered Jewish intellectuals traveled into the German students. Completely eerie. But precisely in a true Freudian sense, it is also terribly familiar'.[115]

During his American exile, Adorno remained entirely a foreigner. His rigid and stable European distance allowed him all the more clearly to recognize the dark side of America's apparent progress. But upon his return to Europe he began to see the old continent with American eyes and from the alienating distance of his exile he noticed all the more strongly the barbarity of its remaining peculiarities.

Adorno was in opposition even when he returned to Germany. He was in opposition to the so-called *Geisteswissenschaft* which claimed to be value-neutral and not political at all. The *Geisteswis-senschaften* provided German professors with an ideology closely connected to the 'inner emigration' (*innere Emigration*) during the Hitler times. The Nazi past was repressed and the former Nazi professors became overnight mere scientists, who were never interested in politics and proclaimed they had been in 'silent opposition'. From the very beginning Adorno in Germany was more or less identified with 're-education', even if he himself was always deeply rooted in German cultural traditions. But Adorno now emphasized the enlightened and materialistic sides of that culture, even stronger than before 1933 and during his exile. The enlightened sides in German idealistic and romantic culture from Kant to Heine were still alive, but de-emphasized by the German mandarins, the professors from the *Geisteswissenschaften*. In their first great survey after 1945 in Germany Adorno and his fellow researchers from the Institute in Frankfurt – published as *Gruppenexperiment* (Group-Experiment) in the 1950s – one major result was that anti-Semitism in Germany even after the war was most significant in two social strata: the academic elites and the peasantry.

So Adorno at the beginning sharply criticized the *Geisteswissenschaften*, and only later, in the 'positivism-debate' of the late 1960s, returning to some of their approaches. Since the Frankfurt School had returned to the University of Frankfurt, Adorno rarely passed up an opportunity to emphasize that the newly opened Institute for Social Research was the avantgarde of empiricism. He also touted the superiority of modern statistical methods and analytic techniques over the old historistic belief in the world-disclosing power of the understanding (*Verstehen*). Ironically, as his scepticism about social-scientific empiricism steadily increased, he developed a career as a sociologist.

It was a long time before Adorno became a full professor in Germany. The position he finally received in 1957 was humiliatingly referred to as the 'consolation chair'. Adorno and Horkheimer were shunned and exposed to their colleagues' anti-Semitism. Adorno would never attain an entirely 'normal' position at a German university. Horkheimer bitterly noted: 'the majority of Germans who sympathized with National Socialism are today better off than those who opposed Fascism'. In 1959 Adorno – at the age of fifty-seven – became Horkheimer's successor as director of the Institute and after 1965 was twice chosen as chair of the Deutsche Gesellschaft für Soziologie. The positivist controversy became a key cultural-political topic. By 1968, it was evident that this controversy was an integral part of the cultural upheaval of the time. Adorno opened the Frankfurt 'Soziologentag' conference that year with the brilliant paper 'Late Capitalism or an Industrial Society?'[116] Adorno there defended the basically Marxian thesis that in its means of production modern society was an 'industrial' one, but in its class relations it still remained a capitalist society.

In his controversy with Karl Popper Adorno did not want to reduce the theory of society to a bundle of hypotheses for empirical falsification. Popper's basic ideas about social sciences were at that time connected with three ideas: (1) the idea of fallibilism that all theories had to expose themselves to falsification by withstanding experience; (2) the rejection of historicism: the idea that no historical prognosis is possible for reasons of the permanence of new inventions and new knowledge, which changes the course of history unexpectedly; (3) the idea of an objective understanding of history as a course of ideas that have become better and better, and more and more appropriate to objective truth by means of falsification. Adorno on all three levels had some agreement and some criticism.

He did not reject falsification, but he rejected the idea of binding *all* theory back to empirical research programmes or mere analytic tautology. For Adorno social theory could not be analysed like a deductive system. It was just the *critical* character of his theory that was opposed to empirical falsification by data from a *false reality* and a *false consciousness*. Adorno's fallibilism, different from that of Karl Popper, was not only fallibilistic in the attitude to his own theory but in the attitude to the social facts themselves. Facts, which were made by the historical praxis of a class-rooted society, themselves could be *false* in the sense of representing a wrong form of life. Insofar as they were false, critical theory had to oppose them instead of revising its own propositions. For Popper the direction of fit between theory and society was only from theory to society; for Adorno both directions of fit were possible. Theory could fit the facts, or reality could fit the critical and normative horizon of the theory. In the first case theory could be falsified, in the second 'reality' as a realm of social praxis should be falsified.

To Popper's second idea, expressed in his *Poverty of Historicism*, Adorno had no objections. The emphasis of his aesthetic and his political theory was the invention of new experiences, new views of the world, new knowledge and new social stuctures which were never predictable. But unlike Popper, Adorno, the co-author of *Dialectic of Enlightenment*, apprehended a state of human affairs in which new inventions could no longer be possible: his completely negative state of affairs that he called the 'administered world', the nightmare of the modern society. To Popper's last thesis about 'objective understanding' Adorno addressed the objection that progress in the history of ideas never could be conceptualized in terms of a cumulative appropriation to truth. Adorno did not deny the objectivity of 'progress' (as we have seen), but he conceived of 'progress' as a revolutionary process with breaks, 'jumps' and the permanent threat of regression which often enough became true. Adorno's idea about understanding ideas therefore was much more dialectical than that of Popper. (For the probable stance of Adorno towards the Kuhn–Popper controversy about a post-analytical philosophy of science see below, Chap. 3, s. 3.).

Adorno's message, communicated with marked success in the 1960s through his ever stronger criticism of mass culture, reached a broad range of editors who published his work and listeners who greedily awaited his next radio talk. Adorno was present in the cultural pages of the serious newspapers, lecture halls, and even occasionally on the televisions of the young republic. Intellectuals like Enzeusberger, even before Marcuse, strengthened Adorno's influence by popularizing his critique of culture. Adorno's friendship with cultural figures, like the Max-Planck Director Hellmut Becker, opened up access to the educational system. Moreover, the work of Jürgen Habermas secured for critical theory an academic reputation for years to come. Habermas and Oskar Negt developed new political dimensions of Adorno's economic critique, including even a radicalized form in the German Socialistic Student Organization. The latter, the SDS, formed the core of student radicalism which revolted against the institutions of late capitalism in the 1960s. With Alexander Kluge, Adorno's ideas set in motion the beginnings of the new German cinema. Adorno himself published an ongoing series of short pieces that appeared in the all leading German-speaking publications, such as *Akzente, Merkur, Neue Rundschau, Hessischer Rundfunk*, the *Sender Freies Berlin*, the

Frankfurter Allgemeine Zeitung, Frankfurter Rundschau, Die Zeit, Der Spiegel, and the *Neue Züricher Zeitung.* His work also appeared in more local newspapers like the *Darmstädter Echo* and the *Frankfurter Neue Presse,* in which he patiently responded to questions such as: 'What do you expect from the new year?' He protested against the emergency laws, speaking to the organizational committee for the Christian Jewish coalition, to meetings of the SDS, to conferences of the German council on architecture and functionalism, and to the European pedagogy conference on education after Auschwitz. He published in smaller journals as diverse as the business-orientated *Deutsche Post,* the *Rundfunk und Fernsehen,* and the *Volkshochschule im Westen.* To the idiotic query, 'About what did you laugh the most in 1966?', Adorno, the unrelenting critic of the German condition, responded with seriousness: 'An elected NPD official said in an interview: your laughter will soon disappear. For me in this year, it has already been long past. Couldn't you have expressed it better than with that ominous phrase?'[117] The NPD was the German Nationaldemokratische Partei, which was in fact a Neo-Nazi party with a lot of members of the old Nazi Party. They had surprising success in the elections during the 1960s, getting their members into the German Bundestag, the parliament. This is what had made Adorno's laughter disappear long before the ominous threat of the elected NPD official.

On 8 August 1969, shortly before the completion of *Aesthetic Theory* and while on vacation in the Swiss Valais, Adorno died of a heart attack, aged sixty-seven. His wife Gretel survived him. They had no children. In his writings, which with his increasing age were frequently written on the occasions of the birthdays or deaths of close friends, Adorno not only railed against the idea of a 'gerontocracy', or the intellectual dominance of an aged cultural elite, but also against the equally antiquated clandestine alliance between metaphysics and death. In the *Gratulor* on the occasion of Max Horkheimer's seventieth birthday, he recalled Kant's idea of immortality in a positive light. It gives us 'strength for opposition to nature's deterioration . . . , which is united in sympathy for oppressed nature'.[118] On the occasion of the death of his old friend Siegfried Kracauer he noted:

> the only thing that this life of thinking did not reflect upon, truly his blind spot, was death. Since it has now overtaken him, it pays back

what his own intentions struggled against: against all completive totality. Since he had to die, the most individual of all things, the universal
clamors.[119]

10. Advocate of the non-identical

The last citation crystallizes the most important themes of
Adorno's negative dialectic: the emphasis on the self-reflective conscious life, the metaphysical critical invective against all comprehensive and against speculative systematic thinking, and the plea
for the 'open' and 'experimental'. Adorno set this against false
totality and *extorted reconciliation,* an expression he used to char-
acterize Lukács's false compromises with a totalitarian totality.
The 'non-identical', the guiding motive of his thought, is the individual that recoils from being subsumed under universal concepts
and norms. The denials of the individual and the 'injury' against
the 'non-identical' became for Adorno a strong protest against the
existent (*das Bestehende*). Albrecht Wellmer correctly called
Adorno an *advocate of the non-identical.*[120]
    As we have seen in the Introduction, the 'non-identical' is the
individual that can never be completely fixed by any universal
description; it can always be newly described. Adorno here
sometimes refers to Spinoza's famous phrase: 'Individuum est
ineffabile', and explains the 'ineffabile' of the 'individuum' in his
words as the 'non-identical'. The 'blinding coherence' (*Ver-
blendungszusammenhang*) of which Adorno speaks refers to that
blinding of the subject that imagines itself to be in possession of
absolute truth and to be able to give a *definitive* description and
conception of the individual. In this critique of the overemphazised
subject that claims absolute truth or 'pure reason' for itself,
Adorno obviously follows the lines of a Kantian criticism. Another
aspect of the meaning of the *non-identical* is that it is the 'particular' over against the laws of the 'general'. The blinding of a simple
'subjective' centred upon the perspective of the ego and upon a
one-sided projection of a limited 'reason' Adorno also called *identitarian* thinking. Provided that it left its mark on a 'collective consciousness' (Durkheim) or a much broader 'occidental rationalism'
(Weber), Adorno could speak of a 'blinding coherence', with reference to comprehensive doctrines and world-views.

Claims about absolute or totalizing knowledge are presumptions about a human reason that is not conscious of its own limits. The claim of absolute enlightenment (certainty) always remains that of a finite, individual, and nature-enslaved being. In this respect human reason, if it believes it has understood the absolute truth and 'the whole', is forever not identical with itself. It is never completely transparent to itself, for our reason is itself something individual, a product of a process of individualization. Totalizing identitarian thinking is deceived about itself and its own history. But what eludes the identitarian self-knowledge of reason is the way in which reason itself has remained an opaque and impenetrable piece of 'nature'. Adorno thus understands the *Dialectic of Enlightenment* as an 'awareness of nature in a subject', that should recall for our reason the cognitively repressed 'primal history of subjectivity'.

Such achievements of memory in no way lead us back to the 'dull oppositionlessness' (Hegel) of nature-bound individuality. In *Negative Dialectics* Adorno writes that 'the illusion that we can get hold of the many immediately', in that we simply achieve a renunciation of reason, science, and the reflective power of the identitarian thinking, 'would smack of a mimetic regression into mythology and back into the horror of the diffuse'.[121] Worse than the blindness of identitarian thinking would be a regression into the barbarity of dull life without opposition. Therefore we can escape from the forgetfulness of our thinking and the blindness of our reason only inasmuch as we seek to make identitarian thinking visible with the tools of constructive rationality: the self-eluding individual of our nature-bound finite existence. Adorno thus demanded not a dismissal of reflection, but a development of a *second reflection*: not a return into the immediate and undivided, but a continuation of the mediations and differentiations of thinking to the point of a *second immediacy*. This occurs inasmuch as it also demands not the romantic cessation of affirmative art, which clarifies and glorifies what exists, but the bold construction of a *second language*. Adorno's main examples here are as elsewhere works of art. They gain a *second language* only through *more* technique and complete domination of material, not through pretechnical expressivity (see Chapter 4.)[122]

Adorno had developed these philosophical views much earlier in several works. Most notable among them was his 1931 inaugural lecture on the *Actuality of Philosophy*.[123] Preceding this was his (never to be submitted) post-doctoral thesis first published post-humously as the *Begriff des Unbewußten in der transzendentalen Seelenlehre*. Similar ideas were also developed in the post-doctoral thesis (the German 'Habilitation') he did later submit entitled *Kierkegaard's Construction of the Aesthetic* and published in 1931, which owed much to Kracauer and Benjamin. Adorno's inaugural lecture was – as Susan Buck-Morss has shown – his first blueprint of the idea of a negative dialectic.[124]

Since Adorno saw the *Actuality of Philosophy* as a practice of thought, he distinguished it sharply from scientific explanation. Philosophy is a second *reflection*, but as an interpretative activity it remains related to the first reflection of scientific explanation. Philosophy is no less experimental and constructive than science, since it operates with 'models' and develops new 'orders of research'. It relies not upon original forces, but only upon the knowledge, reflection, and identitarian thinking that had long since dismantled and divided up 'prefounded' actuality into its 'elements'. The aesthetic paradigm of that method is the principle of collage. You have first an 'idea', a 'theory' of constructing an image (e.g. a neo-Kantian philosophy like some of the cubist painters), then on the background of that 'idea' or 'theory' you have to destroy an old and conventional unity (e.g. tear up a newspaper), then to put some of its parts into a new context (e.g. pieces of newspaper in a more traditional painting) and vary it until (with good luck) a new figure with some new interpretative sense appears out of the decontextulized old material (e.g. an early Picasso). *Interpretation (Deutung)* always begins with the *difference* (Hegel's *Entzweiung* or '*bifurcation*') between identity and non-identity or between reflection and the thing. What the detachment of reflection shows is the contingency of the old unity, things must not be as they are, they could be different, you can change the arrangement of elements. What is in the end disclosed to interpretation as truly 'by convincing evidence' *is only* the result of an experimental and operative praxis, since it takes everything that it arranges for investigation from pre-established actuality. Thus the *essay* is, in the true meaning of the term 'research' (*Versuch*), the proper form of philosophical interpretation.[125]

Decades later this gave rise to the publication on the *Essay as Form* which Adorno in 1958 published before his *Notes on Literature*. The essay technique of exposition, which Adorno's work

utilized even in his large systematic texts, meant to preclude every
representation of a 'second distant world developed through the
analysis of the apparent world'. This representation was the core
of the subjectivist projection of an absolute truth in the world from
without. In this scheme, the true is disclosed to us more as simply
the result of our own praxis. Out of the pre-found elements it 'crystallizes' a new constellation that fits exactly our problems and
inner-worldly 'puzzles', like the correct 'combination' of the lock
of the 'well-secured safe'.[126] In his inaugural lecture, Adorno
argued that 'whoever interprets by seeking a world in itself behind
appearances acts as one who wants to find in a puzzle the representation of a deeper Being, which the puzzle mirrors'.[127] This is the
age-old platonic method, which Adorno rejects. For the

> task of philosophy is not to research the hidden and immediate inten-
> tions of actuality, but to interpret the intentionless actuality, inasmuch
> as the power of the construction of figures . . . sublates the questions
> out of the isolated elements of the actuality. These are the questions
> whose pregnant composure is the task of science; a task to which philo-
> sophy always remains bound, because its illuminatory power is not
> capable of illuminating anything other than those hard questions.[128]

From Adorno's earliest writings, a pragmatic theory of truth, as
close to American pragmatism as to the early Heidegger, replaced
the platonic image–reproduction–representation relation of the
correspondence theory of truth with an action–experience relation.
Adorno here follows an active view of knowledge on the lines of
Kant and Marx. *Negative Dialectics*, conceived over thirty years
later, is in essence the exposition of this idea whose seeds Adorno
had sown in his inaugural lecture. While still in exile in England
Adorno worked on a lengthy study of Husserl, which appeared in
1956 with the title *Zur Metakritik der Erkenntnistheorie*. It clearly
rejects all philosophy of origins (*Ursprungsphilosophie*) and all
claims to final grounds and final justification.[129]

   The mistaken metaphysical idea of a foundationalism for
Adorno is the result of a subject-centred projection. This type of
projection is also at the centre of Adorno's interest in social
research. His questioning of egocentrism is not (as in Heidegger or
Husserl) restricted to philosophical critique and a critical reading
of the history of ideas. As important, and maybe more so, is

normal scientific research in the field of projection and prejudice in everyday life.

In the New York Institute under the direction of Horkheimer, Adorno worked primarily on his study of the culture industry and on the social psychology of prejudice. Particularly notable is his 'The Fetish Character of Music and the Regression of Listening', in *Zeitschrift für Sozialforschung* from the later 1930s, which was his pessimistic reply to Walter Benjamin's more optimistic essay on 'The working out in the epoch of its Technical Reproduction'. The studies of the 1930s ushered in those of the 1940s, especially his chapter on the culture industry in the *Dialectic of Enlightenment*, and then later his study of the *Authoritarian Personality*. The latter made the Frankfurt School instantly famous in the academic world and is the reason why the inclusion of the F and A scales of character types he developed is still a stable component of research on prejudice. These character types were the subjects of a whole series of research projects in America in the 1950s and 1960s.

Another important object of Adorno's empirical research was the mechanism of the subject-centred projection of objective truth onto the foreign and alienating world of others (races, peoples, minorities, foreigners, intellectuals, etc.). He summarizes this socio-psychological research of the Institute in a chapter in the *Dialectic of Enlightenment* co-authored with Leo Löwenthal: 'Anti-semitism is based upon a false projection. Mimesis imitates the environment, but false projection makes the environment like itself.'[130] 'Mimesis' for Adorno is a complex notion, to which I shall return in Chapter 4, section 2. Here it means an attitude to one's natural and social environment and to other people and other things that does not compel this otherness to be under one's own will. Mimesis in the sense Adorno is using the word here means to do 'justice' to the otherness of the other, and to react adequately to the latter's own aptitudes and concerns. 'False projection' conversely means the projection of an image that does not fit with the otherness of the other, one's own egocentric image of the world. False projection makes everything its own image.

Horkheimer and Adorno interpreted the false projection of anti-Semitism as an extreme case of identity thinking. While they see in 'true mimesis' a strong ego's achievement of a genuine decentring, false projection harshly turns one's ego into the centre of a world that is either the 'weak or all powerful total concept of all that is projected onto it'.[131] Thus the racist represents a person crazed by the complementary drives of both greatness and success. 'The closed circle of eternal sameness becomes a substitute for omnipotence. It is as though the serpent which said to the first men "you will be as God" had redeemed its promise in the paranoiac. He makes everything in his own image.'[132]

In social research as well as in art criticism or in philosophical interpretation Adorno turns out to be an advocate of the non-identical – an advocate of the difference of 'the other' and the knowledge and acknowledgement of such difference. Thought can never entirely capture being. But we have to try: 'to transcend our conceptual framework only by means of its own concepts' (*im Begriff über den Begriff hinausgelangen*).[133]

11. An ethic of damaged life

At the end of the Second World War, Adorno finished *Minima Moralia* and the *Dialectic of Enlightenment*. Both books contained an extremely pessimistic diagnosis of the times. The hopes provided by science and enlightenment in the 1930s appeared irrevocably dashed:

> Even though we had known for many years that the great discoveries of applied science are paid for with an increasing diminution of theoretical awareness, we still thought that in regard to scientific activity our contribution could be restricted to the criticism or extension of specialist axioms . . . However, the fragments united in this volume show that we were forced to abandon this conviction . . . In the present collapse of bourgeois civilization not only the pursuit but the meaning of science has become problematical in that regard.[134]

But appearances deceived. Both works tried in such conditions to hold onto the enlightenment without any idealistic illusions and metaphysical hopes, which appeared virtually to exclude an actualization of enlightenment reason. One should read them, as the subtitle of the *Dialectic of Enlightenment* reminds us, as 'philosophical fragments', so neither as an ongoing history of philosophy nor as a simple negative. For a correct understanding one must keep in mind Adorno's method, the essay as form, and read these as philosophical interpretations, models, and attempts at ordering.

Then they are disclosed in their double function as *diagnoses of the times* and as a radical *thought-experiment* that investigates the limit of an enlightenment under conditions of its opposite. The *Dialectic of Enlightenment* has to do with the historical and social conditions of the reason justified by it. Under these conditions, theory threatens to be assimilated to technique, praxis to universal accommodation, and art to industry.

The aims of *Minima Moralia* are immediately practical in a similar way: the aphorisms sketch an ethic of damaged life. The question is how correctness can possibly exist in the damaged life of modernity. The answer is apodeictic: 'there is no true life in a false one'. But that does not mean that there is no possibility of right *action*; the thesis confirms only that there is no *entirely* true life in a false life. But thus it is still a long way from the claim, as Nietzsche suggested, that everything is allowed. Every individual act can still be judged as to its rightness or wrongness. Moreover, the actions and characteristic traits of modern man and the various aspects and all individual moments of his lifeworld are accessible to moral evaluation. *Minima Moralia* is nothing other than a collection of such judgements, for example, the judgement, that 'In many people it is already an impertinence to say "I" '. (One thinks of a German economic minister who, opening an automotive show, declares: 'everyone knows that *I* am fond of large and fast cars'.[135])

Moreover, Adorno's thesis only confirms that *no true life* would be possible in the case of a completely false life. But this does not mean that a *non-forfeited* life cannot be imagined. The *double negation*, Hegel's logical insight that always guided Adorno, is in no way identical with a simple affirmation concerning our ethical relationships. Moreover, *Minima Moralia* are 'reflections from damaged life', as the subtitle confirms, and the damaged life *is not yet* the completely false life. The message is that one must prevent damage from becoming complete destruction. It is similarly true of frequently cited aphorisms like: 'The whole is the untrue'. This phrase does not mean that there is no truth in the world, no true statements, and no right actions. The content of the sentence simply takes deadly aim at the core of Hegelian metaphysics by proclaiming that truth cannot be expressed as a whole either by society or by history. Adorno thus presents first and foremost a critique of a metaphysics that represents a totalizing reason. Such a critique of totalizing reason, though it is in many ways similar to the critiques of Nietzsche, Heidegger, and the postmodern deconstructionists, is just as far from them as it is from the old transfiguring metaphysics.[136] Adorno's rejection of the claim 'The whole is the true', is primarily Kantian, with the polemic converse: 'The whole is the untrue'. Adorno makes explicit the antinomy that is latent with Hegel's famous statement.

The critique of metaphysics in *Negative Dialectics* is salutary, not damaging, aiming to determine the truth of metaphysics in the process of overcoming it. The critique 'is in solidarity with metaphysics in the moment of its fall'. But it wants neither an exaltation of the new nor a rehabilitation of the old. 'It has to do with the absolute, but one broken and intermediate', without any claim to 'completive unities'.[137]

In Adorno's sociological deliberations on the social structure of late capitalism the tension between pessimism and hope, which is at the core of Adorno the philosopher, is concretized as the tension between the cultural potential of *modernism* and the reified social structures of *modernity*. Next I provide some explanation of this important distinction.

12. Modernism versus modernity

In 1968, at the peak of the student's revolt, Adorno gave an interview to the German periodical *Der Spiegel*. The notorious question *Der Spiegel* asked was: 'And what about a positive view, Prof. Adorno?' He answered on occasion with Erich Kästner's rhetorical question 'Yes, where has it got to?', thus alluding to social conditions which hardly gave grounds for a positive report. Adorno would also, however, have insisted that negation and critique are some of the best qualities we possess, and that such a negative form of reason was not nothing, but already *here and now* a stubbornly effective power. This power is not 'without a place', not utterly utopian. Its place in society is culture, or, for Adorno, above all the 'counter-institutions' of modern art (see below, Chap. 4).

In his sociology, Adorno combines Marxist themes derived from a radical critique of *modern society* and the form in which its economy is organized, with derived themes taken from a no less radical, *cultural modernism*. His critique of the way modern societies are organized is aimed at far-reaching targets: the social injustice of capitalist relations of production and private forms of appropriation; the imperial power of economic exploitation; the manipulative force of the culture industries; the destruction of the outside world of nature; and the domination of enforced asceticism over humans' inner nature, of a formalistic and technicistic science. This critique, in a nutshell, attacks the 'administered world'. Adorno also always stressed the male and patriarchal character of bourgeois and pre-bourgeois rule. In other words, on many points his critique appeared to go hand in hand with the discomfort with and critique of modern society shown by the protest and emancipation movements of the second half of the twentieth century.

However, Adorno's critique of economy and society tries to remain *immanent*. Immanent critique confronts the potential and normative utopian horizon of a given society with its more or less bad realizations. Critique which is immanent distinguishes sharply, and this is its orthodox Marxist core, between the technological and organizational opportunities and the particularist ways in which they have been implemented. And it distinguishes, this being its heterodox trait, the regulative notion of freedom and the form of reason already realized in *cultural* modernity from the affirmative functions of a traditional cultural superstructure – which Adorno termed the horrific vision of 'traditionalism without a valid tradition'. The materialist cultural critique he offers of the bourgeois superstructure is *orthodox*. A formulation in his *Aesthetic Theory* is typical of this tack: 'The bourgeois wants art to be opulent and life to be ascetic. It would be better the other way round.'[138] The deliberate mobilization of the potential for rationality embodied in cultural modernity in order to enable the (self-)critique of culture and society is *heterodox* in relation to Marxism. Here, the power of a post-traditional consciousness of radical enlightenment to dissolve prejudices is mobilized; it is a consciousness promoted by the critical social sciences and modern art and which is also fostered by such blessed institutions as universal education, for all the latter's disciplining impact. Adorno's critique of society does not *define* itself in terms of the distinction between what, in his Marxist opinion, was long since technologically possible (the abolition of hunger, the minimization of forms of social injustice, etc.), on the one hand, and the repressive forms of *social* progress, on the other. This critique also rests on the affirmative reference to the *cultural* progress already achieved in demystification, and on the factual unleashing of the innovative potential of culture: the 'bold hypothesis' (Popper) of a 'prior' 'project' (Heidegger, Sartre) of 'daring thought' (Adorno).

Whereas modern conservatism now relies affirmatively on the functional order of society in order to denounce cultural modernism as dysfunctional (an example would be Daniel Bell's opposition of *modernity to modernism*[139]), Adorno's critique has the opposite thrust. It is aimed at the dysfunctional traits of functional orders, namely the counter-productive effects of the accumulation of capital and power. The *modernity* of society must be measured in terms of the *modernism* of culture.

Adorno's image of society is by no means as closed as might occasionally appear to be the case. Adorno believes that modern society and its culture together generate the total and totalitarian unity of a completely *integrated system* within which everything could be different, but no one can bring this about. However, the image also includes something quite contrary that perceives the *dissonances* in the monotony of the whole and these *tear* the whole *asunder*, ambivalently threatening destruction *and* enticing us with unconstrained fulfilment. However much society has really become what Adorno terms a 'system', nevertheless its metaphysical 'conclusive' integration into an unalterable totality, and Adorno insists on this fact, is mere appearance. It is merely an overarching context of illusion, a spell, one which can and must dissolve, and which is already shot through with cracks, and is riddled with holes through which occasionally a weak Messianic light of utopia can fall onto the seemingly administered world.

Adorno's negative view of modern society stems from a no less consistent affirmation of its cultural modernism. *This* affirmation is reconcilable with the negativism. For the reflective potential of a methodical negativism has long since been *institutionalized* in cultural modernism. The affirmation of modernism, which renders it possible to criticize modernity from within, amounts to the affirmation of a negative reason already *embodied* in modern culture. In his *Aesthetic Theory*, Adorno therefore insists that freedom is realized to a certain extent in modern art.[140] Such freedom is based on the ever possible, negative stance toward all the pregiven facts of society and the lifeworld. Such a freedom, or so Adorno believed, was not only embodied by art, but also by the autonomous thought of an intellectualist philosophy, by critical social research, by social research based on ideology critique, and also by the cognitive and technological knowledge that defines the productive forces. Yet in the last respect Adorno was much more a sceptic than in the former. If it could not be guarded and corrected by intellectual critique, the spontaneous development of productive forces would lead to 'purposivelessness with a purpose' in culture,[141] and to self-destruction in society.

2 • Enlightenment of Rationality: Critical Remarks on Horkheimer and Adorno's *Dialectic of Enlightenment*

1. Enlightenment as critique

Enlightenment and rationality are intertwined, and they hang together so closely that they could be identified with each other. Enlightenment is rationality and rationality is enlightenment. But the mutual identification of enlightenment and rationality is not beyond its own historicization. It depends on our reading and historical understanding of both terms. Not all paradigms of rationality are compatible with a particular understanding of enlightenment and vice versa. There exists always a variety of readings of what 'enlightenment' and 'rationality' mean, and some of them contradict one another. For example, the metaphorical meaning of 'enlightenment', as it was used in the eighteenth century, follows directly an older reading of 'rationality' as being man's natural light, the *lumen naturale*, which originated in Stoic and Christian philosophy hundreds of years earlier. But this reading of 'rationality' as a natural substance does not withstand the enlightened criticism of the nineteenth and twentieth centuries.

This is a major thesis of the first chapter of the book of Horkheimer and Adorno, where they define 'enlightenment' in Weberian terms as the progress of 'disenchantment' and 'rationalization'.[1] In accordance with Hegel and Max Weber, rationality for Horkheimer and Adorno does not mean a mere conceptual scheme or notion but is conceived as an integral part of the social reality. It is in Hegelian terms an 'existing concept'.[2] For Adorno and Horkheimer – and here they meet Heidegger and Foucault – this means that rationality is always already related to technology, domination and power internally.[3] Technology, they write, 'is the essence' of enlightened knowledge.[4] 'The power of domination and cognition are synonymous terms', and the universal concepts of old

European, platonist or Cartesian philosophy are expressions of the domination over 'women, children and slaves'.[5]

In the course of history completely enlightened rationality has transformed 'Rationality' into 'rationality', or to put it in Horkheimer's terms, enlightenment's radical criticism has dissolved 'objective reason' and left us with 'subjective reason'.[6] Enlightenment is persistent self-criticism and self-destruction of rationality, replacing old and refuted readings of rationality with new ones that fit better the changing problems of history and society. Truth is internally connected with time: *Wahrheit hat einen Zeitkern*[7] ('Truth has a time index'). *Dialect of Enlightenment* is a particular contribution to that enlightenment of rationality by means of its own self-reflective or critical power. It is particular insofar as it claims to enlighten a specific 'blindness' of preceding enlightenment processes. There are a lot of formulations which paraphrase this blindness. They speak of 'blinded pragmatized thinking', 'unreflective enlightened thinking', 'blind domination of nature', 'false projection', 'self-preservation which is unbroken by reflection' or – as Horkheimer called it in another book – 'instrumental reason'.[8]

2. Enlightenment of enlightenment

The attempt by Horkheimer and Adorno to enlighten enlightenment and rationality is directed (1) against the myth or fetishism of technology and the absolutization of mere technological or scientific rationality, (2) against rationality in the service of class-domination, and (3) against the repressive exclusion of the other, the unreasonable, the alien, the idiot, the outsider, and last not least the 'undomesticated' nature or life, what Adorno calls its 'mimetic impulse'.[9]

These criticisms are more or less in accordance with a broad stream of postmetaphysical thinking, beginning with early romanticism and Hegel, whom Horkheimer and Adorno call the very founder of the 'dialectic of enlightenment'.[10] The first criticism of the myth of technological rationality *on the one hand* is a variation of the criticism of the 'reification of universals' and any objectivistic understanding of linguistic meaning.[11] (See below, Chap. 3, s. 3.) The early Horkheimer – as we have seen – vehemently criticizes any idea of ultimate truth and eternal meaning, the 'bifurcation of the world in two mutually independent realms', the 'dualism of thought and being, of understanding and perception'.[12] What he rejects is the demotion of the known world to something utterly external that follows from the hypostasization of logos which is the Cartesian heritage in modern scientific or technological rationality.[13] In one of the aphoristic sketches in the appendix of the book Horkheimer goes so far as to identify the division of life into spirit and object with the original historical cause of the resentment of a gang of Nazi killers.[14] *On the other hand* Horkheimer's and Adorno's criticism of the 'absolutism' of instrumental reason, which blows it up to the one and only type of rational behaviour, is in accordance with the 'postmodern' or 'postmetaphysical' insight that the plurality of different discourses and language games cannot be overcome by one of them or any higher meta-discourse. If blinded or unreflective enlightened thinking takes scientific rationality as the one and only language of truth, then enlightenment becomes 'totalitarian'.[15]

The second criticism which is directed against the intertwining of rationality and domination can be compared with John Dewey's criticism of Plato. Dewey rejects Plato's metaphysical Rationalism (with capital 'R') for being in the particular interest of a ruling elite of aristocrats, but he praises Plato for his utopian project of general education.[16] In the same manner Horkheimer raises the objection against platonic rationalism that it stands in the service of transfiguration of a class-society, but he defends the materialistic tradition of social utopianism against the unholy alliance between optimistic metaphysics and social pessimism.[17] (See below, Chap. 3, s. 4.) This subversive dimension of materialistic utopism is a dimension, Horkheimer suggests, that we can find even in Plato and great idealistic philosophy. Materialistic utopianism is a latent dimension of idealism, often concealed by its rationalism. But the subversive potential of idealism can be discovered by an intelligent criticism of ideology. This motif returns in the *Dialectic of Enlightenment* when its authors draw a sharp distinction between the 'utopia' of enlightenment and the 'rage' of enlightenment's 'Ratio' against that utopian ideal:[18]

> Kant's concepts are ambiguous: As a transcendental, supraindividual self, reason comprises the idea of a free, human social life in which men

organize themselves as the universal subject and overcome the conflict between pure and empirical reason in the conscious solidarity of the whole. This represents the idea of true universality: utopia. At the same time, however, reason constitutes the court of judgement of calculation, which adjusts the world for the ends of self-preservation and recognizes no function other than the preparation of the object from mere sensory material in order to make it the material of subjugation.[19]

The former, subversive concept of reason includes the 'secret utopia' of a 'common interest' that contradicts the surrounding Rationalism of pure scientific rationality and purposive-rational action.[20] Whereas enlightenment's utopia designs a 'community of free men' for the purpose of realizing heaven on earth – 'happiness without power, wages without work, a home (*Heimat*) without frontiers, religion without myth' – enlightenment's 'ratio' 'prepares its object' as 'material of subjugation'.[21] Insofar that 'ratio' is the 'reason of domination' which appears 'completely functionalized in favour of the established bourgeois order', ratio is the iron cage of 'utopia', from which utopia should liberate itself.[22]

The third criticism, the exclusion of the other, originates from romantic sources. Today it constitutes the politics of deconstructionists, poststructuralists and postmodernists. Dazzled by the bright light of enlightenment's Rationalism, we are not able to see those 'who stand in dark' (Brecht). If a society introduces reason as a mechanism of social integration, then it seems to include the exclusion of the unreasonable and the mad, and all the prerational colonial areas of the white man, minors, the primitive, the uncivilized, women. To this category belong all the enemies of civilization, whom Foucault has called the 'infamous man'.[23] One of the central theses of Horkheimer's and Adorno's book is that the history of all social class-domination originates from the repression of women's nature by male rationality.[24] The 'postmodernist' criticism of the excluding mechanisms of Western universalism was anticipated by the *Dialectic of Enlightenment*, and it leads towards a strong commitment to the lost cases of Western societies, those of the humiliated, the impossible, and the expelled. This political criticism of the system demolishes its high-handed identity, an achievement, Terry Eagleton writes, for which one could 'forgive the postmodernists nearly all of their outrages excesses'.[25] Unlike postmodernism and in accordance with Marxists like Eagleton,

Horkheimer and Adorno do not want to give up enlightenment and rationality. The book's last sentence reflects again the declared intention of the preface, to prepare a new positive idea of enlightenment:[26] 'Enlightenment which is in possession of itself and coming to power can break bounds of enlightenment.'[27]

The third criticism of the exclusive mechanisms of rational discourse does not destroy the universal validity claims internal to that discourse. Instead of abolishing the latter, it leads to its extension. Its purpose is – in Adorno's words – to give a voice to all those who are speechless or silenced.[28]

3. History of the origin of subjectivity

The attempt by Adorno and Horkheimer to enlighten the blinded enlightenment of rationality is now connected with a much more problematic foundationalist account. They want to establish the dialectics of enlightenment or the contingent history of enlightenment's self-criticism and self-destruction on the grounds of an 'original history of subjectivity' (*Urgeschichte der Subjektivität*).[29] This original history of the subject is at the same time an original history of art, of modern mathematics, of the *homo oeconomicus*, of bourgeois coldness.[30] Its explanatory power is immense. But what does 'original history' or *Urgeschichte* mean? Its meaning is included in the distinction drawn between contingent and original history, and this resembles Heidegger's distinctions between *Geschichte* and *Geschichtlichkeit*, or later *Seinsgeschichte* or 'history of being' and 'history as usual'. Adorno throughout his intellectual life criticized these Heideggerian distinctions for being foundationalist philosophy or *Ursprungsphilosophie*, and therefore a regression to the metaphysical dogma of the 'two realms' (see above, Chap. 1, s.10). The problem here is that notions like 'history of Being', *Geschichtlichkeit* or 'original history' presuppose that there exists some deeper necessity in history that never can be influenced by societal action, and that is the very origin, source, and drive of all contingent historical change. It constitutes history.

Yet *Urgeschichte des Subjekts* (prehistory of the subject) by Adorno and Horkheimer is more aporetic than that of Heidegger. That they do not repress the aporia brings them closer to Derrida than to Heidegger. Whereas Heidegger always strived to avoid

contradictions at the cost of enlightenment, Adorno, like Derrida –
to the anger of analytical philosophers – praises and defends
enlightenment and rationality just as often and vehemently as he
criticizes and condemns it; Derrida sometimes contradicts himself
several times on one page.

Adorno's original history of subjectivity is worked out in two
steps, combined with the two famous assertions of the *Dialectic of
Enlightenment*. First: myth already is enlightenment. And second:
completely developed enlightenment returns (or reverts) to mythology.[31] The first thesis is explained in the chapter on Homer and
Ulysses, the second one in that on Kant and De Sade. If we isolate
the first thesis from the second it appears to be basically progressive, and it contradicts the criticism by Heidegger and conservatives
of the project of enlightenment. The first thesis means that there is
no way out of enlightenment. No viable alternative exists. Enlightenment, disenchantment and rationalization are co-original with
the societal level of human evolution, a statement that fits well
with progressive intellectual projects like that of Marx, Durkheim,
Dewey or Talcott Parsons. 'Freedom', Horkheimer and Adorno
write, 'cannot be separated from enlightenment'.[32] Though Horkheimer and Adorno offer one of the most dark and pessimistic
diagnoses of the actual crisis of enlightenment, they nevertheless
insist that the only cure for the ailments of enlightenment is more
enlightenment. Despite all the dialectical entwinement of myth and
enlightenment there exists a difference. Whereas mythology is irrevocably bound to violence and cruelty, enlightenment is the recal-
citrant attempt to avoid violence and cruelty, and this is an attempt
that emerges in the midst of mythical thinking.[33] This attempt
sometimes fails, but – on the ground of the first thesis – it must
not.

It is only the second thesis that says enlightenment *must* decay.
This thesis expresses an a priori necessity that enlightenment must
return to mythology once it is developed completely. It is not clear
how we can know when we have reached this state of negative
perfection. If the second thesis is true, enlightenment never has the
chance to get rid of the original barbarism of history. History in
its course follows a tragic design. 'The fully enlightened earth
appears in the glory of triumphal disaster.'[34] Here the difference
between myth and enlightenment, rationality and cruelty, vanishes. All hope for the progress of enlightenment is destroyed.

Enlightenment is not just one mythological narrative among others, but the myth of all mythology. The sentence that draws all consequences from this thesis stems from Horkheimer: 'To derive from reason any fundamental argument against murder is impossible.'[35] And that means that reason – if it is developed in its last consequences – allows murder. With their second thesis Adorno and Horkheimer go along with Heidegger and a broad stream of conservative cultural criticism. Critical theory falls back upon a negative philosophy of the history of decay.

Such an a priori history of decay presupposes a platonic view from nowhere. This is the point of view of a higher truth that allows those who reach it to recognize the unreduced totality of history. Horkheimer's and Adorno's position here is deeply ambivalent. When they confront 'blinded pragmatised thinking' with the 'self-reflection of enlightenment', they normally argue that this is a self-reflection by the means of enlightenment. With Hegel they always call it 'determined negation' (*bestimmte Negation*).[36] Against the blinded rationale of 'mere self-preservation' the enlightened rationale of self-reflection, Adorno insists, 'should not be less than self-preservation; making its way through self-preservation, ratio must transcend it.'[37] But this transcendence should be one that is *internal* to the purposive-rationality of self-preservation. The late Adorno in a supplementary note to his *Negative Dialectics* has called this – as we have seen – 'ratio's moment of universality that raises it above its subjective bearer'.[38] And the *Dialectic of Enlightenment* expresses the same thought in a deliberation on the rationality of the instrumental means of class-domination:

> The instruments of domination, which would encompass all – language, weapons, and finally machines – must allow themselves to be encompassed by all. Hence in domination the aspect of rationality prevails that is also different from it. The 'objectivity' of the means, which makes it universally available, already implies the criticism of that domination as whose means thought arose.[39]

From here, it is only a small step to a positive concept of reason, e.g. by replacing 'purposive-rationality' with any version of 'communicative-rationality'. 'Ratio's moment of universality' and the 'objectivity of the means' then would mean that the assertions implicit in purposive-rational action could be defended against all criticism raised by an open and inclusive audience. Dialogical rationality is that moment internal to all rationality that differs from domination. Or to put it in Adorno's words from the end of the chapter on Odysseus:

> Homeland is the state of having escaped . . . Eloquent discourse itself, language in contradistinction to mythic song, the possibility of retaining in the memory the disaster that has occurred, is the law of Homeric escape, and the reason why the escaping hero is repeatedly introduced as narrator.[40]

Here language becomes the very medium for the escape from mythical violence and for the return home, in the paradoxical stance of a home that continues in having escaped from home.[41]

But in Horkheimer's and Adorno's book we can find another meaning of 'self-reflection of enlightenment' that is much more metaphysical. Here both identify their own thinking with the abolition of all normal scientific deliberation, with *Geist* or 'spirit' as against 'intelligence', or with the 'idea of a totality' or the 'recognition of totality'.[42] The elitist overtones in some parts of the book as well as the projection of enlightenment's history into an unavoidable return to mythology are due to the latter reading of 'self-reflection' as a deeper insight into the totality of history. If we cancel the latter understanding of 'self-reflection' and keep the 'former', we can avoid the regression of the dialectic of enlightenment back to negative metaphysics, and to conservative politics too. The meaning of the second thesis about the return of enlightenment to mythology is then simply that this *can* happen, but it must not. The question again is open to empirical inquiry and political experimentalism, and no space is left for any foundationalist distinction between material or contingent history on the one side, and original history on the other.

If we take that step we must not renounce strong or radical criticism of domination and its cultural superstructure in late capitalism that is an implication of Horkheimer's and Adorno's thesis on the mythological self-reification of enlightenment. This criticism now can be renewed on postmetaphysical grounds.

If we follow this line of argument we can keep the *Dialectic of Enlightenment*'s strong criticism, and avoid the implication of an apocalyptic or tragic history of enlightenment's decay, which would no longer allow a radical reformism to proceed, which is the only chance to *change* self-destruction of modernity into self-correction. And this is the very utopia of enlightenment: to transform all the power of enlightenment's self-destruction into self-correction without domination, a utopia that can fail and fall back to self-destruction at any attempt to realize it, but it must not. At least, it depends on human praxis and its outcome.

3 • Adorno, Heidegger and Post-Analytical Philosophy

Adorno's lifelong opposite was the philosopher Martin Heidegger. Negative dialectic is a programme which is intended to overcome Heidegger's fundamentalistic opposition to modernity by means of a more radical interpretation of modernity as *cultural modernism*.

Cultural modernism for Adorno (as well as for pragmatists like Dewey) is an experimental attitude. This is obvious in all avantgardist movements of modern art, which propagate themselves as '-isms' like 'expressionism', 'constructivism', 'avantgardism', 'cubism' or 'surrealism'. Experimentalism could be taken as a catch-all concept that covers all tendencies of modern art. The experimental attitude in aesthetics is stimulated by the high acceleration of social change in all industrial, technological and scientific concerns. In the latter spheres modernity is made manifest in '-isms' as well (e.g. pragmatism, empiricism, capitalism, industrialism). Schools change quickly by means of new experimental designs. Without exaggeration one could say that the very stability of the social system of modern art is its extreme variability. Variability keeps modernity alive. This is expressed by the '-isms' which mean that one programme of artistic experiments follows the next.

For Adorno 'truth' and not 'beauty' is the basic value of aesthetics. Here he differs from his friend Horkheimer and goes along with Heidegger. Truth is the sublime that emerges out of the thing-like reality of works of art (see below, Chap. 4, s. 3). But for Adorno the aesthetic truth-value is a function of art's experimental modernity and therefore closely connected with the '-isms'. In contrast Heidegger always wholly rejected the '-isms' of modernity as inauthenticity (*Uneigentlichkeit*). Phenomena like 'communism', 'fascism', 'Bolshevism', 'liberalism' or 'Americanism' are indeed deeply ambivalent. They play an important role in politics, and sometimes have utopian, sometimes totalitarian, sometimes democratic connotations. And what is ambivalent in politics is ambivalent in aesthetics too, as both Heidegger and Adorno would claim.

But, as Heidegger puts it, there are no *essential* differences between the '-isms': 'Bolshevism' is 'the same' (*das Selbe*) as 'Americanism' 'individualism' *the same* as 'collectivism', and this would be true for all '-isms'.[1] The differences on the surface do not count. What really counts is the essence. Both America and the Soviet Union, Heidegger argues, are large-size societies, oriented to the wishes of the atomized masses; they are industrial and technological societies, realizations of a supersubjects project of modernity, etc. 'Authentic thinking', like that of Heidegger himself, therefore, can demonstrate that Cartesian and even Kantian 'constructivism' is *the same* as 'Americanism', 'Bolshevism' and eventually 'Nazism'.[2]

Heidegger's philosophical explanation of this sameness differs from Adorno, because Adorno's critique of modern subjectivity is never as fundamentalist as that of Heidegger. Where Adorno envisions dialectical tensions and ambivalences, Heidegger claims a complete forgottenness of the higher truth of 'Being'. (On the meaning of 'Being' or *Sein*, see below, Chap. 3, s. 3.) Descartes and Kant for Heidegger are the 'poets' who have set out the world-disclosing language of the subject as the master of the world and the world as the object of the subject's technical means. The foundation of the United States and the Soviet Union and the development of all modern '-isms' was in essence or in its authentic meaning (*eigentlich*) nothing other than the realization practically and politically of what Kant and Descartes have protected in theoretical terms. In the 1930s Heidegger believed that Hölderlin as the 'poet' of the German people was the poet of a very different language that would overcome subjectivity and modernity, and lead back to the 'origins' of pre-metaphysical 'thinking'. When the German *Führer* came to power in 1933 Heidegger expected Hitler to become the 'statesman' who finally would translate Hölderlin's poetry into politics. 'Nazism' before 1945 or 1943 (before Stalingrad) for Heidegger was the great metaphysical effort to stop the nihilism and the great danger to the meaning of human life which were internal to modern subjectivity, technology, and economy, and which was enforced and re-enforced by Americanism and Bolshevism.

Unlike Heidegger, Adorno vehemently defends the '-isms' of avantgardist modernism. Despite this engagement with modernism Adorno is most sensitive to the deeply rooted *ambivalences* internal to the experimental habit of all avantgardist movements. The term 'experimentalism' signifies the 'painful' and 'the aspect of violence in modernism' (das Gewalttätige am Neuen), which originates from 'the unforeseen' and the 'disenfranchisement' of subjective arbitrariness which happens within the unfolding process of aesthetic 'objectivization' and 'materialization'. There is no feasibility in predicting the outcome of a serious experiment. It can be beautiful, good and peaceful as well as disastrous and evil. To create a new perspective without violating the material of aesthetic formation and without violating aesthetic and moral conventions is not possible. Artistic experiments are balancing acts 'on a knife', and this is the prize of searching for a truth that is new: 'Experimentation . . . designates something completely different, namely that the aesthetic subject uses methods the result of which it cannot foresee . . . – a veritable balancing act of the experimenting artist.'[3]

Experimentation can work, but it need not; and if not, it can have fatal consequences. The attitude of the aesthetic reactionary is to repress the ambivalence of the open, experimental form of modern art-works. What the reactionary wants to avoid is the pain of truth internal to all experimentalism. And, as Adorno claims, the irrational prejudice against experimentalism is the same as the prejudice against all '-isms' of modernity:

> Experimentation is painful, it elicits resentment against so-called 'isms' or groups of artists conciously united by a shared agenda or style. This resentment covers a wide spectrum of people from Hitler, who loved to sound off against 'those im- and expressionists', to leftist writers [like Lukács – H.B.], who are wary of the concept of aesthetic avantgardism because of their zealous desire to be politically avantgarde.[4]

Adorno envisions the truth of the '-isms' in the front line against the ideology of the work of art as an 'organic totality': 'The element of truth that lies in equating art with an organism, no matter what that truth is, has to be mediated by the subject and its reason.' Here again it is not over truth, but the reference to subject and reason where Heidegger and Adorno separate from one another:

> However, since that truth has long been made subservient to the irrationalist ideology of a rationalized society, those isms which deny that truth seem to be truer. It is by no means the case that isms have

shackled the productivity of the individual. On the contrary, they have augmented it, not the least through collective co-operation.[5]

In this chapter I will outline, with the purpose of illuminating Adorno's philosophy, two variations of more or less 'postmodern' thinking: on the one hand, the fundamentalists like Heidegger and some of his French followers, and on the other hand the antifundamentalistic postmodernists like Richard Rorty and a number of post-empiricist philosophers. As we will see, in many – yet not in all – respects Adorno comes close to the latter in his philosophical orientation.

1. Differing narratives

The history of the impact and influence (*Wirkungsgeschichte*) of Heidegger on continental European culture and thought is as unique as it is overwhelming. It was as significant for the existentialism of the free subject as it was for poststructuralist theories of discourse and power which have declared the subject and man to be a mere episode in the history of power. Without Heidegger, or so it seems, there would be no Sartre, no Foucault, no philosophical hermeneutics, no Gadamer, no Merleau-Ponty. Furthermore, Western Marxism drew invigorating energy from *Being and Time* and this stream of thinking, after the 'turn', still feeds the deconstructionist theory of the text. The influence of Heidegger's work has long since extended beyond continental philosophy and Europe's *Zeitgeist* and, in an increasingly distinct manner, has left traces in American pragmatism and has enjoyed a benevolent reception among more and more analytical philosophers. No matter whether one likes or dislikes Heidegger, as a person and as a philosopher one cannot deny his profound influence.

Being and Time, Heidegger's early masterpiece, opened the way for a variety of philosophical enterprises – existentialist, pragmatist, hermeneutic, Neo-Marxist, or neo-metaphysical and theological ones. Heidegger himself has moved more in the metaphysical direction. The late Heidegger tried to overcome modernity by means of a history of the salvation of Being that has a strong Gnostic tendency. All history after a certain point of time at the origin of European thinking is a history of decay. Heidegger calls it the history of the 'forgottenness of being'. Hope is only concerned with the return of Being like a transcendent salvation. We can do nothing to make things better, we only can wait for a rescue.

Since Plato's image of the cave, in Heidegger's story of Being, there have been nothing but newer and flatter variations of that original 'subjugation' of 'humanity' to 'the idea of correctness', the domination of metaphysics as the 'powers of the understanding' are controlled by the will to will.[6] It was only the element of force that Heidegger perceived in the forceless force of better arguments, this element being an animal intellect going way beyond nature's instinct. After the end of the Second World War he saw the 'ratio of humanity' becoming 'identical' with the 'drive of animality' in the planning and calculating intellect.[7] For Heidegger, in his later works, rational argument was, in the strict sense of the term, 'unholy' – the business of 'dealers and brokers' on an earth whose 'desolation' stems from 'metaphysics'.[8] In a unique reversal of old battle fronts, the 'superhuman' becomes the 'exaggerated' 'intellectualism' of the 'subhuman'.[9] In the everyday life of the occidental subject, dominated as it is by reason and science, the narrative grace of myths is usurped by statements requiring rational justification. Modern life, dominated by the 'subject', is totally alienated from its own historical origins in some forms of archaic rural life. 'The customary life of contemporary man', wrote Heidegger in the 1946 lecture 'What are poets for?', 'is the common life of the imposition of self on the unprotected market of the exchangers'.[10] When the rescuer is supposed to come, in order to drive the exchangers/dealers out of the 'temple of Being', is uncertain; but the poets tell of the origin of the holy – the truth of Being is established by the poet, admittedly under the direction of the thinker.

From this perspective, the history of the salvation of Being, all essential distinctions are blurred between the forceless force of better arguments and the coercive force of sanctions, between the autonomy of non-arbitrary freedom and the arbitrary freedom of the self-empowered subject, between impartial justice and the partial self-justice of the will to power. Heidegger's perspective here is – in spite of his radical critique of metaphysical idealism – idealist in a very simple way. He supposes that semantic or philosophical revolutions in the realm of ideas (such as Plato's invention of 'image' and 'idea' or Descartes's and Kant's invention of 'consciousness', 'subject' and 'reflection') are *prior* to changes and revolutions in the social structure, in the forms of relations of production and societal differentiation. 'Thinking', 'poetry' or semantics come first. 'Interest' and 'economy' are of secondary relevance for historical progress insofar as an event in the history of Being is concerned. The thesis that covers Heidegger's history of Being, which is an idealist critique of metaphysical idealism and a broad stream within postmodern philosophy, runs as follows. What is general and conclusive (as a conclusion following from general premises) in theory is general and conclusive in social reality. Internal to social practices *generality* is *repression* of what is not general and *exclusion* of what does not fit to general premises, and *logical conclusions* are, socially and politically speaking, *forms of domination*. It is repression and domination in reality which makes general theoretical premises true. In this idealist perspective, the forceless force of better arguments becomes the essence and origin of all other force – just as 'armanent in the metaphysical sense', i.e. intellectualism, is the origin of (*Ursprung*) all armanent industries.[11]

In its intellectual-historical and political consequences, however, the perspective of the 'responding and recalling' thinker (*andenkender Denker*) connects with important elements in postmodern thinking. The universalistic validity claim of argumentation is (in Heidegger's sense) 'the same' as the real general, the first and highest idea of ancient metaphysics; the moral universalism of the enlightenment is 'the same' as the compulsory uniformity of totalitarian regimes. Yet, at least for Lyotard, the metaphysical armament seems to be more fundamental than the real one, the gentle weapon of critique more primordial than the martial critique of weapons. Accordingly, postmodern thinking is intellectual pacifism. The practical consequence then is to disarm the weapons of criticism first at all, which is, in Lyotard's words, a 'disarming' 'of intelligence'.[12]

Lyotard shares this idealist trait with Heidegger, but not with Richard Rorty's neo-pragmatist postmodernism. For, like Adorno and Horkheimer, Rorty believes that the freedom of the different and the plural, of the deviant and non-identical, of 'abnormal discourse', is not endangered by 'science or naturalistic philosophy' but by 'scarcity of food and . . . the secret police'.[13] It is not only with materialist insights of this kind that Rorty lines up with the

Frankfurt School. Both Adorno and Rorty also relate a different narrative of the emergence of modernity than do, for instance, Heidegger and Lyotard. Whereas Lyotard and especially Foucault conceptualize, with Heidegger, the history of occidental rationality by beginning with the Greeks, Rorty and Adorno favour a perspective enlightened by the sociology of religion and explain the spirit of modernity from its Judaeo-Christian origins. Whereas Foucault and Lyotard, with more or less normative appeal, outline a relativist world of polytheism and heterogeneous discourses or language islands, Adorno and Rorty, along with pragmatism and Marxism, normatively go back to a moral materialism of solidarity among and between different life-forms.[14]

Of course, by way of the reflective turn to a 'totalizing critique of reason' (Apel), both narratives, that of Foucault and Lyotard as well as that of Rorty and Adorno, are at first compatible.[15] Both can be told in a postmodern manner, guided by a conceptual dichotomy that opens an abyss between *Wahrheit* and *Richtigkeit*, truth and correctness (as Heidegger does). This dichotomy must necessarily let all distinctions of forcelessly compelling argumentation be swallowed up in the totalitarian uniformity of compulsion. The latter distinctions between compelling forms of argumentation and repressive power for Heidegger and postmodernists like Foucault are distinctions *within* the realm of mere *Richtigkeit*. From the point of view of *Wahrheit* or the authenticity of the History of Being (Heidegger) or the transcendental order of things (Foucault) or the world-disclosing power of language games (Lyotard), mere *Richtigkeit* (e.g. the truth of theoretical or moral argumentation in everyday life or in science) is *always already* entwined with 'untrue' or 'false' forms of life, with repression, domination and relations of power. Heidegger and postmodernists like Foucault or Lyotard are theorists of the dialectics of enlightenment, but in a much more idealist manner than Adorno.

Heidegger always works with dichotomously designed distinctions between truth and correctness, between picturing (*Vorstellen*) and thinking, between the will to will at one's disposal, and the destiny (*Geschick*) beyond one's disposal, between the 'grasping' (*Zugriff*) of the concept and the 'gesture' (*Gebärde*) adequate to Being, between 'frantic measuring' and 'moderation', between language as instrument and language as 'governing force'. These and numerous other conceptual distinctions, which as a rule Heidegger

merely construed as an inverted relation of instrumental domination, correspond to analogous differentiations in postmodern
thought. Lyotard's guiding difference between meta-narrative and
narrative, Rorty's alternatives of objectivity and solidarity, of realism and pragmatism, of philosophy and democracy, Foucault's (at
least) implicit division between power and the counter-power of
subversive knowledge, these all aim in the same direction, toward
a totalizing critique of reason.

This also applies to the standard readings of Adorno: here the
basic distinction seems to be that of the non-identical and identifying thought – a distinction which usurps everything else including
all universal validity claims. In place of this I will defend a different
reading of Adorno. As we already have seen, Adorno continuously
relativizes the rigid dichotomy of aesthetic mimesis and instrumental reason, of the non-identical and identifying thought, at
the retained vanishing-point of rational identity. We here should
draw a contrast between a mere *distinction* (including 'extreme'
differences) between identifying thinking and non-identical, mimetic impulses, and a *dichotomy*, which means a fundamental
opposition or an unbridgeable gap between different world-
pictures or 'paradigms'. At this point Adorno comes very close to
pragmatists like Dewey or Putnam, and he shares the basic methodological idea with Rorty. There is, as Putnam[16] once put it, not
only a common element between pragmatism and the thinking of
the new Frankfurt School of Apel and Habermas, but also pragmatism and the old thinking of the Frankfurt School of Adorno
and Horkheimer.[17] Where Heidegger sees a great divide that yawns
between *truth* and *correctness*, between the 'Being' and 'being just
there' (*Dasein*), between *authenticity* and the *inauthentic* life of the
ordinary man (*das Man*) or between poetry and everyday language,
Adorno, along with Dewey, Putnam and Rorty, sees a *continuum*.
Adorno calls it a *constellation*. There are dialectical tensions, even
contradictions and paradoxes, *within* a continuum or a constellation of everyday language and philosophical interpretation,
between 'constructivism' and 'mimesis', between 'spirit' and 'material', between authentic works of art and inauthentic products of
the cultural industry, between identifying thinking and the non-
identical. But there are *no hierarchies* and here is no unbridgeable
gap, no dichotomy between two distinct metaphysical realms.

For Adorno constructivism and mimesis, 'spirit' and 'material', identifying thinking and the non-identical are opposed. They contradict one another. But at the same time they interpenetrate, they are – to say it in the jargon of modern systems theory – 'structurally coupled'. The non-identical of mimetic conduct presupposes internally what it denies at the same time: identifying thinking and instrumental rationality. That at least is the reason why Adorno, like Putnam or Habermas, has a notion of *rational identity* and Heidegger has not. Adorno's notion of 'rational identity' is different from that of Putnam or Habermas, and it is not related to dialogical truth. But it is a flexible and weak, yet positive concept of rationality, which is built by a constellation of constellations. The basic oppositions of Adorno's thinking – mimesis and constructionism, identity and non-identity, general and particular, meaning and material – are single constellations which come together as patterns of constellations, and any plural constellation is a paradigm case of 'rational identity' (see below, Chap. 3, s. 5).

By rational identity Adorno understands something like a non-Hegelian, detotalized overcoming (*Aufhebung*) of the non-identical and identifying thought. It is precisely this idea of a rational identity which enables Adorno to make plausible those fundamental and normatively substantive distinctions which Heidegger and some postmodernists are forced to surrender: the difference between world-market imperialism and egalitarian freedom, between particularism and pluralism, between closed and open societies, between atomism and individualism (see below, Chap. 3, s. 5). Whereas imperialism, particularism, closed societies, and atomism fall on the side of 'identity thinking', 'rational identity' is claimed by egalitarian freedom, pluralism, a truly open society, and individualism.

To sum this up: what separates people like Adorno and Rorty from Heidegger's and some postmodernists' idealism (rooted in the philosophy of Ancient Greece) is the background of a robust *materialism*, which is rooted in the Judaeo-Christian narrative of the Western world.

2. Adorno and postmodernism against Heidegger's anti-modernism

Heidegger's third period of influence[18] began imperceptibly in the 1960s, reaching its zenith in the last two decades of the century.

The understanding of Heidegger since the 1980s is soberly prag-matic, dressed up with fashionable chic, and essentially cleansed of the exaggerated fundamentalistic expectations of the German thinker. Heidegger's emphasis on difference is now misunderstood as a radical critique of totalitarianism. Politically, the original thinker is moving to liberal politics, towards Popper, Raymond Aron or even John Dewey. Liberal and anarchist readings of Heid-egger suddenly seem possible. Philosophically, the announced 'overcoming' (*Verwindung*) of metaphysics is being taken ser-iously, and metaphysics is being violently removed from its throne. Once again, philosophy finds itself being confronted with a form of life which is gradually ageing. But this time, the colours that philosophy uses are postmodern and bright. One almost hears the tanks of those liberating armies that echoed across the Rhine in 1945 and put an overdue end to the Nazi dictatorship, when Rich-ard Rorty abruptly declares an end to the waiting-for-the-rescue and expresses the view 'that perhaps the rescue may have already taken place behind Heidegger's back – in America'.[19]

Whether in moderate or radical, emphatic or serene tones, with negative or affirmative signs, Rorty, Adorno and Lyotard celebrate the innovative and creative potency of cultural modernism, the new and inventive, the sublime and intensive, the unconventional and the post-conventional, the abnormal discourse and the productivity of the subversive. In Germany Heidegger had a much more bucolic image. He was the magic master of a world of poets, priests, farmers, shepherds and small villages located in areas like the Black Forest. To be in the state of *Eigentlichkeit* and to live an authentic life for Heidegger meant to live in communities of small size, far away from the noisy and busy big cities which are ruled by the anonymous everybody (*das Man*).

But in the age of postmodern philosophy Heidegger's farmer's guard (*Hut*) becomes a lively Parisian vanguard (*Vor-Hut*) for Lyotard. In the non-identical, Adorno informs us of a radical con-cept of freedom which, in its anarchist and libertarian character-istics – its left- and right-wing ones, respectively – is in accord with the anarchism of French poststructuralists and with the moderate liberalism of American neo-pragmatism. In contrast, Heidegger's History of Being resounds with the traditionalist-authoritarian counter-programme, the propaganda of re-enchantment: the return of aura to culture and of the sacred to art. Today's followers of Heidegger's rural images in Germany are poets like Botho Strauß or even more the Austrian Peter Handke. Adorno's sharp polemic conceptualizes such attacks on the spirit of modernity as 'feigned humility'. Heidegger's pagan invocation of the aura of Greek temples is hopelessly bourgeois in view of the newly opened experiential horizons of aesthetic modernity: from Eisenstein's films through Schönberg's music and Newman's paintings up to Harold Bloom's criticism. These artists and critics are deeply influenced by romantic irony, urban experience and the conflicts of the modern age. They do not want to go back to their roots and a nostalgic longing for original forms of life. What they try to do is to make new meaning out of the paradoxes and dichotomies of an irreversible shattered and fragmented existence.

Adorno, like Heidegger and Derrida, but unlike Rorty or Lyotard, defends a notion of aesthetic truth, related to the sublime. Adorno parts from Heidegger in binding the truth import of works of art to the notion of historical progress, to its newest developments and ephemeral manifestations. One here could say with Rorty *and* Adorno that origin is replaced by future: essentialist deepness by the mere surface of contingent constellations of social criticism, political commitment, fashion and intrinsic aesthetic value.

> Paradoxically, the philosophical awareness of truth in works of art is akin to the most ephemeral form of aesthetic reflection, i.e. the manifesto. One methodological principle that seems to me compelling is to try to shed light on all art from the perspective of the most recent artistic phenomena, rather than the other way round, which is the case with history-of-ideas approach.[20]

The distance from all positive concepts of totality, the scepticism about any philosophy of origins (*Ursprungsphilosopie*), and the profane motives of this thinking lead Adorno away from Heidegger and, with Rorty, Lyotard and Foucault, to the front lines of postmodernism. But Adorno's critique of modern subjectivity is less radical; for instance, when he talks about 'consciousness of the non-identical', or even about 'autonomous dissonance' in music or about the 'force of the subject', when he declares cultural modernity to be the 'centre' and 'power-station' of 'emancipation', he is unequivocally introducing categories of idealism and enlightenment, concepts of the conscious life, of rational freedom and individual identity. It is here that the various postmodern roads part.

Rorty initially follows tracks also taken by Adorno. Rorty is insured by language analysis against the pitfalls of metaphors of reflection, but is also more resigned, without Adorno's utopian energy. Lyotard, in contrast, opposes the autonomy of reason to the heteronomy of the sublime, a rational communicative community to a child-like community of feeling. Lyotard tries to make a case for the heterogeneous, 'popular folklore stories', the unforgettable, original 'wisdom of nations', the lively scepticism of many little stories in which real life is antagonistically involved. Its hopes are the small narratives which answer, with many voices, the imperial evil of the meta-narratives and major stories on the French Revolution, on the Declaration of Human Rights, on Bolshevism, capitalism and Nazism, on rational and racist terror.[21] Here Lyotard picks up Heidegger's idea that the French Revolution, Bolshevism, Americanism and Nazism are the *same*.

Concluding one could say that Adorno and most postmodernists share a view of culture that is experimental, ironical and anti-authoritarian. In comparison, Heidegger's point of view is authoritarian, in search of the sacred and the untouchable secret of the culture of a historic people, whereas critique and destruction of the aura and the sacred is common to Benjamin, Adorno, Rorty, Lyotard and Derrida. To say it in Adorno's words from a letter to Benjamin in 1939: 'If music, as in mass culture, becomes comedy, that is something deeply positive, it destroys the sacred feelings of reconciliation. Here I see the great agreement between my work [*on the 'fetish character of music'*] and yours on the mechanical reproduction of art.'[22] And Adorno adds, correcting his own work: 'If like that [*the deeply positive, progressive side of the mass culture – H.B.*] in my text remained unclear, I would regard that as a big mistake.' The contrast with Heidegger here is that of art as (ironical) *disenchantment* and destruction of aura versus art as *re-enchantment* and re-establishing its mystical power over the people. This power over people is the ideological and social function of Heidegger's *Dichter* as *Stifter*, – which now in Germany has returned in the work of poets like Botho Strauß. Both Strauß and Peter Handke have a strong tendency to go back to rural images, the atmosphere of old Greek temples and, most important, the higher message of poetical disclosure. Through poetry they perceive something divine which gives us mere everyday human beings a new order, or a new form of life. Their idea of the poet is, like Heidegger's, the idea of the *Stifter* of the *Sein* of our *Dasein* – the founder of being of our presence.

3. Adorno and post-empiricism against 'the myth of the framework'

Before I return to following the two tracks of postmodernism (taking the term 'postmodernism' in a very broad sense) outlined briefly in the introduction to this chapter, I will deal here with the basic objection of Adorno and others to Heidegger's linguistic idealism. Adorno sums up all his polemics in the famous phrase: *Kein Sein ohne Seiendes*, 'No Being without existence'. The point of this claim is a rejection of Heidegger's very idea of world-disclosure which goes back to Haman, Humboldt and German romanticism. Unlike Humboldt and most of the post-empiricist, Kuhnian philosophers of science, Heidegger overestimates the poetic force of language. And this causes him to attempt to re-enchant poetry.

In their protest against the instrumental theory of language, Heidegger and Adorno, Rorty and Haman, Benjamin and Quine, Kuhn and Schlegel, are in the same boat. The instrumental theory was the metaphysical mainstream from Plato to Hegel and Carnap. Language for these thinkers is an instrument used by a consciousness or a subject to dominate the world of objects. The point of the protest against the instrumental theory of language consists in a categorial distinction between the poetic, signifying and productive force of language as a whole and the referential and instrumental use of individual utterances.

When we make use of language, and utter a sentence, then we 'always and already' (*immer schon*, as Heidegger says in *Being and Time*) have presupposed a whole network of implicit linguistic meaning, implicit theories, grammatical rules and so on. We can say that language as the network of meaning and rules in our background *constitutes* the meaning of the particular utterance that someone actually uses. Philosophers like Herder, Haman, Humboldt or Heidegger have argued that the linguistic context of language as a whole is the mere product of historical inventions, of poets in a broad sense of this word. What we make actual use of, and what are at stake in normal debates on truth or falsity, are always individual utterances, but never our language as a whole, be it a language of a historical people, of a high or low culture, of a specific social class, or be it the language of experts (like lawyers or artists) or scientific schools (like the Copenhagen School of quantum mechanics or the Frankfurt School of sociology). Language as a whole, one could say with Wittgenstein, is the entwinement of life-forms and language games; or, with Adorno, language like a work of art is a 'historical constellation'.[23] Language here is a medium that enables us to make use of meaningful sentences *as well as* meaningful instruments (like a hammer or a signal flag) or meaningful products of our work (like tables or chairs). 'Language' *vis-à-vis* 'individual ulterances' or 'meaningful actions' means the whole linguistic and prelinguistic framework (or social and cultural context) that discloses a world of our life and 'existence' (*Dasein*). To invent a new language therefore means to disclose a new world. In this sense Adorno uses the word 'language' to speak about the 'non-instrumental' 'language of art' or the 'language of music'. Beethoven's musical 'language' is a good example for the creation of a new world of listening and thinking. The following generations of composers do not use it in the way they use single compositions as instruments of their specific work. On the contrary they *presuppose* Beethoven's music as a language that constitutes a new realm of aesthetic (and not only aesthetic) experience.

Given that language as a whole cannot be subjected to any form of instrumental control or calculation, and that language also lays down the scope, framework or 'ground plan' for possible true and false statements (or also good and bad deeds) *from the outset*, the singular subject suddenly breaks out of the centre of the 'always and already' linguistically disclosed world. Instead, the subject always and already finds itself at a contingent position *in the framework* of a linguistic occurrence without a subject. Thus, we forever find that language is 'always ahead of us'. And this is what Heidegger expresses in the famous sentence: 'Language speaks'. And even when we talk *about* language, we only seem to 'master' it, for we are only able to do so by having recourse to an uncontrolled game of linguistic distinctions not made by us. We can only talk *from within* language *about* language.[24] What a 'thing', a social relationship, a toothbrush or a stone is, *what* it shows itself to be to us, and *how* it does this 'comes to us from language'.[25] If we forget this, we 'forget Being' and given that no one can have something in front of him that is behind him, it is hardly surprising that even philosophers have not put the question as to the meaning of Being and have certainly not gone down the path which goes in the direction of the non-instrumental dimension of language. Yoked to the methodologically constructed and mathematically computed 'en-framing', modern science – and with it art, culture and religion – completely loses sight of the historical 'project', the 'Being' of its own technological practice.[26] Whoever uses language 'only as a means of expression', Heidegger argues, *ineluctably* forgets its true, non-instrumental Being, founded by poets such as Hölderlin and Galileo.

This being the case, 'an unrestrained and yet eloquent talking, writing and sending of the spoken word races round the globe. Man acts as if *he* were the sculptor and master of language, while it remains the master of humans.'[27] The 'inversion of *this* relationship of master and servant' is the *egocentrism of the modern subject*.[28] Heidegger admittedly does not speak here of 'egocentrism', but of the 'planetary imperialism' of the 'subjectivism of man'.[29] It is this diagnosis which Heidegger at the first glance seems to share with the authors of the *Dialectic of Enlightenment*.

One of Heidegger's examples of the poetic character of language is the language of modern physics. The great poetry of Galileo and Newton consisted in a new way of talking about things. All natural things are extensive bodies that only move when propelled and, of their own accord, neither aspire to some naturally given goal nor place themselves within a hierarchy of such goals. The creed of this new poetry of nature runs: all bodies are equal. And precisely this is what enables it to tie them into a referential network of mathematics and calculation and to master these things by calculation.[30] The categorial error that generates the egocentric structure of modern subjectivity consists in the world-disclosing language which makes the instrumental mastering language of modernity possible by becoming assimilated to the calculable and disposable bodies themselves. The poetry of modernity is *imagined* to be controllable and calculable. The world becomes a picture. This is the greatest illusion of the modern subject. The subject projects an *imaginary world* for itself. And this projective step into 'error' is to a certain extent unavoidable and 'necessary' – something Heidegger does not tire of asserting. The theory of the illusionary projective structure of modern egocentric subjectivity is in full accordance with Adorno's critique of the reification of subject-centred projections of objective truth onto the external world. As we have seen, for example, the *Dialectic of the Enlightenment* explains anti-Semitism as 'based upon a false projection', which 'makes the external world like itself'. Eventually one could say with Adorno that the 'age of the world picture' is the age of identitarian thinking. The egocentric subject 'makes everything in his own image'.[31]

Again Adorno and Horkheimer could agree here with Heidegger, with the important exception that they would never declare the 'error' of egocentric projections of 'world-pictures' to be something necessary and unavoidable. This would be only the case if we were *assuming* that we are not able to distinguish between the world-disclosing force of language and the instrumental use of random, individual sentences and random 'things'. Now, Heidegger goes so far to assert that this precondition is necessary and, indeed, the 'highest necessity'.[32] This assertion marks him off not only from Adorno and Horkheimer, but also from Popper, Piaget, Quine, Putnam, or Rorty, who otherwise, like Heidegger, believe in semantic holism or at least that 'the language of observation depends on theory' and therefore that we can only ever compare sentences with sentences and can never compare sentences with the world.[33] Heidegger bases his assertion that a clearly unavoidable categorial error has occurred by claiming that Cartesian metaphysics, which reduces *truth* to *certainty*, belongs to the constitutive *ground plan* of the modern sciences and, moreover, of modern culture. Unlike Heidegger, Adorno and Horkheimer reject emphatically any idea of a priori *necessity* related to the blind historical *fact* of instrumental domination and egocentric subjectivity.[34]

Heidegger (and here the paths of diverse tracks part) does not believe that the ground plan of science and the project of modernity as a whole could have been *changed* and (in part) *falsified* by the *experiences* which we have through the emergence of science and the continuation of modern culture. And he is of this opinion because he believes that the truth of a sudden 'occurrence' of world-disclosing poetry is something completely uncorrectable, an 'event' beyond all innerworldly processes of learning. At best, 'demi-gods' (poets, thinkers and founders of states), but never common 'mortals', access this occurrence of truth. The respective historical constitution of Being of an entity – or, to compare it with Kuhn, the 'paradigms' of 'normal science' – are *created* by the 'demi-gods'. This theory of *founding creation* (*Stiftung*), which Heidegger elaborated in his Hölderlin lectures of 1933 and 1934, presents the 'ontological difference' of *Being and Time* as an elitist social difference between 'demi-gods' and common mortals.[35] The decisive feature of the ontological difference is now transposed onto this latter difference. It consists of the hypothesis which Heidegger upheld throughout his life, namely that Being always grounds all entities and that the process is never reversible.

However, one should not allow the teleological semantics of 'grounding' to mislead us here. Heidegger correctly rejects the egocentric categorial error here. To the extent that the word 'Being' stands for 'discourse' in Foucault's sense or for 'paradigm' as Kuhn understands it and thus for non-instrumental language as a whole, Heidegger's hypothesis is quite accurate: 'Being *is* not'.[36] 'Being' does not exist like an object, 'Being' tries to avoid being identified by a controlling and dominating subject. Here one could say also with Adorno: 'The non-identical is not', and that is just the (paradoxical) meaning of talking about something that is not identical with itself. And this is precisely the meaning of 'Being' which Heidegger here brings in if he says 'Being *is* not'. This corrects the categorial error of egocentric projection which treats the perspectival section of the world which we respectively have before us as if it were the whole world. The world in which we 'represent' ourselves is not necessarily the world in which we *are*. In other words, Heidegger is right when he repeatedly emphasizes that we have a *different* access to Being from that which we have to what is 'given' in the world.

But Heidegger does not stop at that. Contrary to Adorno he believes that there is *absolutely no access* from existence to Being. There is no path which leads from a knowledge of matters of fact to that higher 'knowledge' of the 'incalculable'. For 'man' only knows of that non-instrumental dimension of language 'in creative questioning and shaping out of the power of genuine reflection . . . Hölderlin knew of this'.[37] But Hölderlin's knowledge is not that of a 'mortal'. Therefore all those events and all those innerworldly learning processes which common 'mortals' experience are also of no consequence for the history of the basic linguistic condition of Being. Therefore they are as 'inessential' as the mere material suffering of anyone under the burden of the daily reproduction is for the productive and creative suffering of Heidegger's 'demi-gods'.[38] Only the latter have placed part of 'the path of authentic history concealed to the common eye' behind them.[39] The reason for this completely one-sided definition of the lower by the higher truth is to be found solely in Heidegger's assumption that the 'truth of Being' is absolutely irreversible.[40] This truth always already determines '*what* the things are'.[41] The higher 'truth of Being' (that is not the lower truth of a proposition) predefines the yardstick of correctness for every individual judgement, both in moral practice and in scientific theory alike: 'Ontic truth is necessarily oriented toward ontological truth.'[42]

That means that the truth of our real-world, 'material' existence ('ontic') completely depends on the higher truth of a History of Being ('ontological truth'). Sometimes it seems as if Heidegger wanted to say that the ontological truth of Being determines all ontic existence. In his monograph on Kant of 1929, Heidegger used this statement on the necessary orientation of ontic towards onto-logical truth to reformulate a higher transcendental truth, but with a substantive difference. Whereas Kant presumes a *universal* a priori which can clearly be experienced in common everyday prac-tice, Heidegger *relativizes* the transcendental truth, making it a no less unalterable historical truth. And, in the 1930s, it was this which to Heidegger's mind was the truth of a 'historical people', e.g. the Germans.[43] It is accessed respectively in historically rare, ontological 'decisions', which take a 'different shape at different times and among different peoples'.[44] This is *extreme* relativism, it is even solipsistic on the level of collectivities. Ideology for Heidegger is at the foundation of truth.

Heidegger's historical a priori, which causes the 'highest and hardest revelation of Being' to occur, has in common with Thomas Kuhn's notion of the 'paradigm' (and Foucault's concept of 'dis-course' or Adorno's 'historical constellations') not only a linguistic holism but also a categorial differentiation of language as a whole from its individual utterances. Heidegger shares with Kuhn, Fou-cault and Feyerabend above all the confusing and rightfully highly controversial *incommensurability hypothesis*.[45] This is the hypo-thesis that the language of Aristotelian physics never could be truly translated into the language of Galileo's mechanical universe, or that the language of Newton's physics could never be translated into that of Einstein, not even partially. Aristotle and Galileo (this is, for example, Heidegger's thesis in his lecture course from 1936 on 'Das Ding') are living in completely different worlds. So one could not argue that Galileo's reconstruction of the movements of planets and other bodies is better than that of Aristotle, or that Galileo's is true and that of Aristotle false. Kuhn has made the same point with regard to Newton and Einstein or Priestley and Lavoisier.

Nevertheless, here again differences can be discerned. In his more sober statements, Kuhn remains a pragmatist and opposes scientific paradigms of all higher truths. They cannot be disproved, let alone verified, by methodological processes of logical deduction of the experimental inquiry into nature, because, so Kuhn suggests, no claim to truth can be raised for common statements. 'Long battles' must, like Heidegger's 'projects of Being' and 'clearings' (or Foucault's 'discourses'), 'give them control'.[46] However, and this is the difference, they are by no means therefore *independent* of the innerworldly processes of learning used in normal scientific practice. For the cumulation of anomalies that eventually leads to a crisis, in which a mixture of social struggle and world-disclosing new descriptions finally wins out, is *first* the result of a *rational*, normal scientific practice. And this result, which a historical community of scientists always comes up against, which they *discover* within the world and at the same time repress, can, *second*, not be repressed ad infinitum. At some stage the cumulation of anomalies compels them to concede *rationally* that they are in a crisis and no longer know a way out.[47] In other words, common rationality and reason impact on the paradigm, so that we could turn here on Heidegger with Adorno's phrase: 'No Being without existence'.

And Adorno's famous materialist aphorism also holds, if with a grain of salt, for the theories of language, culture and science put forward on the basis of a holistic understanding of meaning in recent philosophy from Quine to Putnam. One could say that Heidegger, too, in his struggle against transcendental philosophy overcame the dogmas of empiricism and, above all, of the analytical method. The concepts of 'historical Being' and of 'language as a whole' have long since obscured the boundary lines which once carefully separated a knowledge of the world from a knowledge of meaning. The historical language of a concrete community is, as a whole, the smallest semantic unit but *at the same time* it is a factually substantive world project, which lends expression to the community's understanding of itself, something that is as deeply rooted in the 'unconscious' background of a community as is know-how for a skilled person.[48] Given, however, that Heidegger, as we have seen, merely wanted to revive the one-sided constitutive 'ontological difference' in the somewhat aged transcendental 'doctrine of two realms', in order to use them afresh (partly in a third realm or *Reich*) he rigidly clung to the 'necessity' and 'hardness' of a priori truths and immunized them against it being possible to revise them through rational learning. Language is the home of Being and the gates are shut: it is a 'cage of obedience'. With even greater justification than in the case of Kuhn, Karl Popper might well have warned against the 'myth of the framework' in the case of Heidegger.[49]

The genuine message of the hermeneutic-linguistic philosophy of our century from Heidegger and Wittgenstein up to Gadamer and Quine and Kuhn is: do not overlook the context. Remember the historical point of view from which you are observing and describing selective parts of the world and its symbolic order. This is true but it becomes mere ideology or – as Popper puts it – a 'myth of the framework', when we *reduce* truth to our point of view and to our particular context of life. What we claim to be true from our historical point of view *is* a *claim* of truth that does *not* change with the context. The same is true with respect to 'reference'. There is no reference without meaning and interpretation, but (against Heidegger and Kuhn in the reading of Kuhn criticized by Popper) reference is not completely determined by meaning, or in Heidegger's words but against Heidegger: 'ontic truth' is not completely determined by 'ontological truth'. And this statement has a political and social implication. It fits much more with democracy and egalitarianism than Heidegger's counterpart. 'Ontic truth' is the truth of normal science and everyday language, it is basically egalitarian, whereas the 'ontological truth' of world-disclosing revolutions of the totality of meaning is extraordinary and in some respects it can be 'elitist'.

Post-empiricist thinkers like Hempel, Quine or Putnam have gone further down the other, egalitarian and more democratic path taken by Kant. They have taken seriously Heidegger's wholly justified warning that we must heed Being and ensure that our statements concur with language as a whole if we are not to experience each sentence as a paralysing falsification. However, they have linked this to a hypothesis on the *reversibility of all knowledge*. Since there can be 'no Being without Entities', the relation between our utterances and statements, on the one hand, and innerworldly experience and new discoveries when dealing with things, on the other, must be taken just as seriously as the non-instrumental concurrence within a language.

If we want to solve the categorial error of modern egocentrism we have to draw a clear distinction between *reference* to things and the *descriptions* of them.[50] Reference does not – as Heidegger claims – depend completely on description. Whether things are *as* they are is not determined by our descriptions of them. Heidegger and other linguistic idealists are right when they argue that there is no access to a real world of objects and objective relations other than through our descriptions that always and already are part of the whole network of a historical language. But the linguistic idealists are wrong when they extend this thesis to 'reference', and argue that things *are* the way they are because of our descriptions. Here Adorno always was a linguistic 'materialist' insofar as he claimed for a strict distinction between subject and object, description and reference. The 'object' never can be covered completely by the 'subject'. The late Adorno has called this the *Vorrang des Objekts* ('priority of the object'): materiality is not to be dissolved into meaning, which latter is the category-mistake of all linguistic idealism. Insofar as Heidegger goes back to a historical a priori which can never be an object of *immanent critique*, his own thinking neglects and represses the non-identical of everyday experiences in life, art and science as well. Not being fallibilist, Heidegger's History of Being becomes itself a paradigm of what Adorno calls 'identity thinking'.

Heidegger, who was prey to an extreme intensionalism (the thesis that meaning determines reference, that language determines truth, etc.), did not succeed in solving the problem of reference in the final analysis and relapsed into the higher-level egocentrism of poetry and thought, since things had not gone so well with Adolf Hitler, the German 'founder of state'. It is not until we open ourselves, to put it slightly metaphysically but vividly, to what Hugo Dingler (or even Charles S. Peirce) calls the 'resistance of the real' and thereby give the entities that have not been identified in advance by Being space to breathe, that we have the innerworldly *experiences* which compel us at some point to renounce the ego-centric projection of an *imaginary world*. And precisely that is the experience which we *have always made* in the factual developmental process of modern science, art and culture. The egocentrism of the *modern age*, the metaphysics of a subject certain of itself, has long since crashed on the rocks of *modern* art and science. Adorno has demonstrated this – as we will see in Chapter 4 – in the case of art that is modern. The 'clearing' of the modern understanding of self no longer reveals a higher, a priori truth, but merely knowledge which, in Quine's sense, is more central than everything else and therefore is more rarely brought into question, but, like all knowledge, is open to question. Fallibilism has become a deep-seated understanding of self, an 'essential feature' of the clearing of Being and the ground plan of Western culture and its normal sciences.

As we have seen here, Adorno goes along with Heidegger in rejecting the instrumental theory of language from Plato to Kant and replacing it with the notion of 'historical constellations'. But his 'historical constellations' are no longer historical a prioris like Heidegger's world-disclosing poetry. They do not determine the realm of contingent, empirical, and material entities, which Adorno also calls the 'non-identical'. The world-disclosing power of great poetry (like that of Jesus, Hölderlin, Newton or Marx) is not power enough to overcome the dialectical tension between language as a whole and particular material entities. And it is precisely this tension that *opens* world-disclosing poetry and the 'historical constellation' determined by this poetry for innerworldly experiences of falsification, immanent critique and learning processes. Here Adorno and post-empiricist philosophers are at one in criticizing Heidegger's metaphysics of *Seinsgeschick* ('historical destiny').

4. Adorno, Horkheimer and pragmatism against philosophy

Materialist insights and moral motives separate Rorty and Adorno from Heidegger and all postmodern polytheists. For them, unlike for Heidegger, Christianity and the history of the rationalization of the world religions is much more than a mere footnote to Plato. The Protestant heritage of American pragmatism – no different from a Weberian Marxism enlightened by the sociology of religion, not to mention the Judaeo-Christian roots of Marx himself – suggests a different reading of occidental rationalism than that of the rise and fall of Greek metaphysics as understood by the history of philosophy. It is the history of the individualizing and egalitarian forces of monotheism and Judaeo-Christian morality.

Right up to Kant's non-stop polemic against passivity, the rationalism, rejected by myth, of the prophetic redemptive religions discredits the 'leave things as they are' attitude. *Looking on* is replaced by the henceforth constitutive portion of human *contribution*: work, praxis, solidarity, subjectivity. Pagan fate, Heidegger's Greco-Germanic *Geschicklichkeit* ('destiny'), is replaced by the utopian universalism of the idea of a justice for all – a universalism denounced by Lyotard as 'meta-law'. This idea, unlike the more aristocratic philosophy of Heidegger and others, seizes the masses. Max Weber writes: 'The annunciation and promise now, naturally enough, address the masses of those who are in need of salvation. They and their interests come to the fore.'[51]

Under 'the pressure of typical and ever-occurrent distress',[52] the narcissistic particularism of the pagan theodicy of good fortune shatters. It becomes obvious that this theodicy was above all created for the good conscience of the rich. From the very beginning, however, in the new Judaeo-Christian theodicy of suffering, the plebeian motives (Weber) of the oppressed and burdened combine with the rationality of moral insight. The older theodicies of luck contributed greatly to the good conscience of the ruling classes. Accidental success was interpreted as divine destiny, and those at the top were the few chosen by the gods. Theodicies of suffering turn this ideology on its head. The question now is, why do we at the bottom of the society suffer whereas they, who are not good and just – even by their own terms – get it all? In particular the prophets, beginning with a Messianic theodicy of suffering, combined moral universalism, social utopianism and the engagement for the poor and disempowered people. It is precisely at this point that the monotheistic religions surpass the standard of a rationality of Greek philosophy. It is to this reading of the history of rationality that Adorno refers when he writes: 'The smallest trace of senseless suffering in the empirical world belies all the identitarian philosophy that would talk us out of that suffering.'[53]

The principal objection which critical theory in Adorno and Horkheimer raised against European thought from Plato to Hegel was that it stood essentially 'in the service of transfiguration'.[54] One should add here some differentiations, which Horkheimer and Adorno sometimes but not always acknowledge. Most important is the difference between Hegel and Kant. Kant is much less affirmative than Hegel, if he is affirmative at all. Adorno knew well that one never could say about Kant that his philosophy was 'in the service of transfiguration'. The opposite is true. But not with Plato, Aristotle, Hegel or Heidegger. Here we find the idealist overtones which neglect the suffering of the human beings.

The real sufferings of history and of real individuals, Horkheimer writes, 'utterly ephemeral in all seriousness', were degraded by metaphysics into something supposedly inessential and accidental which could not touch the higher truth of the 'Whole' and the ultimate meaning of history as a 'Totality'.[55] Thus metaphysics, which is for Adorno the paradigm of identifying thinking, merely transfigures the real state of affairs, coerces a false reconciliation and procures a good conscience for the beneficiaries of the existing order. The spontaneous impulse toward freedom that is immanent in the 'non-identical' and the actual suffering which is condemned to speechlessness in the horizon of transfiguring thought, all this is ignored and falls by the wayside. The very possibility of giving utterance and expression to differences, alternatives and utopias finds itself repressed. Metaphysics, identifying thought and instrumental reason serve to circumscribe narrow limits to what community means, especially when they are in league with the contemporary dominant order as they so often are. Then, in Rorty's words, which could easily be those of Adorno or Horkheimer in this context, we lose the capacity (1) 'to listen to outsiders who are suffering' or (2) 'to outsiders who have new ideas'.[56] This comes close to two central aspects of the meaning of Adorno's notion of the 'non-identical': (1) the suffering of the particular bodies, (2) the utopian force of new inventions against established discourses. In similar vein the young Horkheimer used to polemicize particularly violently against the reactionary alliance between 'optimistic metaphysics' and 'social pessimism'.[57]

If Adorno criticizes identifying thinking and makes himself an advocate of the non-identical thought, then one could compare this with John Dewey criticizing philosophical intellectualism from a modernist, scientific and experimental point of view, which he calls experience. 'Experience' for Dewey is closely related with experiments whose results cannot be prognosticated. 'Experience' is related to *future* and *new* ways of life which are not covered by old and past and eternal ideas. 'Intellectualism' therefore can be compared with Adorno's 'identity thinking'. Both meanings coincide with Freud's and Marx's critique of the domination of the present and the future by the past.

Adorno's notions of the 'non-identical' and 'identity thinking' are both deeply ambivalent, as we have seen. On the one hand, identity thinking is the mere expression of the 'administered world' and a deep-rooted domination over people and nature. On the other hand, there would be no emancipatory idea of the non-identical without its reflection within the techniques and categories of discursive logic and identity thinking. By means of a second reflection (Adorno), which tries to do justice to the non-identical (even if it never can reach such justice finally) identifying thinking becomes transformed into an element of true experience. And the same is true seen from the other side of the difference, which parts the non-identical from the identical. Without being reflected in the disenchanted light of identifying thinking, the non-identical is, as we have seen, 'the horror of the diffuse' (Adorno). Through the second process of reflection the non-identical becomes itself an experience which is mediated by abstraction's universal reason. By means of a second reflection the non-identical is transformed – as Adorno puts it – into a second immediacy.

Being transformed by reflection into a second immediacy, Adorno's notion of the non-identical comes very close to Dewey's notion of experience, because the second reflection overcomes the dualism between the non-identical of the first immediacy and the first-level reflection of identifying thinking. The idea of a second immediacy presupposes a continuum instead. In Dewey's work we find a distinction which is comparable with Adorno's 'first vs. second immediacy'. In *Experience and Nature* Dewey draws the line between 'primitive' (= first immediacy) and 'cultivated naiveté' (= second immediacy).

There remains a difference: for Dewey 'experience' is closely connected with modern science, and his notion of 'experience' covers both realms, art and science, and brings them together. For Adorno, true experience or a 'second immediacy' is closely connected to art and opposed to science. For Adorno modern empirical science as a whole is identity thinking, and the term covers both modern science and platonism. Here Adorno, the negationist thinker, comes closer to Heidegger than to Dewey.

'Identity thinking' is what the pragmatists and the early Horkheimer call 'metaphysics'. And metaphysics is dualistic, bound to passive vision and the 'god's eye perspective' (Putnam), and grounded in a correspondence theory of truth. What Horkheimer and Adorno so vehemently attack is the idea of an ultimate and finally 'closed' truth. 'An isolated and definitive theory of reality is utterly inconceivable' wrote Horkheimer in 1935 and thereby repudiated, like the pragmatists, the thought of a theory detached from the context of praxis within the lifeworld.[58] Theory does not relate to reality like a copy or reflection of an original (as we have seen in Adorno's inaugural lecture quoted in s. 10 of Chap. 1). No theory and no science can pretend to a God's eye perspective from which reality could reveal itself as 'it is and eternally is', in Hegel's words.[59] The optical metaphor becomes an image of what is to be avoided, a warning sign of a path that leads into 'error', as one could say with Heidegger. And in this regard Heidegger and Horkheimer, Adorno and Dewey, are as one. (Already for Hegel there is some irony in his statement on eternity, because at the same time Hegel defines his own philosophy as being 'its own time brought into thoughts': 'Philosophie *ist ihre Zeit* in Gedanken gefaßt'.)

In critical theory, as in Quine, a certain robust realism here becomes the instrument of ideology critique whose purpose is to expel the idea of 'eternal meaning' from metaphysics.[60] Quine is, not only in political terms, far from any 'critical' theory. Despite this, not only is his holism familiar to critical approaches, but his robust realism is also an antidote to metaphysical idealism, an antidote that is already present in critical theory from Marx to Horkheimer. Horkheimer the materialist mistrusts mysticism and the recourse to silence. It is true that he concurs with Wittgenstein when the latter, like Husserl, claims that the genuine problems of our life are not solved by finding answers to all our scientific questions. But Horkheimer refuses to follow the early Wittgenstein in abandoning the meaning of life to that which cannot be said, in which the mystical shows itself: 'Materialism too believes that the problems of life are not soluble in a purely theoretical manner, but it also denies that "the meaning of life after longstanding doubts" can possibly be clarified in some other way. Neither "the mystical" nor "the meaning of life" exist'.[61]

For Horkheimer and Adorno there is no meaning of life which could exist 'alongside' or 'beyond' the everyday praxis of life, knowable to those who possess, as Plato and Aristotle put it, 'an eye' with which to perceive it. For Adorno and Horkheimer, as well as for pragmatists like Dewey, critical practice is the key to theoretical and practical problems as well. Just as resolutely as Horkheimer or Adorno, Rorty repudiates the idea that 'finite, mortal, contingently existing human beings might derive the meaning of their lives from anything except other finite, mortal, contingently existing human beings'.[62] Whereas the early Wittgenstein seems to share the Greek experience of 'wonder' about what can hardly be grasped, Horkheimer and Rorty demystify this sentiment by transforming it into a practical insight into the limitedness of the means at our disposal for realizing our intentions. But that is something which can be changed, and we can hope to do better in the future.[63] Horkheimer argues that science only eliminates ignorance but it does not eliminate the meaning of life. Consequently science can make a very considerable contribution to the solution of the real problems of life. This is not diminished by the fact that science has nothing to say concerning the 'ultimate questions', nor by the fact that science frustrates the 'metaphysical need', something which both Horkheimer and Dewey regard as a false need. The early Horkheimer, the later Adorno and John Dewey also agree with one another in not regarding the 'technical means which help human beings to happiness' as somehow secondary in any way to the ethical purposes of life.[64]

The inner affinity between the anti-philosophical ideology-critique of the young Horkheimer and Adorno on the one side and the positions of Dewey, the early Heidegger and the later Wittgenstein on the other results from their shared rejection of dualism of reality and thinking, surface and essence, and so on. Co-operative praxis, the ready-to-hand character of our 'being-in-the-world', the intricate interconnection of thought and life-form in the language-game, all these lead to a radical overcoming and relativization of those hierarchical relationships which have been erected by ontological and epistemological thought since Plato. Horkheimer argued that it was the exemplary illusion of metaphysics to believe that Logos and Spirit belonged to a higher, theoretically knowable sphere separated from the realm of praxis and empirical experience. For Horkheimer, as we have seen above (Chap. 1, s. 4), 'the bifurcation of the world in two mutually independent realms', 'the Cartesian isolation of spiritual thinking substance from spatial reality', 'the dualism of thought and being, of understanding and perception', is all part of the fatal flaw of philosophical thought.[65] What Horkheimer here rejects is the 'demotion of the known world to something utterly external'.[66]

As in Judaic monotheism, ethics takes the place of that ontology which determined the pagan thought of the Greeks and the Egyptians.[67] Critical theory, which overcomes the fixed dualism of thought and being, represents therefore a critical relationship which obeys a practical 'existential judgement' and thus remains connected to 'the contemporary situation' and the possibility of changing it.[68] Horkheimer's anti-platonism, like Dewey's, has an essentially social and ethical motivation. He explicitly praises the anti-elitist character of the pragmatic principle of instrumental confirmation. The

> critical significance [of this concept] *vis-à-vis* the assumption of a transcendent, more than human truth (which instead of being in principle accessible to experience and praxis is reserved only for revelation and the insight of the elect) turns it into a weapon against any and every kind of mysticism.[69]

This critical theory is Heidegger without the historical a priori of the fate of being (*Seinsgeschick*), and Marx without the confident philosophy of history. The programme of critical theory is in the first place a continuation of the nominalist critique of reification, one which overlaps not only with Kant, Marx and Jewish thought, but also with the post-empiricism of Quine and his critique of the 'reification of universals'.[70] Even if Adorno sometimes used the term 'nominalistic' to criticize positivism, in a broad sense Adorno himself belongs more to the nominalist's than the platonist's tradition. Nominalism in this respect means the rejection of a second realm of ideas that constitutes all appearing reality, material corps and organic bodies. Plato's 'idea' – his 'soul, which is a prisoner of the mortal body' – for Adorno is the historical result of a reification of identity thinking, whereas the appearing reality, material corps and organic bodies are the non-identical that is repressed or blinded by the bright light of Plato's ideas. Like Adorno, nominalists emphazise the role of critical practice and criticize the reifications of universals in identity thinking.

The permanent critique mounted by Horkheimer and Adorno (and today by Habermas) against all forms of 'foundationalist thinking' which seeks for final justifications, and of the idealist absolutization of truth, forms part of a comprehensive critique of reification which also includes the social and political spheres. That is why Adorno demands 'utter fidelity to the ban on images, one which goes far beyond what this originally intended in its place'.[71] Adorno here does not only think of philosophy, theology and social theory. Here he bans especially the images of a realm of utopia. But of equal importance for Adorno is the ban of images in aesthetics, which correlates with Adorno's preference for abstract painting (like Pollock) or sense-destructive and meaning-disturbing poetry (like Beckett). Adorno does not want to rule out photography and cinema by that ban on images, but the ban is relevant here too. Photography and cinema fulfils the ban on images if it is 'negative', 'shattered', 'fragmented', and the paradigm here is the technique of collage. Photography is art as a perspectivic construction of its own reality, and not as depiction of a pregiven reality (or its ideal form).

The ban on images goes back to the Bible and there we can find the origin of all Marxist and pragmatist critique of ideology. Originally, in Isaiah, this argument, so entirely alien to Greek thought, is formulated in a single sentence: 'Who hath formed a god, or molten a graven image, protects him not and is use for nothing.'[72] Rorty also pursues precisely this line of thought when, confronted by those philosophers who kneel down in homage to 'such things' as 'the truth of man', he constantly asks the question: 'What use is it?'[73] The prophetic enlightenment is the common source which nourishes the critique of metaphysics up to the present day in Adorno, Dewey, Habermas, Putnam or Rorty. The idol – Isaiah argues – is but a piece of wood. In part the wood is useful, and serves to warm us and roast our food, but the other part, from which the wooden idol is carved and before which the ignorant kneel has no such practical value, is nothing but a useless piece of wood.[74] According to Jeremiah, the graven images 'are only wood cut down from the forest'. They are 'like scarecrows in the field; they cannot speak and must be born because they cannot move; ... they are beaten silver ... the work of goldsmiths and carvers; ... they are all but the work of skilled men's hands'.[75] Rorty simply applies this rhetoric to philosophy:

> When we go, so do our norms and standards of rational assertibility. Does truth go too? Truth neither comes nor goes. That is not because it is an entity that enjoys an atemporal existence, but because it is not an entity at all. The word 'truth' in this context is just the reification of an approbative and indefinable adjective.[76]

In the critical theory of Adorno and early Horkheimer an anti-dualistic critique of reification is connected with an ethic of social equality instead of a hierarchical ontology of aristocratic distinctions. They repudiate a privileged and theoretical model of knowing in favour of the project of practically transforming the world, a materialist this-worldly negativism and fallibilism, all these are central themes in the critical theory of Adorno and early Horkheimer. It is these themes which they share with Habermas and the pragmatists from Dewey to Putnam. And they are also themes which distance them from Greek thought and its contemplative metaphysics, along with the correspondence theory of truth, all of them ideas which must be ascribed to the other tradition of European self-understanding, that deriving from the biblical thought of Jewish and Christian monotheism.

From the biblical perspective of the 'rational theodicy of suffering' (Weber), even the Greek ethics of the 'good life' gives the impression of a cleverly rationalized theodicy of luck, renewed by philosophy on the highest of levels. This is an ethics, bereft of equality, of cleverly and well-administered privilege. Only the theodicy of suffering and misfortune is successful in breaking through to a higher rational standard of moral consciousness. In redemptive religions, the privileged access to moral insight is destroyed and exposed as the ideology of the propertied male classes. In order to experience injustice, it is not necessary to have the wisdom of well-to-do, worldly-wise old men experienced in matters of power who, as Aristotle writes, 'have an eye'.[77] Only the theodicy of suffering pushes through to the true, the moral, and egalitarian concept of justice; injustice which has been experienced becomes the foundation of a moral insight accessible to everyone.[78] Insight into experienced injustice is the privilege of the underprivileged. Behind the veil of ecstasy, the redemptive religions articulate the reflective force of this insight.

Putnam, as well as Horkheimer, Adorno and Habermas, regards the ethical turn towards equality as the decisive step forward in the awareness of freedom. In his Paul Carus lectures Putnam says:

> The value of Equality is, perhaps, a unique contribution of the Jewish religion to the culture of the West. Greek ethics, as we know it in Plato and Aristotle and even in the Hellenistic Period, has no notion of universal human equality . . . This is connected with some features of Jewish legal code, for example, the fact that the life of one Israelite is worth as much as the life of any other Israelite . . . and so on. What makes this point of view a radical innovation when compared with the Code of Hammurabi and to other ancient codes, is that these latter applied the idea of 'equal penalties' only to social equals: a nobleman who killed a slave only had to pay a money fine. The idea of a set of penalties that should ignore social class, the idea of a justice which in the biblical idiom does not 'respect persons', that is, show partiality, was a concretization of equality.[79]

To sum up this section, where Adorno and Horkheimer meet pragmatism is primarily:

(1) the anti-essentialist rejection of metaphysical dualisms;

(2) the replacement of these dualisms by networks of relations, which include binary oppositions, even contradictions – Adorno here uses the term 'historical constellation', and that means objects and concepts become what they are only in relationship to other concepts and objects and only within a larger socio-historical process, but these relationships and this process are 'intrinsic to the object's own identity';[80]

(3) the (nominalist) critique of all reifications, following here the biblical ban on images;

(4) the practical turn from hierarchical ontology to an egalitarian ethics, which is internal to the critique of earlier philosophical ideology which transfigures the bad existence and keeps within the scope of an 'affirmative culture'.[81]

5. Rational identity and negative dialectics

Adorno always thought that rationality could not be reduced to mere purposive or instrumental rationality. At the same time he refused to renew the old idealist or transcendental distinction between reason (*Vernunft*) and rationality or understanding (*Verstand*). The latter seemed to him to be much too dualistic. For Adorno reason and rationality are entwined. There exists no realm of subjective freedom that is free from all nature and that is not connected internally with the domination of nature by the same subject's purposive rationality. Against Kant he insists that our rational freedom is based on nature. But against Nietzsche and the fundamentalistic critics of enlightenment Adorno holds true that there is an element of 'objective' rationality internal to mere subjective reason. The subject can transcend subjectivity (and the negative dialectic that binds it to instrumentalism and domination) on its own, and only by its own subjective reason. What is 'objective' in subjective rationality, and what can be discovered in self-reflection, is ratio's moment of universality: 'The ratio's moment of universality raises it above its subjective bearers.'[82] But – different from Kant's doctrine of virtue – ratio's moment of universality is a Hegelian 'moment'. It is a moment of a whole constellation of moments, which do not all belong to a Kantian realm of pure purposes. Adorno's idea of 'ratio's universality' therefore cannot be separated from drives, nature and mortality.

Adorno calls his idea of 'ratio' that transcends subjectivity the 'rational identity' of the subject. 'Rational identity' is opposed to (but not completely separated from) 'identity thinking', and it is synonymously used with 'full' or 'non-violent rationality'.[83] Adorno never really clarified these concepts. But one can find a number of remarks and examples which highlight various aspects of its meaning. I would like to mention at least a few of these.

'Rational identity' for Adorno is (1) *consciousness of the non-identical* in contrast to the 'horror of the diffuse'. 'Consciousness of the non-identical'[84] is to be understood first (*a*) as an appeal to open discourses for all possibly essential experiences, i.e. experiences which lie in the interest of those affected. The appeal to excluded, non-identical experiences can, for example, be ignited by the systematically restricted universalism of supposedly universal 'world-pictures' (*Weltanschauung*) as described by Heidegger in

'The Age of the World-Picture'. Of course the mistake of such world-pictures, lacking an appropriate consciousness of the non-identical, is not their universalism, but rather the fact that they are not universalistic enough and, like scientism, exclude entire dimensions of rationality and human experience. Consciousness of the non-identical also includes (b) anamnetic solidarity (*Eingedenken*, or the reflective memory, that we have not forgotten) with those who have suffered – a suffering which can never be made good. Anamnetic solidarity is a limiting concept which refers to the irredeemable, but legitimate, claims of those interests which were irreversibly violated in the past and which can no longer be articulated in practical discourses; it is now impossible to safeguard these interests. Only memory can do this.

'Rational identity' for Adorno is (2) *the correction of such real abstractions of identifying thought* that find expression for example in the reduction of freedom to 'free wage labour' in modern capitalism. The exchange abstractions of the liberal idea of freedom contradict the egalitarian meaning of the modern concept of freedom.

> When we criticize the barter principle as the identifying principle of thought, we want to realize the ideal of free and just barter . . . If no man had part of his labour withheld from him any more, rational identity would be a fact, and society would have transcended the identifying mode of thinking.[85]

Adorno's concept of rational identity rests on (3) *the integration of elements of instrumental and mimetic-aesthetic rationality*. The central and basic concept of *Negative Dialectics*, moral freedom, is explicated by Adorno as the utmost tension between the antagonistic extremes of mimesis and self-preservation. Only the strong subject of intellectual character is free, the one identical with itself. In the integration of intelligible freedom and ego strength, Adorno follows Kant and Freud. Autonomy, for Adorno, is the result of the compulsion to form an identity and the drive for self-preservation. Only the strong ego is able to withstand the impulses of the empirical character that overcome the ego as if it were a piece of blind and alien nature.[86]

Adorno's paradigm case for 'rational identity' is the *artistic form*. Just as *Negative Dialectics* does not want to eliminate the whole family of identifying thinking of 'concepts', 'discursive logic', 'instrumental rationality', 'subjectivity' or 'communication' from critical theory, so *Aesthetic Theory* does not want to exclude 'form', 'formalism', 'construction', and 'technique' from aesthetic modernism. On the contrary for Adorno artistic form is a rational identity 'that makes the non-identical less alien but lets it remain distinct'.[87] The aesthetic form is an anti-essentialist formation against its own totality: 'An aesthetic of form therefore is feasible only if it breaks with an older kind of tradition which was spell-bound by form because it had to totalize it.'[88] Rational identity of the non-identical does not enforce an identity of formal unity and the transcendence of the specific, manifold material. Its integration of subjectivity *is* its disintegration: 'Disintegration is the truth of integral art . . . the law of form of an art-work stipulates that each of its moments as well as the unity of all moments together be organized in accordance with their specific makeup.'[89] Thus works of art are 'not the unity of a manifold but the unity of the one and the many'.[90]

The speculative motif in Adorno's negative dialectics is the notion of the *reconciliation of reason and nature*. This can only be construed dialectically, in the form of paradoxical phrasing. Unlike Kant, Adorno thought that reason and rationality were not *per se* foreign to nature. Adorno shares the premiss put forward by Piaget and other theorists of evolution (anticipated by the late Schelling) and shared by Dewey and the pragmatists that the history of the development of reason is a natural history. Intellect detaches itself in the course of time from nature, the notion of what should be becomes detached from what is. But what is detached keeps part of the process of nature. We need to have a somatic existence, a body in time and space, to be able to take an affirmative or negative position towards that existence. To transcend nature and to sever mind from body is itself a natural process. Adorno felt that Kant's philosophy constituted the irreversible codification of this severance and the 'detachment' of the mind from the body. But Kant ignored the fact that such severance did indeed take place, forgetting to reflect on its genesis. The divisive negation of one's own intuitive nature by the rational freedom of the subject represses the fact that such negation, as Hegel said quite unmeta-phorically, is quite literally pain and labour. 'All pain and all negativity', which are, and here Adorno concurred with Hegel's 'materialist' insight, 'the motor behind dialectical thought', have inscribed themselves in the mind itself as 'the multiply mediated, at times unrecognizable shape of the physical'.[91]

A rational view of the difference between reason and nature (between what is and what should be, between freedom and necessity) therefore includes a speculative hypothesis on the history of human development, that is Schelling's 'materialism'. In his late philosophy Schelling had developed in speculative terms of a philosophy of spirit the thesis that all spirit stems from nature because nature itself has an internal tendency towards spiritualization. Thus for Schelling organic forms are 'paleosymbolic' or 'paleospiritual' forms of nature which tend to evolve in the direction of a broader, more differentiated and more autonomous spiritual order of things. Yet spirit, even in its most autonomous manner, remains modified nature and part of its historical evolutionary process. Adorno writes: 'Everything of the mind is modified bodily instinct, and such modifications are the qualitative shift into something which is not that which simply is. An urge is, according to Schelling's insight, the prior form of the mind.'[92]

Conscious life can only be imagined as the *self-transcendence of organic life*. However, this process of becoming conscious is accompanied by a dialectic of what Piaget calls the *cognitive repression* of all earlier stages of evolution.[93] This dialectic, which ultimately seduces the mind into thinking that it is absolute, can only be clarified by means of a second stage of reflection, which Horkheimer and Adorno termed *Eingedenken*, 'bearing in mind the nature in the subject', and which Piaget called the 'decentering of subjectivity'.

The free subject has to tear itself free of its own historical and organic genesis. It has to presuppose that it has become an 'intelligible character'. This consciousness of freedom constitutes the specific virtue of being a human subject. However, it contains an overestimation that leads to a false absolutization of the subject. Therefore the subject's consciousness of freedom has to be decentred by the painful insight that all our freedom is not only constrained but *enabled* by nature. For Adorno the conditions of possibility of freedom are natural (and social) conditions, which are external to the subject's consciousness and therefore represent an irreducible element of alienation. Freedom is as much grounded in our rational will as in our prerational 'impulses'. Insight into that 'necessity' of nature constitutes a 'higher' level of rational, self-reflective freedom.

> Without the unity and the compulsions of reason, nothing even similar to freedom would have been thought of, let alone existed . . . No model of freedom is available other than that involving consciousness, as in society as a whole, intervening in this manner in the complexion of the individual through society. This is by no means chimerical, because consciousness is itself rechanneled instinctual energy, itself also impulse, also an element of that in which it intervenes . . . If this affinity did not exist . . . then neither would the idea of freedom.[94]

The 'unity and compulsion' of reason are elements of identifying thought which 'intervene' in the 'non-identical', namely in the conceptually inaccessible ('ineffable') complexity of the individual. As non-identical, the individual is an opaque complexity of diffuse instincts and impulses. However, from the perspective of a rational identity at a higher level, the 'affinity' (a category derived from mimesis[95]) of identifying thought and non-identifying impulses can be experienced as the non-compulsive integration of the Ego. The Self is born. We can at least imagine it, for the primordial relation of reason and nature, the affinity between them which we can bring to mind, is just as constitutive of the 'idea of freedom' as is the (Kantian) opposition, the sharp juxtaposition of reason and nature. Kant himself made an important first step in the direction of overcoming the fundamental oppositions of his first two 'Critiques' in the *Critique of Judgement*, to which Adorno sometimes returns in his theory of aesthetics, which is (as we will see in the next chapter) his very theory of freedom.

4 • Freedom, Critique and Transgression in Adorno's Theory of Aesthetic Modernism

According to Adorno, genuinely modern art is experimental, fragmented, shattered – and irreconcilably opposes false consciousness. Modern art is an art of reflection – to borrow an expression from Robert Musil in *Mann ohne Eigenschaften*, 'shining mysticism'. Modern art for Adorno is directness given intellectual form and fragmented by reflection.[1] From the moment Kant's *Critique of Judgement* appeared, Adorno believed it possible to pinpoint an increasing intellectualization of art: 'extremely intellectualized art which could be traced back to Mallarmé and achieved its apex in the dreamlike confusion of Surrealism'.[2] Mallarmé's 'l'art pour l'art' for Adorno is a paradigm of intellectualized art, that has become completely 'self-reflective' or – as one could say today in the language of systems theory – 'self-referential'. Art becomes completely intellectualized if it refers merely to itself. 'That consciousness kills', Adorno writes in *Aesthetic Theory*, 'is an old wives' tale. False consciousness alone is deadly.'[3] Irreconcilable and 'without an image to model itself on',[4] a rapidly ageing yet persistently new art stands opposed to life and its reification. Yet the irreconcilability of modern art is not only directed outward. It is also turned against itself, driving modern art's own contradictions to the fore so that the works 'crumble with necessity and rigor' until – as Adorno says of Beckett's *Endgame* – they conduct a 'play with elements of reality, free of all direct representation'.[5]

The aesthetic image stands under the ban of images. Adorno's reference to the biblical ban on images has two aspects that go back to the biblical tradition, but now have become completely secularized. The ban on images was a major means of rationalization and disenchantment for the old prophets, and it continues in modern art's preference for abstract forms. In the Bible the created world and all human products have lost any sacred meaning, and the same has become true for art in the twentieth century. All premodern art was bound directly to religion, and even bourgeois art had produced a secondary religious meaning as a religion of education and formation (*bürgerliche Bildungsreligion*). Bourgeois art was – for the first time in history – autonomous art, but at the same time it was a purifying mirror of bourgeois class consciousness. Art had become a sacred image of the ruling class. It is precisely this image that has been banned by modern art techniques of shock-effects, montage and abstraction. Adorno here is broadly in accordance with Benjamin and Brecht.

The second aspect of the ban on images that has a similiar function in the Bible and in modern art is to produce a direct, unreduced experience of the object. There should no longer be any access to the true reality of works of art that is mediated through (beautiful or ugly, more or less perfect) copies. If we compare this with the Bible, the similarity becomes evident. If there exists no valid copy or image of God in this world, then the only access man or women have to God's realm must be direct and unmediated, e.g. through the ear of the prophet or whoever it is to whom God speaks. The ban on images in both cases, that of the Bible and that of art, ensures that any true experience of the divine or the artistic reality must be an experience of the sublime or its counterpart. Therefore Adorno speaks paradoxically of the *nicht abbildlichen ästhetischen Bilder* ('non-copying aesthetics pictures') of art that is authentic.[6] He always draws a strict distinction between *Bilder* and *Abbilder*, pictures and copies.[7] Pictures can be sublime or humble and degraded, and the same is true of the biblical God, who appears as the sublime or (as in Jesus) humiliated. Copies of an original can be beautiful or ugly, more or less perfect, but they never can be sublime or humble. Adorno argues that only pictures which constitute a reality *sui generis* are able to be art's authentic projects, projects that can make a claim to truth. Authentic art (as well as an authentic individual life), Adorno argues, should try to avoid being a copy.

Such art inevitably transcends the boundaries of art and challenges the concept of art itself, as Adorno claims both German expressionism and French surrealism do.[8] This trend of art is violently opposed to all 'realistic' illusionist art which seeks to reflect and transform the world. Adorno concurs on this point with his conservative opponent Arnold Gehlen, if not in the prognosis, then at least in the diagnosis. Painting which has become absolutely non-representational radically renounces 'a duality of levels', as Gehlen calls it, and instead overcomes all the dualisms of the old platonic metaphysics in the aesthetic.[9] Indeed, Breton's surrealist manifesto already considered precisely this to be the peculiar *pragmatism* of the most recent avantgarde of that time.

What Breton calls surrealistic 'pragmatism' is opposed to any art that is representational, that is art that first has a meaning in the appearing *Gestalt* which is only a surface that points back to a deeper second meaning of essence behind the appearance. The basic philosophical meaning of 'pragmatism' in the American context is to cancel the distinction between essence and appearance, and this coincides with the objective of the surrealist revolution. This also coincides with Adorno's understanding of aesthetic modernism. An important consequence is that the fundamental opposition between dream and reality vanishes. Dream, fantasy and imagination are part of our practical and real-life experience, not another realm.

Breton asks why should one separate dream and reality and dissect them into two ontological layers: 'Is a dream less pragmatic than the rest of our life?'[10] Surrealism, according to Adorno, 'expels the images of antiquity from the Platonic heaven'.[11] As Gehlen sharp-sightedly observes, in order to renounce the aesthetic reflection of a truly real nature and thereby 'duality', 'but seek to retain the artistic means of images having a direct impact', there is 'only a single way of pin-pointing reflection by the observer: to alienate the represented object itself and associate the reflection with the object – by denying that one can recognize oneself – this is surrealistic painting'.[12] A man glances in the mirror and sees himself from behind, and beneath the image of a pipe is written 'this is not a pipe'. Surrealistic paintings have a double aim. First, they irritate, puzzle and negate the spectators' usual expectation of seeing a copy of a well-known world, which appears on the canvas in another, different, illuminated, transfigured, or alienated light. Second, instead of referring as a sign to an external reality outside the painting, they present themselves as new things, never seen before, or as objects *sui generis*, which have an internal force to ban and disturb the spectators' gaze and self-assurance. Essentially or *per se*, Adorno thus gives Gehlen's theory a sharper edge: surrealistic painting is already non-representational and abstraction is a direct extension of the same process. The idea of the surrealistic shock gives birth to a new manner of painting.[13] Surrealism is itself a new philosophy of art, and a philosophy that is realized in surrealistic paintings and objects.

Modernity brings the destruction of sense, unity, fixed meaning and 'conclusive' orientation to unreconciled expression 'without itself taking a position'.[14] Things are not as the realist Lukács had hoped from socialism. Were society to master its catastrophic constitution and to emancipate itself from superfluous domination, the great bourgeois novel would not return, nor would the narrative bursting with life or the classical symphony, as though nothing had happened and all were well now. Why not? New social structures call forth new forms of art, and the light of these new forms falls back on previous art and gives it a new aspect. Modern experiments with dissonant, shattered and fragmented works of art lead us to become sensitive to the fragmentation and the dissonant sounds that already exist in classical works of art. From surrealist novels we can become aware of the surrealism which is latent under the representational surface of realist novels.

Adorno argues that the shattered form of open works, the incessant struggle never recognizably rounded off into totality, into which the countless endgames of modernity have incurably disintegrated, *is* as such *also* a moment of *successful* emancipation from the constraints of totality and from the triumphal gesture of affirmative art and culture. As Adorno sees it, art from the beginning had already participated in 'all injustice'. For Beckett's 'game with elements of reality, free from all representationality, that takes no position', finds 'in such freedom from the prescribed business' 'its happiness'.[15] It *is* real freedom, 'the materialization of the most advanced consciousness'.[16] Adorno defends Beckett's *Endgame* not simply as a protest against senseless life under the rule of capitalism and the 'commodity form', but also as of value in itself. Beckett's dramatic work liberates itself from an old and more repressive form of art, and it discloses a world of a new experience of freedom.

Art emancipated from the spell of 'blackmailed reconciliation' and 'disreputable affirmation', from the constraints, the 'lies' and the 'ideology' of traditional art, *needs* a place in an emancipated society. Indeed, it is possible only in a society in which the relations of reaching understanding (*Verständigungsverhältnisse*) are at least somewhat accommodating to it.[17] 'One is not to believe', suggested

Adorno 'unconstructively' (*zur Ungüte*) at the 1959 Baden-Baden art symposium, 'that modern art is the way it is because the world is so bad, and that in a better world it would be better. That is a hotel-art perspective.'[18] Adorno fears that Lukács with his exaggerated love of classical art might be drawn to this decorative perspective.

It is no accident that Adorno's *Aesthetic Theory* closes with lines which show how much Adorno held to the letter and spirit of aesthetic modernity, even against his own construction of history:

> It is possible that the art of the past, which has today become an ideological moment of the unfulfilled society, would devolve upon a fulfilled society; but that the newly emerging art would thereby return to rest and order, to affirmative representationality and harmony, would be the sacrifice of its freedom. Were the art of the future to become positive, then the suspicion of the real endurance of negativity would be acute; so it is always, relapse threatens incessantly, and freedom, which would be freedom from the principle of possession, cannot be possessed.[19]

Adorno recognized in Lukács's opinion of Beckett's work – that it is merely the mirror of late capitalist pathology and 'worldlessness' enlarged into anthropological dimensions – nothing but the 'philistine cliché that modern art is as ugly as the world in which it arose'.[20] No surrealistic art could possibly outdo the comment of a communist functionary made on a pornographic text of Dali's: 'You are only trying to complicate the simple and healthy relationship between a man and a woman.'[21] For Adorno one of the functions of art is always to question the nature of so-called healthy relationships.

1. Experimental freedom

Adorno's 'positive' idea of freedom that emerges within the new non-representational, shattered and open forms of art is the idea of 'experimental freedom'. It is the anticipation and tentative realization of freedom in a truly 'open society', whose 'openness' is not reduced to capitalism plus parliamentary democracy as in Karl Popper's political work.

Unlike Brecht and Lukács, Adorno insists on the unequivocal

autonomy of art. Yet, he is no apologist of 'l'art pour l'art'. Art is autonomous in society, but not autarchic. A certain extra-aesthetic understanding of freedom is associated with aesthetic modernism. In Adorno's understanding of aesthetics, freedom is neither arbitrariness nor rational control and planning of one's own life – in other words it is neither a Hobbesian negative nor an Aristotelian positive freedom. Freedom is neither an uncontroversial pursuit of the good life nor a simple absence of external coercion. Instead, Adorno's model of freedom seeks a conscious exposure of the self to the contingencies of situations which the subject neither dominates nor controls. I would call this an experimental understanding of freedom, and autonomous modern art is the institutional location of such freedom.

This connection between aesthetic modernism and an extra-aesthetic, experimental understanding of freedom is largely concealed behind a different, negatively theological or abstractly utopian layer of meaning in Adorno's writings which refers to the image of a completely 'peaceful society' and holds to the belief that reification in the present is complete. But there is no necessary connection between these two layers of meaning, which consistently overlap and penetrate one another in Adorno's works.[22]

How utopian is Adorno really? I would argue here for a post-utopian reading of his work. But, in my opinion, the post-utopian version must still retain a utopian element in order not to fall victim to the postmodern destruction of reason apparent in writers like Derrida and Foucault. This element links art and society and makes the aesthetic a critique of society. It is post-utopian in that it gives up any hope of a final redemption from all evil; but it is utopian since it nevertheless does not surrender the right to a fundamental critique of *all* socio-political institutions, indeed of the very principle of the institution. Irritation and the deliberative use of strategies of paradoxical communication are among the main purposes of modern art-works. Manifestations (exhibitions, happenings, demonstrations) that protest vehemently against the banning of art from the walls of the museum are shown in the museum. There exist a lot of paintings whose purpose is to introduce the question whether they are paintings at all – and not script (like the cryptograms of Paul Klee from the early 1920s) or accidental results of damage in transit (as the many scratches on Dubuffet's paintings). The institutionalization of open and fragmented, fleeting and anti-realist works of art with disturbingly paradoxical messages confronts us with the paradox of art as an institution of radical institutional critique.

From the standpoint of this critique everything could be different, although on a day-to-day basis of course it remains the same. Art shows that it must not. The painting could become text, the stage could become a public assembly, or – conversely – the revolution on the streets could become a performance on the stage. The critique regards everything as contingent, and art disturbs our perception insofar it confronts us with this contingency. As an institution of radical institutional critique art is always counterfactual and 'utopian' and can never achieve totality. The experience of this critical point of view links the experimental freedom of the aesthetic sphere to modern life as an experimental form of life. Instead of allowing real life to become paralysed by the tragedy of mortality and of consoling all hope for some future utopian reconciliation, aesthetic modern art refers to the extra-aesthetic freedom of an experimental life as *one* of the institutions of radical institutional critique. This links even the most radical and esoteric art with public critique and utterly profane *learning processes* in an egalitarian society.

At this juncture it is necessary to differentiate further, for the institutionalization of radical institutional critique is not peculiar to aesthetic modernism, rather it is simply a characteristic of modern society *per se*. Modern science can also be defined as institutionalized institutional criticism, as can the political legislation of democratic sovereignty. But in art a specific element is added, which is its reference to an experimental understanding of freedom. In addition, the pitiless, distanced view of the art objects is worth mentioning.[23] Art shares this aloofness with science. Yet from romanticism right through to surrealism, there still seems to be a motive which is characteristic of aesthetic modernism and marks it off from science, morals, law, and so on. This motive is not, however, the idea of a 'rebellion against the normative' which Karl-Heinz Bohrer borrows from surrealism, Benjamin and Adorno (or according to Baudelaire: 'evil as an aesthetic category').[24] This only leads to a negative obsession of art with the sphere of the moral.

The critical-ironic distance of modern art from life does not aim at a specific value sphere or institution of modern society; rather, it creates distance in all its institutions, even distance in the meta-institutions of language. That this has been shown is, I believe, the greatest achievement of deconstructivistic literary criticism.[25] Modern art, one could say along the lines of Adorno, reflects with its expressive means the cognitive thesis of deconstructionism that all idealized meaning is contingent and depends on its utterance in time and space. Therefore already language *per se* is internally related to domination. The speechless is excluded from speech once man has reached the social level of a talking animal. Art is a speechless speech that brings the speechless, preconceptual and non-identical to speech ('das Sprachlose zur Sprache bringen'). That which is silenced by the medium of language as such comes back to language by means of the sublanguage of art that is modern. This is the political meaning of the shattered form of the creatures of modern art. But the aesthetic inclusion of that which is speechless and silenced is not its inclusion in our ethical life, because art that brings the 'other' and 'excluded' to the fore does not ask for the justice or injustice of the exclusion. The aesthetic inclusion of the excluded other, the non-identical, does 'justice' on a higher level only, would include justice in what is unjust in normal justice (see the remarks on the 'non-identical' in my Introduction).

I will initially use the example of Adorno's analysis of the transition from great affirmative to truly modern, romantically inspired art. This example shows how both factors are intertwined and mutually determine each other: first, the post-utopian element of the autopoietic closure of art, to form a self-referential system, an autonomous institution and, second, the anarchistic-utopian aspect of radical critique of *each* institutionalization. I understand this interconnection of institutional affirmation and institution-shattering impulses as an alternative to the historical metaphysical understanding of art, one that can also be found in Adorno and which projects a type of negative theology into art.

The aesthetic culture of modernity, which Adorno, in avantgarde fashion, always identifies with *modernism*, is thus also irreconcilably opposed to its own – and Adorno's – tendency to abstract utopia and to the cognition of totality, to final reconciliation and ultimate grounds: whether *ex negativo* in an 'ontology of the false condition' or as the devastating insight that the 'whole is the false'.[26] Precisely *as* consistent modernism, it comports itself irreconcilably toward its own historical self-understanding: that it is the already completed end of history, or a culmination of history to be brought forth.[27] Thus the consistent consciousness of aesthetic modernity already becomes in Adorno himself the falsifier of a construction of history turned negative. The way Adorno analyses modern art opposes his own tendency to interpret this art as a utopian appearence of a completely different and completely reconciled world. What I want to do is to make a sharp distinction between Adorno's theoretical or philosophical self-understanding and his praxis as interpreter and critic of modern art. His self-understanding is that of a negative philosophy of history which links art in the manner of negative theology with the imageless otherness of a transcendental realm of freedom and reconciliation. Here Adorno always comes very close towards a history of decay. Yet his interpretation and critique of modern art shows another reading of modernity, that allows a more immanent critique of modern society from the point of view of its culture and art. Adorno the critic and interpreter of modern art is more radical in his critique of metaphysics and more a consistent modernist than Adorno the negative philosopher of history and utopian thinker of the 'complete other' (*das ganz Andere*). Adorno's analysis of modern art allows us to understand art as part of the radical critique of society, even of language as such. But this critique can be productive within society, and enlarge its own potential of liberties. It need not be a view from nowhere to fulfil its critical function.

Just as *Negative Dialectics* allows itself the thought of universal solidarity only at the moment of the *collapse* of metaphysics and in the face of its remaining ruins, so art participates in the utopian gleam of reconciliation only in *departing* from the metaphysical thought of its final sublation (*Aufhebung*) in life. Music overcomes on the threshold to modernity the idealistic and early romantic *expressive model of the spirit*, which condenses everything singular and particular into an organic form of life.[28] Art now becomes an expression of difference and multiplicity. Adorno's example for passing this threshold from unified spirit to decentred difference is Schubert's confrontation with Beethoven and the classical tradition.

Schubert's music is so sorrowful because it does not find its way back to the integral expression of musical complexity and loses itself in the freedom of the particular and the detail. Adorno recognized in the romantic outburst of unmastered sorrow that makes

an impromptu of Schubert's sound 'so incomparably more sorrowful than even the darkest pieces of Beethoven', an essential motif
of modernity, indeed its first breakthrough.[29] Schubert is more sorrowful than Beethoven to the degree that he is more modern. The
reason, for Adorno, is that sorrow follows immediately from the
'release of the particular' from the compulsion to dialectical reconciliation of the whole with the parts. The 'persistence of the particular' – embodied by Beethoven in music and by Hegel in philosophy – is freed from the compulsion to a higher, superimposed
unity. The *loss of reconciliation* is inseparably bound to this *emancipation* from the compulsion to totality. Hence the sorrow: 'The
Schubertian sorrow depends, accordingly, not merely upon the
expression (which is itself a *function* of the musical complexion),
but upon the release of the particular.' Yet the 'emancipated detail
is also abandoned and suffering, negative'.[30]

A passage such as that quoted here from the sketches for the
Beethoven book clearly emphasizes how distant Adorno's radical
individualism is from all forms of communal or collective identity.
Adorno was never an enthusiastic class warrior. Whereas, for
instance, the 'communitarianism' fashionable today in the West
consists in a renewal of the expressive model of collective life
developed from Herder to Hegel, for Adorno *all* freedom of modernity begins with criticism of that model's metaphysical character
of compulsion, which the inner logic of Beethoven's composition
still follows. The 'dual character' of 'totality' is proper to the
organic expression of the particular in the universal:

> the totality has the character of the *persistence* of the particular (which
> is missing from Schubert and from all romantic art, including Wagner);
> and something ideological, transfiguring, which corresponds to the
> Hegelian doctrine of the positivity of the whole as the epitome of all
> particular negativities; thus the moment of untruth.[31]

Adorno is, unlike Lukács, free of nostalgia. Schubert's sadness is
more like the highly conscious, almost intentional consequence of
the liberation from the spell of bourgeois subjectivity. It is the
destruction of that subjectivity which first makes such sadness possible and opens it up to aesthetic experience. The direct object of
mourning is not what is past, but rather it itself, namely mourning.
If new music as in the late Schönberg, as Adorno claims, culminates

in an expression of weeping, then this is not a well-disciplined, methodical 'act of mourning'. Any intention and any reserved self-control is washed away in the expression of weeping.

Adorno's conception of freedom is entirely directed toward the experimental play of 'blind somatic' impulses and overcomplex 'material' variety, which does not let itself be understood, mastered, interpreted.[32] The metaphors of streaming and flowing that dissolve the rigidity of self-identical subjectivity are aimed at this interplay. These metaphors are not intended primarily to convey emotion; they are intended as an expression of a new way to experience and disclose the world, and besides as a new moral outlook.

Modernity emancipates itself from tradition at the point at which it *willingly* 'lets itself be carried along by the rushing current of the tones themselves', as Hegel put it with a sharp turn of phrase aimed against all romanticism.[33] Adorno uses nearly the same words, but he reverses the evaluation. What Hegel execrates and represents as a loss of freedom becomes for Adorno the vital ideal of freedom for modern music, and in his apology for an informal music it is the 'desideratum of musical freedom'.[34] For Adorno spontaneity is vitally contrary to oppression, both in music and politics. The unity of melody and the regularity of metre, 'the finite recognition of a harmonic position, and above all of the tone' (Schopenhauer), were for Hegel and Schopenhauer the guarantee that what Adorno once called the 'tempting sensual' would not exceed the bounds of the musical. For Hegel, melody guarantees the popular pedagogical contribution of music to 'the free being-with-itself of subjectivity'; for Schopenhauer, the harmonic position both reflects and reinforces 'man's sober life and striving'.[35]

Adorno confronts this tradition with the idea of freedom which is oriented toward an experimental disposition. The subject finds his/her freedom precisely in the fact that he/she puts itself into danger, abandoning itself to the force of its own *impulses* just as it exposes itself to a multiplicity of principally uncontrollable *situations*. Experimental freedom is the creation of new alternatives which 'crumble the crust of convention' – as Dewey would put it. Experimental freedom is the freedom of chance to open or disclose new realms of freedom. The roots for such an experimental understanding of freedom lie without a doubt in the actions and anti-art works of the avantgarde and post-avantgarde, and not in philosophy (here again Adorno comes much closer to Schelling and the romantic tradition than to Hegel and the classical period). Modern freedom *is* experimental freedom: the sublation of duality, the destruction of meaning, the liberation of poetry from prosaic relevance and from the constraints of practical commitment, the transgression of the borders that separate art from life. Adorno applauds the surrealistic installations of 'cut-off breasts, mannequins' legs in silk stockings' and other 'objects of partial desires' as the 'child's picture of the modern age' which 'rescue' the 'consumption fetish' and the rapidly 'obsolete' from technical objectivity.[36] Psychoanalytic theory does not do justice to this movement because it itself is too harmless. One figure of surrealism is the *exhibitionist* whom Adorno compares in *Minima Moralia* with the artist:

> Artists do not sublimate. That they neither satisfy nor repress their desires, but transform them into socially desirable achievements, is a psycho-analytic illusion; incidentally, legitimate works of art are today without exception socially undesired. Rather, artists display violent instincts, free-floating and yet colliding with reality, marked by neurosis. Even the philistine's dream of the actor or violinist as the synthesis of a bundle of nerves and a tugger of heart-strings, has more truth than the no less philistine economic theory of instincts, according to which the favourite children of renunciation get rid of the stuff in symphonies and novels. Their lot is rather a hysterically excessive lack of inhibition over every conceivable fear; narcissism taken to its paranoiac limit. To anything sublimated they oppose idiosyncrasies.[37]

Here again, Adorno is denying the theory that art is the expression of something different from art, be it ideas (Plato), class-interests (Marx) or unconscious sexual drives (Freud). There is no 'duality of levels' (Gehlen) in art that is authentic. All authentic (modern) art is a praxis *sui generis*. This is better expressed by surrealist provocative actions or the unsublimated narcissism of a third-class violinist in a coffee house than in those harmonist works that try to express something that is higher or deeper than the art-work in itself. Because it destroys this illusion and expresses heterogeneous instincts much more immediately, Adorno prefers dissonance in music and all other art. In Schönberg's music, in the wrong notes of a 'tugger of heart-strings' or in surrealist happenings, it is the moment of dissonant abbreviation that breaks the norm and the normative of the 'affirmative culture' (Marcuse).

2. Farewell to theory

Should Adorno in fact be, as Rüdiger Bubner once remarked, the 'most important aesthetic thinker of a century rich in artistic production, but rather impoverished in the theory of art', then his importance rests in my opinion in the fact that Adorno *took an aesthetic view of aesthetic theory* – whether idealistic, romantic, materialistic or, like his own, negativistic.[38] In so doing, Adorno traced the *movement* and *dynamic* of modernity, the *temporal core* of its truth and the rapidly transforming 'symptoms of a powerful tendency', without smoothing over the contradiction between the actual movement of the arts and the *concept* ascribed to them by philosophy.[39] Adorno, the 'advocate of the non-identical' (Wellmer), here starts with the observation that philosophical or theoretical *concepts* never can capture the totality of the individual works and movements of art.

The ambivalence of Adorno's *Aesthetic Theory* is the ambivalence which exists between philosophical theory and aesthetic critique. The *theory* is conservative and hopelessly utopian, related towards a negative philosophy of history: 'The whole is the false'. But that is not the whole Adorno. Adorno as a *critic* of aesthetic modernism criticizes his own theory, because even Adorno's theory remains theory, and that means a constellation of *concepts* that never can reach the non-identical without identifying it, and in identifying does violence to it. The only *critic* who comes close enough to his/her object to communicate with it in a free manner is the one who does not violate it. Adorno here follows a line that starts with early romanticism and ends up with Walter Benjamin.[40] Schlegel, as a critic of *Wilhelm Meister*, understands criticism as going on with the work of art on another level, that transform the work of art into the open form of a work in progress. Wilhelm Meister's cultural voyage of discovery (*Bildungsreise*) for this reason never ends; every critic that follows in the course of time from generation to generation gives it a new turn. The subject of the classical formation is decentred step by step on this road of criticism so that the works 'crumble with necessity and rigour'.[41]

Whereas Goethe needs the romantic critic to open his *Wilhelm Meister*, which is a classical novel of cultural discovery (*Bildungsroman*), Beckett's *Endgame* and other avantgardiste modern art from the very beginning have internalized the romantic critic. They permanently reflect themselves and do not need the external critics to transform the work to an open form and to decentre its subjectivity. On the other hand the critic does this with theory. It 'crumbles' in the open form of the essay (see below, s. 3). As critics, Schlegel, Benjamin or Adorno overcome the metaphysics of the subject.

Paradigmatic for Adorno's aesthetic stance *vis-à-vis* his own theory is the *transgression theorem*. It expresses best what Adorno wants: *neither* to subsume and adjust to theory the aesthetic stance of the critic opening itself to the new, *nor* to allow theory to become aesthetic and to decay into 'conceptual poetry'. The aesthetic stance of the critic is not aesthetic production but a form of non-violent communication with works of art. Adorno developed the 'transgression theorem' in the 1960s. 'Transgression' means the transgression of borders between music and painting, sculpture and text and so on, or between 'high' and 'low' culture, between art and life, theory, philosophy and art. Adorno's word for 'transgression' is 'infringement' (*Verfransung*). 'Transgression' does not mean 'regression' that cuts down all differences and overcomes all limits. As Christine Eichel has shown in an important study of Adorno's aesthetics of music, the theorem replaces the model of the subject with a synthesizing sublation of the arts in art and of art in life.[42]

Adorno gives the name *Verfransung* (literally, 'infringement'), which we here call 'transgression', to the internal dissolution of the boundaries between the individual art forms and between art and life, which was long ago anticipated by surrealism and has become ubiquitous since the 1960s. The explosive dynamic between classical modernity, neo- and post-avantgardism forces *art of its own accord* to transgress the particular boundaries of its forms. Music, the classical temporal art, spatializes itself by consciously renouncing its expressive force, and painting gives itself temporal form by becoming expressive and non-representational. Adorno was always interested in the transgressions and overlapping moments on the boundaries of poetry and music, music and writing (the silent reading of the score as the ideal of listening to music), of philosophical essay and art, notes and literature. It is a process to which he himself contributed, for example, in ironic titles for his essays or books: 'Words without Songs', 'Notes to Literature'.

Adorno's sensitivity to the violation of borders and to transgressions shows that by no means everything falling under the rubric 'postmodern' falls outside the horizon of his late aesthetic. It is of decisive importance for the concept of transgression that no Wagnerian *Gesamtkunstwerk* arises out of it, and that life does not become an art-work, as in fascist and Stalinist mythology. The tendency toward overlapping and infringement is partial, subversive, spontaneous, but it is never total nor in a totalitarian manner aimed at the whole. 'Transgression' is an alternative to the model of sublation (or overcoming) that oversteps the autonomy of art without destroying it. Transgression or *Verfransung* therefore can be taken for a negative dialectical reading of Hegel's positive or affirmative dialectical sublation (*Aufhebung*).

Sometimes the polemics of the late Adorno against *some* examples of avantgardist art (as concrete poetry) have made it seem as though Adorno had become anti-avantgardist. This should be corrected. From the perspective of Adorno's lecture in July 1966 on 'Art and the arts', a new light is shed by the concept of transgression on his *Aesthetic Theory* which, at least in the first phase of its reception, was connected too strongly with a notion of the art-*work*, an emphasis on higher aesthetic truth, the rehabilitation of semblance, even of natural beauty. Adorno, who was hardly free of prejudices against America and the culture industry, and showed just as strong a prejudice in favour of Austro-German music, had distanced himself noticeably from the avantgarde and the 'latest developments'.[43] But the subterranean surrealism of *Aesthetic Theory* poses a consistent contrast to that position. Through the entire book Adorno emphasizes the truth-shattering force of semblance, and vice versa, the impact of the aesthetic material which dissolves the semblance. Adorno declares as the 'fundamental layers' and 'invariants' of modernity 'dissonance', 'explosion', and 'construction', and his consistent emphasis upon 'suddenness' and 'subversion' is supplemented with the idea of an 'infiltration of the aesthetic with the moral'.[44] Finally Adorno postulates the 'normativity of modernity', which grounds itself solely in the 'antitraditionalistic energy'[45] of the works of modern art. The diagnosis of 'anti-avantgardism' is at any rate false and must be corrected

and differentiated in light of the transgression theorem.[46] Adorno
rejects only the avantgarde's *imperial* claims of sovereignty, which
encroach upon life and destroy autonomy, on the ground that they
still follow the false metaphysical model of *sublation*.

The insight into the simultaneous necessity and impossibility of
a *theory* of the aesthetic is of decisive importance for Adorno's
judgement and attitude towards informal and serial music, toward
the conscious blurring of the boundary between image and tone,
towards the dissolution of fixed spatio-temporal systems and the
classical genres, towards the introduction of the principle of chance
and of improvisation in various forms, towards the return of montage, towards happening and film. As Gertrud Koch and Miriam
Hansen have recently shown, Adorno wanted to posit an emancipatory potential even in a mass cultural phenomenon like film.[47]
For him, the cinematic mimesis of expressive bodies suggested a
prelinguistic experience prior to the conscious articulation of the
ego. A *theory* of art is necessary because art has stimulated our
thoughts and has had a *moralistic-practical impact* through the
public controversies it provokes. But at the same time such a theory
of art is impossible because art cannot be reduced to *understanding*
or to *morality*. Sensuality resists being couched wholly in concepts – the mimetic impulse is in conflict with its rational reconstruction, and mimesis loses any exemplary instructive character.
Mimetic expression in Adorno's sense does not mean to imitate
something (as in Plato or Aristotle), but to create new similarities
between expression and something. It is more a somatic reaction
than a form of lower level cognitive reflection (or mirror of
nature).[48]

Adorno's insight into the antinomies of aesthetic theory goes
back to Kant. Art stimulates thought, sets the concept in motion
and lets the murmur of the recipient audience's voices become
louder. Yet no thought can entirely grasp the meaning of art, the
movement of the concept comes to an end and the many voices
contradict one another. Concept and meaning of art, understanding and sensibility, contradict and interpenetrate each other at the
same time. By way of this conceptual comprehension and intuitive
sensibility there can be built a frequently changing variety of 'constellations'. Whereas Kant speaks of 'concept' and 'understanding',
Adorno in his philosophy gives preference to 'rationality' and 'construction'; and in place of 'intuition' and 'sensibility' steps the word

'mimesis'. Yet this is an antipathy to 'mediation', indebted to Nietzsche, that differentiates Adorno from Kant. In the *Critique of Pure Reason* it is the doctrine of the schematism which so reconciles understanding and sensibility that the latter learns to see and the former receives *something to see*. In the *Critique of Judgement* it is the notion of 'beauty', and it is the receiving, communicating and reasoning audience that forges public meaning out of the sense-distant 'idiocy' of the art-works, that refines taste and lets itself be ethically impressed by the beautiful symbols. Adorno rejects this sort of communicatively rational reconciliation and replaces it with a negative dialectic that has no centre, and is oriented more to the 'sublime', which is out of reach of human understanding, than to the 'beauty', that can be understood communicatively. A 'dialectic in standstill' that lets all contradictions stand unreconciled, is one of the favourite ideas of Walter Benjamin that Adorno has taken over. Adorno's dialectic 'constellations' are like photographic 'stills'. But these abruptly changing 'stills' will never come together in the illusion of one 'movie' telling a closed story.

In this manner, Adorno radicalizes Kant's critique of objective unity. There remains no unity as a realm of regulative reason internal to the subject or the art-receiving public. Adorno deepens the abyss, sundering and dividing concept and sensuality, construction and mimesis. In the aesthetic there is no schematism, no mediation; and the meaning upon the *extra*-aesthetic determinacy of which the possibility and effectiveness of art itself rests remains indeterminate *in* art. The works stimulate the senses and the understanding, they excite sensual perception and provoke the comprehension of meaning. Yet the more closely one looks, the more distantly they return the gaze, and with each recognized meaning another collapses. Referring to Kafka's work Adorno writes: 'Gestures are counterpoint to the words', in his work the 'traces of experiences that are covered over by meaning'.[49] Kafka's first principle is: 'Take everything literally, cover nothing from above with concepts. Kafka's authority is that of texts'.[50] Adorno construes texts here literally as their dense materiality, different from letter to letter, opposing the meanings of words and sentences that are always and everywhere identical.

Because understanding always falls short of the aesthetic reality it experiences, the light that focuses the 'explosion' of the works into a 'tongue of flame' falls upon an eye going blind.[51] The art-works keep narratively comprehensible meaning at a sharp distance from themselves, or 'damage' it through 'small acts of sabotage'.[52] Adorno sets the 'hermetic principle' of 'inimitability' against the hermeneutics of the fusion of horizons.[53] The act of sabotage directs itself not only against moral standards and the normative. This is still construed in far too strong a moralistic and normative sense. The sabotage is directed against meaning and significance *per se*, it is the meta-institution of language itself which is damaged.

To the extent that art itself becomes conscious of its own autonomy, it loses its *ability to become theory*. A modern art which has become completely reflective cannot be reduced to any one idea. The only appropriate stance that remains is criticism. Adorno understood this contradiction between theory and criticism but, as a philosopher of history and a utopian, held onto a theory which he believed had become impossible. As an art critic, however, he reacted spontaneously to these art-works and sabotaged his own theory. When Adorno interprets as a critic Mahler's symphonies or Beckett's *Endgame*, he shows himself as a truly negational thinker. He not only rejects the claims for a reconciliation that already has taken place in history, which for Adorno are the illusions of classical art-works and classical philosophy of history (like that of Hegel). Adorno also consistently destroys utopian hopes for a *final* reconciliation, when he rejects the idea that art in a better society than this could again become affirmative. The 'nonidentical' cannot and should not be covered by concepts and reconciled with instrumental reason, neither in this nor in another society. Social criticism and the indirect expression of a political utopia (without final reconciliation) might be one important aspect of great works of art. But these works are not primarily the presemblance (*Vorschein*) of a utopian society (as they are in Bloch's *Prinzip Hoffnung*). This latter idea for Adorno would be a regression to platonism and the dualism of 'essense' (now 'utopia') and 'appearance' (now the present history).The art-works *themselves* are, as Adorno says, 'a second reality which reacts to the first'.[54] One needs only to interpret this literally, as the Manifesto of Surrealism interprets the expression 'surrealism': as a description of a reality *sui generis*. Breton 'equates the surreal facts with real or independent ones'.[55] If art, in its 'play with the elements of reality', already represents its own second reality, then it loses its character as mere *appearance* of a future reality: 'The unique essence of music, of not being an image, and not being for a different reality, but rather existing as a reality *sui generis*.'[56] Art, or so Paul Liessmann has put it, 'creates no reflection of the world in one way or the other'.[57] This is exactly what Adorno the aesthetic theorist shares with the surrealists and it is what marks him off the utopian Bloch. Here the aesthetic critic breaks away from the idealistic theorist. This becomes clearer once we turn to Adorno's deeply ambivalent expression of *aesthetic truth*.

3. The time for criticism

What then does *aesthetic* truth consist of? One answer that Adorno gives – which I would like to term the *theoretical* (or philosophical) answer – reads: aesthetic semblance is true as the pre-semblance of an absent reconciliation. Art is true as 'the impression, the obverse of the administered world'.[58] The dissolution of the contradiction between appearance and reality would be found then in a utopia of reconciliation indistinguishable from negative theology. In semblance, the *higher* truth of art would appear. Understood in this way, the theory of art would remain platonically contemplative. And some of Adorno's formulations suggest such an interpretation, all the way up to the distinction of the *bios theoretikos* as the highest form of life: theory is for the Adorno of *Negative Dialectics* the 'lingering gaze of thought',[59] and already in the *Minima Moralia* he defines thought as the 'forceless contemplation, from which all happiness of truth stems'.[60] The theory has completely withdrawn from the reality of what Marx termed the 'people who deal and interact with each other'.[61]

Yet this interpretation is contradicted by the fact that Adorno understands theory throughout as *critique*, and couples it in art with an *aesthetic-practical, experimental conception of freedom*. In the *Introduction to the Sociology of Music*, he writes: 'The common ether of aesthetics and sociology is critique.'[62] And the *Aesthetic Theory* postulates a 'critique of culture through art'.[63]

It is of decisive importance that criticism follows art and *not* theory. It lets itself in for and exposes itself to the experience of contradictions and antinomies, complex and uncontrolled situations and impulses. It transgresses itself in them and in the

execution of critique behaves aesthetically toward the pre-
fabricated *solutions* of theory, which in the end it allows us to see
through as illusion and false generalization. In criticism – in this
respect similar to aesthetic comportment – the communicative
everyday reality is simultaneously proximate and distant. Yet
critique is not withdrawn from reality, has not left this world for
the forceless gaze upon the thing itself in order to retreat into the
shadow realm of pure ideas of reason, or into the dream of a complete satisfaction of drives and the salvation from all evil. In essays
like that on 'informal music' or on the transgressing tendencies of
the arts, Adorno behaves *one-sidedly* as a critic, so that in such
texts the tension between a negative-utopian motivated construction of theory and the materialism of criticism comes remarkably
to the fore.

What Adorno interpreted in 1966 as the process of transgression
is a development that initiates *inside the particular works* and
crosses over the boundaries with other art-forms and with life *from
the inside out*. As Adorno sees it, the 'latest development' contradicts in this manner the all too superficial tendency of the
avantgarde to align itself with the model of sublation (or overcoming the object). The sublation model does not speak the language
of the works, but rather the comprehensible, communicative language of propaganda, and it approaches art and the arts from
above, with the logic of subsumption. Film, despite all criticism of
the culture industry, is paradigmatic for the 'latest development':
'While film would of immanent necessity cast off its artistic
aspect – almost as if that aspect contradicted its artistic principle –
it remains in this rebellion art and expands it.' This contradiction –
which Christoph Menke, drawing on Derrida and Adorno, has
defined as a contradiction between *autonomy* and *sovereignty* – is
the 'vital element of all genuinely modern art'.[64] What Adorno
observes is related to the inner logic of the aesthetic language,
which escapes every extrinsic, comprehending and instrumentally
classifying grip. 'What tears down the boundary posts of the art-
forms is moved by historical forces which awakened inside the
boundaries and finally overflowed them.'[65] In Adorno's interpretation of the prose of Hans G. Helm, of Calder's mobiles, the 'swell-
ing paintings of Bernhardt Schulze', and the compositions of Dona-
toni, Ligeti and Varese, the art-forms 'seem to delight in a sort of
promiscuity that violates civilizing taboos'.[66]

The process of transgression by which boundaries are rendered fluid brings the *proper* language of art and its anarchistic impulses to the fore in the world and opposes the unitary logics of subjectivity, the *Gesamtkunstwerk* as well as communicative reaching of understanding. The concrete shape of the sound of language, its thing-like, dense materiality, does not let itself be transformed into identical meaning: 'The Same, which the art-works mean as their What, becomes, through how they mean it, an Other.'[67] This persistent Other of the arts that *escapes* the intersubjective reaching of an understanding remains none the less in its vicinity. For it is not equivalent to the 'entirely Other' (*ganz Andere*), which the solitary *thinker* draws from an 'ontology of the false condition', but is rather an Other that the arts *place* in the real public space of our everyday world. It is the 'second-order thing'[68] which the critic comes across, to which he comports and exposes himself, yet about which he must none the less speak in an unavoidably communicative language.

Adorno shares an observation with Gehlen: because the works of modernity pry loose their thing-like substratum from the horizon of great representative orders, from their connection to an ethics, religion, culture and nature comprehensible to all, because they finally contradict all ordinary understanding and become abstract, intellectual (*geistig*) and reflective, they are in *need of commentary* to a degree as yet unknown. Yet the more understandable the commentaries become, the less comprehensible the work; they demand 'interpretation', yet interpretation only lets their 'puzzle-like character' emerge ever more clearly and metamorphizes in the end *all* art, even the putatively understandable old art, into consistently new puzzles.[69]

Criticism experiences 'second-order things' as things in-the-world. And at this point Adorno seems to correct even his previous criticism of Heidegger. Heidegger's text on the origin of the artwork in his *Holzwege* 'has the merit of soberly describing the thing-like aspect of the aesthetic object, which, as Heidegger with good reason ironically notes, even the much-touted aesthetic experience (*Erlebnis*) cannot get around'.[70] Beyond that, Adorno praises Heidegger for forcefully emphasizing the 'linguistic character of all art'.[71]

But Adorno and Heidegger cross paths at a decisive point: the relation of *thing* and *language* – or, in Heidegger's terms, the conflict between 'ground (for the earth) and the world' – which sets in motion the transgression of the arts out of the peculiar linguisticality common to them.[72] What Heidegger identified in his essay on art as the side of art-work facing the ground, Adorno refers to as its thing-like character, or as the 'aesthetic material'. It is without voice or language, as is a stone which has been dug up from the ground, but the temple which people have built from the stones discloses a 'world' which is for them understandable (Heidegger) – and it is exactly this that constitutes the works of art's 'linguistic character' (Adorno). In the fissure between the earth (or ground) and the world, between thing and language, the works become 'enigmatic' (Adorno).

The 'linguistic character' (Adorno) of the art-work is the work's comprehensible, world-disclosing (Heidegger) aspect that can be expressed in explicit linguistic phrases. Adorno refers to this 'linguistic-' or 'world-aspect' of the art-work also in terms of 'construction'. We can understand what we have constructed. This meaningful aspect is in works of art confined to dense 'material' (Adorno), to the uninterpreted 'ground' or 'earth' (Heidegger) from which it is made. The point is here that the artist's 'construction' can become a work of art only if it is realized in a specific 'material', e.g. colours on a canvas. But these colours despite the construction will never lose their multiple meaning. The incomprehensible aspect of the earth or ground or material remain in reflectively constructed art-work as 'puzzle' (Adorno) that gives endless reason for further interpretation, because it never can be expressed completely in the one interpretation.

In its 'enigmatic' character, in the simultaneous presence of meaningful discussion and material that is foreign to meaning, the language of art is at once understandable and yet not to be understood. Modernity brings the character of the work to the level of consciousness by staging the productiveness as well as the pure destructiveness of all paradoxes as an endless game, an endgame, between the loss of meaning and and the act of pinpointing a meaning. This language of works of art is both anti-traditional and anti-instrumental, and thus *uncommunicative*: it is neither informative and objectively understandable, nor the expression of an always already comprehensible event of tradition. We learn with it neither to master the world nor ourselves. It affords us neither knowledge nor a vitally necessary point of orientation. Instead it works through disorientation and by causing confusion.

Heidegger emphasizes just as forcibly as Adorno the *alienness* of the works and the *rift* that yawns between the mute earth – upon which they contingently stand or are displayed – and the public world – into which they are interpreted and in which they are always already linguistically disclosed.[73] Their productiveness, their innovative force and their mysterious alienness depend on the uncalmable and irreconcilable strife that is enflamed with that rift. Adorno speaks similarly of an 'objective contradictoriness in the phenomena'.[74]

Nevertheless the language of 'second-order things' cannot be escaped in colloquial or ordinary language and the understanding and learning processes peculiar to it. This makes understanding more difficult, but does not destroy it. In works of art which are great the 'puzzle' that emerges out of *formed non-identity* never vanishes. Yet there is nothing sacred and taboo in art-works, every side art shows to the gaze of the observer can be interpreted in the discursive, instrumental language of concepts. Conceptual comprehension that never can grasp the art-work's fluid, dense and opaque 'material' is nevertheless the only 'chance' it has to come out with its 'truth content'. The work of art can realize this 'chance' of conceptual understanding only in the communicative process of its public reception. And it *can* reach conceptual and communicative understanding *because the work of art itself cannot avoid communicating*. It is (even by silence and non- or anti-communication) 'Kommunikation . . . mit dem Auswendigen . . . , mit der Welt.'[75] In English translation the complete quotation is: 'The manner in which art communicates with the outside world is in fact also a lack of communication, because art seeks, blissfully or unhappily, to seclude itself from the world. This non-communication points to the fractured nature of art.'[76] In other words, Adorno wishes to say that art communicates to us both inside and outside the boundaries of received linguistic meaning.

By its own autonomy art *is* a 'fait social'.[77] Works of art oppose understanding but cannot avoid it: 'As artefacts, works of art communicate not only internally but also with the external reality which they try to get away from and which nonetheless is the substratum of their content.'[78] All the means available to works of art have to reject the 'false condition', but all art-works stem from articulable, expressible concepts, and constructive and technical means which are internal to the 'false condition': 'Thus, because

of the technical procedures inherent in works of art, concepts are
not only an inner necessity helping them to decode themselves but
also the chance to transcend that necessity.'[79] The constellation
that transcends this world is only a set of relations from the 'material' of this existing world and its ordinary language.

This is where critique comes in. Adorno is no linguistic idealist,
which is what distinguishes him from Heidegger. Critique mediates
between the ordinary, everyday human understanding and the art-
work's world-disclosing powers. This is exactly the public role
which Adorno ascribed to the 'Essay as Form' in the ongoing process of enlightening a real public. In his vague appeal to a higher
'truth' of art, Adorno may have just as much in common with
Heidegger as in his judgement of the character of the works, which
is at once thing-like and yet 'language-like'. But 'critique' and the
'essay' or even public intervention are just as foreign to Heidegger
as the pedagogical notion of enlightenment that characterizes
Adorno's exoteric writings. This difference goes back to a difference in what characterizes the meaningful, 'linguistic' or 'world'-
aspect of the art-work. For Adorno meaning is a function of
'construction', and that means instrumental or subjective reason,
mainly the product of reflection and theoretical design. The linguistic aspect of art is the subject's project. In contrast Heidegger
conceives meaning that is disclosed to a human being (*Dasein*) in
the clearing (*Lichtung*) of the world, as the *objective meaning* of
Being. This Being (with a capital 'B') is completely dissolved from
our subjectivity, and therefore needs no interpretation by critics
who make comments in newspapers, books, radios and so on.
Heidegger's 'thinker', who hears the silent voice of Being, has no
need for interpretation by intellectual critics in a marketplace of
ideas. The gap that divides esoteric thinking from exoteric talking
with others remains unbridgeable. Not so in Adorno.

Adorno categorically forbids hypostatizing the opposition of
exoteric and esoteric. His philosophical ideal is in fact a text from
which all sentences are equidistant from their centre. It is the ideal
of a decentred world which would overcome all deductive hierarchies: 'One of the tasks of dialectical logic is to eliminate the
last traces of a deductive system, together with the last advocatory
gestures of thought . . . In a philosophical text all the propositions
ought to be equally close to the centre.'[80] Here again we are confronted with one of Adorno's formulations which try to overcome

metaphysical and ontological dualisms and to transform them into *innerworldly* differences or constellations of contradictions, tensions, and so on.

Only new art which completely breaks away from the accustomed understanding and breaks away from the horizon of everyday ethical life needs critique which ensures it is *experienced* by the public as provocation and innovation. Criticism of art as art's perfection is a romantic invention.[81] The role of criticism is not to render incomprehensible works comprehensible, but rather to put up mutually contradictory contributions for discussion, to let the provocations become *effective* and to salvage new, surprising and overwhelming experiences which slip our controlling grasp. Criticism links hermetic works to the learning processes of a public which can no longer orient itself to the authoritative guidelines of meaning or the dogmatic certainties of firmly established value communities. Just as the public cannot rely on traditional meanings, nor can the critic build upon a secure, privileged access to truth through non-contradictory and valid theories. She can only hold on to the 'works', the 'creations', on to the *objects themselves*, although they hardly provide a foothold. And that is the real reason why Adorno – not as a platonic theorist distanced from the world, but rather as a polemicizing, erring and irritating critic who distorts the perspective – retrospectively defends avantgarde movements like surrealism against their own self-confident interpretation in the light of psychoanalytical theory and its truths, which are as uninspired as they are out-of-date. Just like that theory which is metaphysics, so too criticism is in conflict with theory, whether the surrealist theoretical claim to psychoanalysis, or Adorno's own commitment to a philosophy of history.

By subsuming works of art under theory, all that happens is that what 'is estranging about them . . . is explained away by reference to the already familiar'. Pyschoanalytic theory as well as ordinary hermeneutic interpretation denies the objectivity, the impact, even 'the violence' which arises from the creations of art, in which its 'rampant variety is reduced to a couple of flimsy categories like the Oedipus complex'.[82]

4. Critique of culture by art

The 'critique of culture by art' leads down the path of exemplary self-critique to the absolutizations of one's own theory. Whereas 'theory' – hardly differently from Heidegger's 'thought' – banishes the 'linguistic character of all art' beyond ordinary language, theory-oblivious criticism shows how the language of the things is 'entwined in a single line' with that of ordinary humans.[83]

Criticism rests upon a premiss that the extra-aesthetic, objective-realistic truth content of the works discloses itself alone through an immanent analysis of 'technique' and 'form', 'compositional' or 'poetic process' and 'procedure'.[84] This leads Adorno in his analysis of Beckett's *Endgame* to the central thesis that I have mentioned already, and quote in its entirety here: 'The game with elements of reality, free from all representationality, which takes no position and finds in such freedom its happiness as freedom from the ordained business, unmasks more than an unmasker who takes a stand.'[85] Thus Adorno makes it clear that the *objective truth* of the works of art, insofar as they have one, does *not* consist in the representation of the false condition. The work *represents* neither a positive nor a negative truth. 'Beckett silences out of tenderness the tender no less than the brutal.'[86] Reference to reality lies only in the game with its elements. This game has social content, but no cognitive truth. After all, the mass media inform us incessantly of the world's condition. Adorno emphasizes repeatedly that Beckett's *Endgame* would be fundamentally misunderstood as a valid representation of current horrors. This is expressed in the metaphysical misunderstanding of the existentialist interpretation current in Adorno's day, which presents the play itself as a 'simultaneously stereotypic and erroneous prattle of self-alienation'.[87]

If criticism has dissolved the work's *objective* truth to the point of negating every objective propositional meaning, then in a second, subsequent step it destroys the *aesthetic truth of semblance*. In this two-stage negation, criticism exposes the anarchic feature of the works, their negative character which pushes them on to become a critique of *all* institutions. Adorno tirelessly demonstrates in hundreds of cases how the work of art causes the world 'to crumble', to demolish each existing institution, each symbolic form, and that includes also that of the work of art itself. But they do this and can only do this when they institutionalize themselves *as art-works* and differentiate themselves as form and appearance in a play with the ruins: 'The explosion of metaphysical meaning, which alone guaranteed the unity of the aesthetic structure of meaning, allows the latter to crumble with a necessity and rigor in no respect less than that of the traditional dramaturgical formal canon'.[88] What is exploded here is Gehlen's hard, archaic institution: namely, metaphysical meaning. Art thus destroys its own basis. But by effecting its act of destruction, it remains art and becomes a productive *renewal*, a *new beginning* of the institution: 'a necessity and stringency . . . which is not inferior to the traditional code of form'.

The aesthetic destruction of meaning attains cultural stability through its 'necessity and rigor', and can become an element of the rational self-understanding of a social collective. While the explosion that tears life asunder *annihilates* the truth content of metaphysical meaning, the artful aesthetic crumbling of meaning *rescues* many possibilities for truth, without any longer binding itself together into *one* truth. The aesthetically controlled destruction of meaning unchains instead a pluralistic, multidimensional 'truth potential' of art; not – as Adorno and Heidegger believed – its *one* truth.[89] The 'truth' of the works thus by no means disappears in the aesthetic destruction of appearance; rather it decomposes into multiple, mutually contending dimensions, which can then indeed, in the public criticism and reception of the works, become effective both for ethical self-understanding and for an emancipatory learning process, that free themselves from tradition and bring an aesthetically experimental conception of freedom to the fore within social reality. In *Aesthetic Theory* Adorno calls this the 'infiltration of the aesthetic by the moral'.[90]

Even the 'formalistic radicalism' of autonomous modern art contains a 'social moment': 'Conservative apologists of culture view as decadent the suffusion of aesthetics with morals'.[91] The autonomy of arts as *social* autonomy within the societal totality is fragile; and on the other hand *artistic* autonomy over against society as a whole is from the very beginning transgression of borders:

> This conservative penchant for purity and non-contamination reflects the toil that went into the drawing of these boundaries throughout the history of art, never succeeding fully, as can be seen in the case of art's relation to diversion. Still, anything that seems to remind the conservatives strongly of the shifting quality of these boundaries, anything that suggests the possibility of hybrid art, provokes a strongly negative response on their part.[92]

Adorno's example here is the aesthetics of the ugly: 'The condemnation of ugliness in conservative aesthetics finds support in a subjective inclination that has been verified by social psychology, namely the inclination to equate – justly – ugliness with the expression of suffering in order then to berate it projectively.'[93] Prejudice against *entartete Kunst* – here the socialist realist Lukács comes very close to Nazism – is the differentiated entwinement of true propositions and false projections. Aesthetic experience would be the destruction of such disastrous entwinement. It is here that critique comes in with a *double function*: to interpret works of art which resist interpretation and understanding and to criticize prejudice which makes forceless understanding and free expression impossible.

This peculiar achievement of destruction, which criticism makes recognizable in art and life, is bound up with characteristics of our ordinary everyday language. Thus art remains dependent upon ordinary language, even if it has become specialized in the material and moral quality of ordinary language, the objectively tangible and therefore incomprehensible aspects of it.

Adorno showed through examples such as Eichendorff's lyrics and Beckett's *Endgame* how *both* dimensions of our ordinary language – the irreducible sound shape and the prosaic literal meaning, the opaque materiality of the words on the one hand, and on the other hand communicative speech, which transforms meanings and raises universal truth claims – have intertwined themselves into a collapsing 'toppling movement out of the meaning'.[94] In *Endgame*, the social relation of master and slave, an 'element of reality', is transformed into a purely linguistic role game in the dialogue between Hamm's communicative offer of meaning and Clov's communication-breaking reply.

> It sounds as if the law of its progress were not the reason of speech and counter-speech, not even their psychological hooking together, but rather listening, related to the law of music that emancipates itself from preordained types. The drama listens to hear what sentence will follow upon the last.[95]

Here too the 'fraying' (*Verfransung*) of the arts shows itself equiprimordial with their peculiar 'linguistic character'.

The scene with the alarm clock in *Endgame* is exemplary. Just as Clov has in other passages consistently punctured the overblown poetic clichés of the poet-lord Hamm by taking them literally in slavish prose, so he plays in this scene an ironic game with the informative linguistic meaning of the alarm, to which he listens as though it were a piece of music. Thus Clov transforms the earnest reaching of an understanding concerning the informational content of the communicative medium 'alarm clock' into a gourmet discourse upon the aesthetic quality of the sound.

> CLOV: I'll go and see. *(Exit Clov. Brief ring of alarm off. Enter Clov with alarm-clock. He holds it against Hamm's ear and releases alarm. They listen to it ringing to the end. Pause.)* Fit to wake the dead! Did you hear it?
> HAMM: Vaguely
> CLOV: The end is terrific!
> HAMM: I prefer the middle.

The art-work tears apart any communicative understanding being reached in experimentally arranged, 'released self-motion of the linguistic material'.[96] The meaning content is dashed to pieces on the materiality of the sounds and the hills of ink. It is in this sense of a thing-like language resistant to all understanding that 'great music' is 'eloquent beyond all words'.[97] But it is none the less not language that here – as Heidegger says – 'thinks', or – as Adorno says – 'speaks'. We can only know that something is 'eloquent beyond all words' because we have already experienced and practised it in the *ordinary discursive use* of the words and sentences of our everyday language. It is not language itself but rather we who speak through the works. But we abandon ourselves spontaneously in aesthetic comportment, whether as producer or as consumer or recipient, to the flow of language and its conflicting games. It is in this manner that we make language speak, as though it spoke to us itself through second-order things, through hills of ink and sound shapes. But it is still clearly only our own experimental freedom, a freedom to experience and expand the borders of that freedom, which is drawn by the uncontrollable complexity of our own life.

In every ordinary reaching of an understanding, however banal and clichéd, these two moments – sound and sense – enter into a relation of tension. Normally the understanding of meaning, which

refers by means of validity claims to the universal communication
community of all those who could object, functions relatively without compulsion or significant disturbances through the opaque
materiality of language. Art sets its peculiar linguistic character in
motion at those places where the ordinary functioning of language
has been penetrated by violence and become indistinguishable from
pathological rigidity. It is in this sense that art opposes the 'false
condition' of society. It objectifies the communication-breaking
power of language into 'second-order things', in order, though
without doing violence, systematically to 'demolish' and 'shatter'
the only apparently living meaning of culture. Thus modern art
remains the art of an egalitarian society. In the face of the constantly mounting bleatings of the conservative intelligentsia it
insists on the older revolutionary impulse of an egalitarianism
without conformity.[98] This is its objective truth:

> Jacobinean, the lower music storms into the upper . . . The self-satisfied
> polish of the mediate form is demolished by the disproportionate sound
> from the pavilions of military bands and the palm-garden orchestra . . .
> Symphonic music digs for the treasure that alone the roll of distant
> drums or the murmur of voices promises ever since music established
> itself domestically as art. It would seize the masses that flee from
> culture-music, yet without conforming to them (*gleichzuschalten*).[99]

In early 1940 Adorno identified popular music as part of the
effort of late capitalism to transform man into an insect. But he
was not completely pessimistic about the efficiency of this effort of
the manipulating, prejudice-reinforcing machinery of the cultural
industry. In some respects Adorno always believed in the recalcit-
rant power of the resisting 'non-identical'. We are not ants. Therefore he closed his essay 'On Popular Music' with the hypothesis:
'To become transformed into an insect, man needs that energy
which might possibly achieve his transformation into man.'[100]
The resisting energy of mimetic impulses on the other hand does
not stem from high culture and culture music. Insofar as it rejects
the idealism of culture music, the military bands, and palm-garden
orchestras, and the jitterbugs of popular music may be a first step
in the right direction which will put an inverted idealism on its feet
or – again – in Adorno's own words: 'The bourgeois would have
art be sumptuous and life ascetic; the opposite would be better.'[101]

Conclusion

Theodor Adorno was a most complex figure in modern political thought and German philosophy in particular. A person of his time who made a lasting impact on the modern intellect, he was deeply influenced by the burgeoning of modern art which took place around the outset of the First World War. His developing artistic interest merged with his preoccupation with music. Adorno was very close to Schönberg's circle when that was at the height of its influence and was himself an accomplished musician. His bourgeois adolescence and early manhood was then rocked to its foundations by revolutionary Marxism which took hold of Adorno in the early 1920s, although he was never to become a party-political person. He sought always to escape any form of institutionalized Marxism. In the course of his intellectual career he was indeed to produce a profound defence of the individual brought up in the bourgeois family. In keeping with his Marxist impulses he criticized this subject very strongly, but at all times tried to preserve what was emancipatory within it. Adorno did not want to contemplate a society which did not preserve all that was positive within the modern middle-class subject. The strong criticism of established philosophy – which had at its core the bourgeois subject – went hand in hand with the defence of all its non-idealist tendencies. Both in politics and philosophy Adorno preferred the spontaneous to the orthodox, and the experimental to the conventional. Above all, Adorno wanted to preserve insight into the dark side of the enlightenment whilst at the same time rescuing its positive and emancipatory moment. His life's work was a testimony to a rejection of the twentieth-century capitalist order which was an equally strong affirmation of its creative cultural achievements. True to his own principle of non-identity, Adorno's programme was bound to remain radically incomplete.

Notes

Introduction

[1] With respect to the first meaning of 'non-identity' there is a point where Adorno meets Heidegger's 'forgetfulness of being' (*Seinsvergessenheit*). But there are a lot of other aspects of meaning in Heidegger's notion with which Adorno would disagree completely. These are especially the meaning variants of Heidegger's *Seinsvergessenheit* which are closely connected with a 'philosophy of origins' (*Ursprungsphilosophie*) and a 'History of Being' (*Seinsgeschichte*).

[2] Niklas Luhmann, *Soziale Systeme. Grundriß einer allgemeinen Theorie* (Frankfurt am Main: Suhrkamp, 1983), p. 134.

[3] See for an instructive and insightful comparison of Luhmann and Adorno: Stefan Breuer, 'Adorono, Luhmann. Konvergenzen und Divergenzen von Kritischer Theorie und Systemtheorie', *Leviathan*, 15 (1986), pp. 91–125.

[4] Theodor W. Adorno, 'Fortschritt', in *Stichworte: Kritische Modelle* (Frankfurt am Main: Suhrkamp, 1969), vol. 2, p. 42: 'Der Fortschritt der Naturbeherrschung, der, nach Benjamins Gleichnis, im Gegensinn jenes wahren verläuft, der sein Telos an der Erlösung hätte, ist doch nicht ohne alle Hoffnung. Nicht erst die Abwendung des letzten Unheils, vielmehr in jeglicher aktuellen Gestalt der Milderung des überdauernden Leidens kommunizieren die beiden Begriffe von Fortschritt miteinander.'

1 Between Frankfurt and New York

[1] Reprinted as an addendum in Friedemann Grenz, *Adornos Philosophie in Grundbegriffen. Auflösung einiger Deutungsprobleme*: Theodor W. Adorno and Arnold Gehlen, 'Ist die Soziologie eine Wissenschaft vom Menschen? Ein Streitgespräch' (Frankfurt am Main: Suhrkamp, 1974).

[2] On the culture of the German mandarins: Fritz K. Ringer, *The Decline of the German Mandarins: The German Academic Community 1890–1933* (Cambridge, MA: Harvard University Press, 1969); Hauke

Brunkhorst, *Der Intellektuelle im Land der Mandarine* (Frankfurt am Main: Suhrkamp, 1987).

[3] Grenz, *Adornos Philosophie*, p. 250.

[4] For further information on the distinction between functionalist ('modernity' with respect to the functional order of the society) and cultural modernism ('modernism' in the context of cultural autonomy), see below, Chap. 1, s. 12 and Chap. 4, s. 1.

[5] Grenz, *Adornos Philosophie*, pp. 245–6, 248.

[6] Ibid., p. 250.

[7] Theodore W. Adorno, *Autobiographie aus Zitaten* (Frankfurt am Main: Suhrkamp, 1978), p. 1.

[8] Adorno, *Minima Moralia: Reflections from Damaged Life* (London: New Left Books, 1974), p. 161.

[9] Adorno, *Noten zur Literatur* (Frankfurt am Main: Suhrkamp, 1981), p. 72.

[10] See Leo Tolstoy, *Anna Karenina* (Zürich: Diogenes, 1985), p. 96. The novel's first sentence is: 'All happy families resemble one another, each unhappy family is unhappy in its own way.'

[11] Adorno, *Erziehung zur Mündigkeit* (Frankfurt am Main: Suhrkamp, 1971), p. 112.

[12] This will become an important constructive element in Adorno's *Aesthetic Theory*. I shall come back to the point in Chap. 4, s. 1.

[13] See Max Horkheimer and Theodor W. Adorno, *The Dialectic of the Enlightenment*, tr. J. Cumming (New York: Herder and Herder, 1972).

[14] Adorno, *Minima Moralia*, pp. 22–3.

[15] Ibid., p. 23.

[16] Adorno, *Negative Dialektik* (Frankfurt am Main: Suhrkamp, 1973), pp. 240, 244, 278 ff.

[17] *Theodor W. Adorno and Walter Benjamin: Briefwechsel 1928–1940*, ed. Henri Lonitz (Frankfurt am Main: Suhrkamp, 1994), pp. 388–9.

[18] Adorno, *Minima Moralia*, pp. 22–3.

[19] Adorno, *Ästhetische Theorie* (Frankfurt am Main: Suhrkamp, 1970), p. 334.

[20] Cf. also Herbert Marcuse, 'Über den affirmativen Charakter der Kultur', *Zeitschrift für Sozialforschung* (ed. Max Horkheimer), 6/1937; Münich: dtv-reprint, 1980, pp. 54–94.

[21] Adorno, *Ästhetische Theorie*, p. 335, English trans. by C. Lenhardt: *Aesthetic Theory* (London: Routledge & Kegan Paul, 1984), p. 321.

[22] Adorno, *Ästhetische Theorie*, pp. 518–19; trans., p. 478.

[23] Adorno, *Zur Metakritik der Erkenntnistheorie. Studien über Husserl und die phänomenologischen Antinomien* (Frankfurt am Main: Suhrkamp, 1970), p. 47. English trans. from: idem, *Against Epistemology: A Metacritique. Studies in Husserl and the Phenomenological*

Antinomies, trans. Willis Domingo (Cambridge, MA: MIT Press, 1983), p. 39. The 'Late Quartets' referred to are by Beethoven.

24 Adorno and Horkheimer, *Dialectic of Enlightenment*, p. 37.

25 Ibid. About the difference between Adorno and Heidegger in this respect see below: Chap. 3, s. 3.

26 Ibid.

27 The thesis that instrumental reason is purely subjective is the more one-sided, undialectical thesis of Max Horkheimer in his lectures from 1944 at the Columbia University, which were first published in English in 1947 under the title *Eclipse of Reason* (New York: Oxford University Press, 1947) and later in German: *Zur Kritik der instrumentellen Vernunft* (Frankfurt am Main: Fischer, 1967).

28 Horkheimer and Adorno, *Dialectic of Enlightenment*, p. 37; my emphasis.

29 This root, which goes back to Benjamin, is discovered by Susan Buck-Morss in her brilliant book: *The Origin of Negative Dialectics: Theodor W. Adorno, Walter Benjamin, and the Frankfurt Institute* (Hassocks, Sussex: Harvester Press, 1977). I will come back to that point and Adorno's 'inaugural address' on 'Die Aktualität der Philosophie' (1931) in Chap. 1, s. 10, below.

30 On Kracauer see now Gertrud Koch, *Kracauer zur Einführung* (Hamburg: Junius, 1996; English trans. forthcoming: Princeton University Press).

31 Adorno, *Notes on Literature*, vol. 2, tr. Shierry Weber Nicholsen (New York: Columbia Press, 1992), pp. 58–9.

32 Cf. Martin Jay, *Marxism and Totality* (Berkeley: University of California Press, 1974), p. 250; Theodor W. Adorno, *Nervenpunkte der Neuen Musik* (Reinbek: Rowohlt, 1969), pp. 19, 29.

33 Georg Wilhelm Friedrich Hegel, *Phänomenologie des Geistes* (Hamburg: Felix Meiner, 1952), p. 20.

34 For a comparison of Adorno and Piaget see Hauke Brunkhorst, *Theodor W. Adorno: Dialektik der Moderne* (Munich: Piper, 1990), pp. 9, 15 ff., 219 ff., 242 ff. See also: Susan Buck-Morss, 'Piaget, Adorno, and the Possibilities of Dialectical Operation', in H.J. Silverman (ed.), *Piaget, Philosophy, and Human Sciences* (Evanston, Ill.: Northwestern University Press, 1997), pp. 103 ff.

35 Rolf Wiggershaus, *Theodor W. Adorno* (Munich: Beck, 1987), p. 37.

36 Adorno, *Drei Studien zu Hegel* (Frankfurt am Main: Suhrkamp, 1963), p. 162.

37 See Thomas Kesselring, *Die Produktivität der Antinomie: Hegels Dialektik im Lichte der genetischen Erkenntnistheorie und der formalen Logik* (Frankfurt: Suhrkamp, 1984), p. 119.

38 Siegfried Kracauer, *Geschichte – von den letzten Dingen*, being vol. 4

of *Schriften*, ed. and tr. by Karsten Witte (Frankfurt: Suhrkamp, 1990), p. 229; see also Koch, *Kracauer zur Einführung*, p. 140.

[39] Kracauer, *Geschichte*, vol. 4, p. 229.

[40] Adorno, *Drei Studien zu Hegel*, p. 89.

[41] Michael Theunissen, 'Begriff und Realität', in Manfred Horstmann (ed.), *Dialektik in der Philosophie Hegels* (Frankfurt: Suhrkamp, 1978), p. 340.

[42] Adorno, *Drei Studien zu Hegel*, pp. 86–7.

[43] Georg W. F. Hegel, *Werke*, vol. 20, *Vorlesungen über die Geschichte der Philosophie III* (Frankfurt: Suhrkamp, 1971), p. 356.

[44] Adorno, *Drei Studien zu Hegel*, p. 52.

[45] Ibid., p. 52, my emphasis.

[46] Horkheimer and Adorno, *Dialectic of Enlightenment*, p. 187, amended trans.

[47] Ibid.

[48] Ibid., p. 190, amended trans.

[49] Ibid., amended trans.

[50] Adorno, 'Vers une musique informelle', in *Schriften*, vol. 16 (Frankfurt am Main: Suhrkamp, 1973), pp. 501, 537.

[51] Adorno, *Minima Moralia* (Frankfurt am Main: Suhrkamp, 1964), p. 102.

[52] Adorno, *Noten zur Literatur*, p. 300.

[53] Siegfried Kracauer, 'Minimalforderungen an die Intellektuellen', in *Deutsche Intellektuelle 1910–1933*, ed. M. Stark (Heidelberg: Schneider, 1984), p. 366.

[54] Adorno, *Ohne Leitbild* (Frankfurt am Main: Suhrkamp, 1967), p. 9.

[55] Adorno, 'Henkel, Krug and frühe Erfahrung', in *Henkel, Krug and frühe Erfahrung: Noten zur Literatur* (Frankfurt am Main: Suhrkamp, 1974), pp. 556 ff.

[56] Adorno, 'Über den Fetischcharakter der Musik', *Zeitschrift für Sozialforschung* (1938), p. 354.

[57] Adorno, 'Mahler', *Schriften*, vol. 13, pp. 184 ff.

[58] Adorno, *Notes to Literature*, vol. 1, ed. Rolf Tiedemann, tr. Shierry Weber Nicholsen (New York: Columbia University Press, 1991), p. 64.

[59] Ibid., p. 66.

[60] Ibid., p. 71.

[61] Leo Löwenthal, *Mitmachen wollte ich nie* (Frankfurt am Main: Suhrkamp, 1980), pp. 248 ff.

[62] See below, Chap. 4.

[63] Max Horkheimer, 'Zum Rationalismusstreit in der gegenwärtigen Philosophie', *Zeitschrift für Sozialforschung*, 3 (1934), pp. 50, 46; idem, 'Traditionelle und kritische Theorie', *Zeitschrift für Sozialforschung*, 6 (1937), p. 254; idem, 'Rationalismusstreit', p. 47.

64 Ibid., p. 48; Max Horkheimer, 'Materialismus und Metaphysik', *Zeitschrift für Sozialforschung*, 2 (1933), pp. 14–15; idem, 'Rationalismusstreit', p. 46.

65 Ibid.

66 Horkheimer, 'Materialismus und Metaphysik', p. 26; idem, 'Rationalismusstreit', p. 50; idem, 'Traditionelle und kritische Theorie', pp. 253, 282, 290.

67 Ibid., pp. 246–7; Max Horkheimer and Herbert Marcuse, 'Philosophie und kritische Theorie', *Zeitschrift für Sozialforschung*, 6 (1937), p. 625 (quote from Horkheimer's part); Horkheimer, 'Traditionelle und kritische Theorie', p. 292 (from the English-language summary of the essay published with the original text in the *Zeitschrift für Sozialforschung*).

68 Horkheimer, 'Rationalismusstreit', p. 33.

69 Max Horkheimer, 'Zum Problem der Wahrheit', *Zeitschrift für Sozialforschung*, 4 (1935), p. 356; idem, 'Rationalismusstreit', p. 47.

70 Horkheimer, 'Materialismus und Metaphysik', p. 32; idem, 'Wahrheit', pp. 330, 332–3.

71 Karl Marx, *Grundrisse* (Berlin: Dietz Verlag, 1953), p. 928, trans. from the German original.

72 Herbert Marcuse, 'Marxism and Feminism', in *Women's Studies* (London: Gordon and Breach, 1974) p. 279.

73 Karl Marx, *Capital I* (Harmondsworth: Penguin, 1981), pp. 163 ff., 301 ff, 367, 644–5, 756–7, 929–30, *et passim*; Alfred Sohn-Rethel, *Intellectual and Manual Labour* (London: Macmillan Press, 1978).

74 Jürgen Habermas, *Theorie des kommunikativen Handelns*, vol. 2, *Zur Kritik der funktionalistischen Vernunft* (Frankfurt am Main: Suhrkamp, 1981), pp. 445 ff.

75 Max Weber, 'Science as a vocation', in H. H. Gerth and C. Wright Mills (eds.), *From Max Weber: Essays in Sociology* (London: Routledge & Kegan Paul, 1948), p. 155.

76 Lukács, *History and Class Consciousness*, p. 88.

77 Max Weber, *Economy and Society: An Outline of Interpretive Sociology*, vol. 1, ed. Guenther Roth and Claus Wittich (Berkeley: University of California Press, 1978), p. 86. Italics added.

78 Max Weber, 'Religious rejections of the world and their directions', in H. H. Gerth and C. Wright Mills (eds.), *From Max Weber: Essays in Sociology*, p. 331. Italics added.

79 Max Weber, *Gesammelte Aufsätze zur Religionssoziologie*, vol. 1 (Tübingen: J.C.B. Mohr, 1920), p. 535.

80 Lukács, *History and Class Consciousness*, p. 89.

81 Ibid., p. 91.

82 Ibid., p. 86.

83 Ibid., p. 91.

[84] Frankfurt am Main: Suhrkamp, 1981. Habermas gives to the Marx-
      ian differentiation between 'living' and 'dead labour' a more abstract
      form with the differentiation between 'system' and 'life world'. For
      further information see Hauke Brunkhorst, 'Paradigm-core and
      theory-dynamics in critical theory. People and programs', in *Philo-
      sophy and Social Criticism*, 24/6 (1998), pp. 67–110.
[85] Adorno/Benjamin, *Briefwechsel*, p. 396.
[86] Cf. for example, F. Grenz, *Adornos Philosophie in Grundbegriffen*,
      pp. 35 ff.
[87] Adorno, 'Über den Fetischcharakter der Musik', p. 355.
[88] Adorno/Benjamin, *Briefwechsel*.
[89] See Buck-Morss, *Origin of Negative Dialectics*.
[90] See Walter Benjamin, *Zur Kritik der Gewalt und andere Aufsätze*
      (Frankfurt am Main: Suhrkamp, 1965); and the critical remarks in
      Jacques Derrida, *Gesetzeskraft. Der 'mystische Grund der Autorität'*
      (Frankfurt am Main: Suhrkamp, 1991).
[91] Wiggershaus, *Theodor W. Adorno*, p. 37; see above, Chap. 1, s. 3.
[92] For this distinction see Jürgen Habermas, 'Bewußtmachende oder
      rettende Kritik', *Zur Aktualität Walter Benjamins. Aus Anlaß des 80.
      Geburtstags von Walter Benjamin*, ed. Siegfried Ungeld (Frankfurt am
      Main: Suhrkamp, 1972), pp. 173–223.
[93] Walter Benjamin, 'Über den Begriff der Geschichte', *Gesammelte
      Schriften*, vol. 1/2, *Abhandlungen* (Frankfurt am Main: Suhrkamp,
      1974), pp. 691–704; Theodor W. Adorno, 'Fortschritt', in *Stichworte.
      Kritische Modell 2* (Frankfurt am Main: Suhrkamp, 1969), reprinted
      in Adorno, *Gesammelte Schriften*, vol. 10/2 (Frankfurt am Main:
      Suhrkamp, 1977), pp. 595–782.
[94] 'Theses on the philosophy of history', in *Illuminations*, tr. Harry
      Zohn (Glasgow: Fontana, 1979), p. 262.
[95] Ibid., p. 263.
[96] Ibid., p. 259.
[97] Ibid., pp. 256, 263, 265.
[98] Adorno, 'Fortschritt', in *Stichworte*, p. 33.
[99] Ibid.
[100] Ibid., p. 35.
[101] Ibid., p. 42.
[102] Benjamin, 'Über den Begriff', p. 699.
[103] Adorno, 'Kammermusikwoche in Frankfurt am Main', *Gesammelte
      Schriften*, 20/2, *Vermischte Schriften II* (Frankfurt: Suhrkamp, 1986),
      p. 771.
[104] See Wiggershaus, *Die Frankfurter Schule* (Munich: Hanser, 1986),
      pp. 88 ff.
[105] Adorno, 'Reaktion und Fortschritt' in *Adorno/Krenek Briefwechsel*
      (Frankfurt am Main: Suhrkamp, 1974), p. 180.

[106] See Ulrich Oevermann, 'Zur Sache. Die Bedeutung von Adornos methodologischem Selbstverständnis für die Begründung einer materialen soziologischen Strukturanalyse', in Adorno-Konferenz 1983, ed. Ludwig von Friedeburg and Jürgen Habermas (Frankfurt am Main: Suhrkamp, 1983), pp. 234–89.

[107] Adorno, 'Wissenschaftliche Erfahrungen in Amerika', in his Stichworte, p. 113.

[108] Adorno, 'Antwort auf die Frage: Was ist deutsch?', in his Stichworte, p. 108.

[109] Herbert Marcuse, 'Reflexion zu Theodor W. Adorno', in Herrmann Schweppenhäuser (ed.), Adorno zum Gedächtnis (Frankfurt am Main: Suhrkamp, 1971), p. 48.

[110] Adorno, 'Traumprotokolle', in his Vermischte Schriften II, being Gesammelte Schriften, 20/2 pp. 573 ff. The 'Schnatterloch' in Miltenberg is a narrow path between Amorbach, where the Wiesengrunds occasionally spent their summer holidays, and Miltenberg, a nearby town on the River Main. The narrow path offers a beautiful view from the crest of the hills over the town nestling on the banks of the river.

[111] Adorno, 'Kein Abenteuer', in his Vermischte Schriften II, pp. 585 ff.

[112] Quote from Wiggershaus, Die Frankfurter Schule, p. 508.

[113] Adorno, Vermischte Schriften II, p. 461.

[114] Ibid., pp. 453 ff.

[115] Leo Löwenthal, 'Erinnerungen an Theodor W. Adorno', in Adorno-Konferenz 1983, pp. 399 ff.

[116] Adorno, Ralf Dahrendorf, Harald Pilot, Hans Albert, Jürgen Habermas, and Karl R. Popper, Der Positivismusstreit in der deutschen Soziologie (Neuwied and Berlin: Luchterhand, 1969); Adorno, 'Spätkapitalismus oder Industriegesellschaft?', in Aufsätze zur Gesellschaftstheorie und Methodologie, pp. 149–66.

[117] Adorno, 'Drei Fragen in der Silvesternacht 1966', Süddeutsche Zeitung, 22/313 (31 Dec. 1966–1 Jan. 1967), p. 2, in Vermischte Schriften II, p. 737.

[118] Adorno, 'Gratulator', Gesammelte Schriften, 20/1, Vermischte Schriften I (Frankfurt am Main: Suhrkamp, 1986), p. 164.

[119] Adorno, 'Nach Kracauers Tod', Vermischte Schriften I, p. 196.

[120] Albrecht Wellmer, 'Adorno, Anwalt des Nicht-Identischen. Eine Einführung', in Zur Dialektik von Moderne und Postmoderne. Vernunftkritik nach Adorno (Frankfurt am Main: Suhrkamp, 1985), pp. 135–66.

[121] Adorno, Negative Dialektik, p. 160.

[122] Adorno, Ästhetische Theorie, pp. 148, 195, 317 ff.

[123] Adorno, 'Die Aktualität der Philosophie', Gesammelte Schriften 1 (Frankfurt am Main: Suhrkamp, 1973), pp. 325 ff.

[124] Buck-Morss, Origin of Negative Dialectics. The thesis of this book is

that Adorno developed the idea of a negative dialectics from his very philosophical beginnings and gained much from his friendship with Walter Benjamin.

125 Adorno, *Schriften*, vol. 2, pp. 341–2.
126 Adorno, *Negative Dialektik*, pp. 165 ff.
127 Adorno, *Schriften*, vol. 1, p. 335.
128 Adorno, *Schriften*, vol. 1, pp. 335 ff.
129 Adorno, *Against Epistemology: A Metacritique; Studies in Husserl and the Phenomenological Antinomics*, trans. Willis Domingo (Oxford: Basil Blackwell, 1982; Cambridge, MA: MIT Press, 1983).
130 Horkheimer and Adorno, *Dialectic of Enlightenment*, p. 187.
131 Ibid., p. 190, on 'true mimesis' see below, Chap. 4, s. 2. For a careful study of Adorno's concept of 'mimesis' see Josef Früchtl, *Mimesis. Konstellation eines Zentralbegriffs bei Adorno* (Würzburg: Meisenhain, 1986).
132 Ibid.
133 Adorno, *Negative Dialektik*, pp. 165 ff.
134 Horkheimer and Adorno, *Dialectic of Enlightenment*, p. xi.
135 On Adorno's moral philosophy cf. Gerhard Schweppenhäuser, *Ethik nach Auschwitz* (Hamburg: Zur Klampen, 1993). 'In many people it is already an impertinence to say "I"' (*Minima Moralia*, tr. E. F. N. Jephcott, London: New Left Books 1974, p. 50.)
136 On Adorno's complex relations within the network of modernism, anti-modernism and postmodernism see below Chap. 2.
137 Adorno, *Noten zur Literatur*, pp. 573, 570.
138 Adorno, *Ästhetische Theorie*, p. 27.
139 Daniel Bell, *The Cultural Contradictions of Capitalism* (London: Heinemann, 1976).
140 See below, Chap. 4.
141 See above, Chap. 1, s. 8, and the chapter on 'cultural industry' in Horkheimer's and Adorno's *Dialectic of Enlightenment*.

2 Enlightenment of Rationality

1 Max Horkheimer and Theodor W. Adorno, *Dialektik der Aufklärung. Philosophische Fragmente* (Frankfurt: Fischer, 1997), pp. 9 ff.
2 This is the meaning of 'Begriff' in the first chapter heading, 'Begriff der Aufklärung'. See Horkheimer and Adorno, *Dialektik der Aufklärung*, pp. 5–6, 9.
3 Ibid., pp. 10, 15, 20, 28, 31–2, 37, 64, 178, 190, 211–12.
4 Ibid., p. 10.
5 Ibid., pp. 10, 28.

6   See M. Horkheimer, 'Zur Kritik der instrumentellen Vernunft', in his *Kritische Theorie der Gesellschaft*, vol. 3, 1968 (Frankfurt: Marxismus-Kollektiv, 1968), pp. 118–279.

7   Horkheimer and Adorno, *Dialektik der Aufklärung*, p. ix. See Richard Rorty, *Kontingenz, Ironie und Solidarität* (Frankfurt: Suhrkamp, 1989), pp. 102 ff.

8   Ibid., pp. 3, 101, 190, 196. On 'instrumental reason' see Horkheimer, 'Zur Kritik'.

9   Horkheimer and Adorno, *Dialectik der Aufklärung*, p. 192.

10 Ibid.

11 Ibid., pp. 31 ff with backing from Husserl's work on 'Crisis'. See William Van Orman Quine, 'Logic and the reification of universals', in Quine, *From a Logical Point of View* (New York: Harper, 1963), pp. 102–30; Paul Lorenzen, *Methodisches Denken* (Frankfurt: Suhrkamp, 1969); and with a retrospective view Albrecht Wellmer, 'Zur Kritik der hermeneutischen Vernunft', in Christoph Demmerling and others (eds.), *Vernunft und Lebenspraxis* (Frankfurt: Suhrkamp, 1995), p. 125.

12 Max Horkheimer, 'Zum Rationalismusstreit in der gegenwärtigen Philosophie', *Zeitschrift für Sozialforschung (ZfS)*, 3 (1934), p. 50; idem, 'Zum Problem der Wahrheit', *ZfS* 4 (1935), pp. 331–2, 334; idem, 'Traditionelle und kritische Theorie', *ZfS* 6 (1937), pp. 253, 282.

13 M. Horkheimer, 'Materialismus und Metaphysik', *ZfS* 2 (1933), p. 26; idem, 'Traditionelle und kritische Theorie', p. 254.

14 Horkheimer and Adorno, *Dialektik der Aufklärung*, p. 249.

15 Ibid., p. 12.

16 John Dewey, *Demokratie und Erziehung* (Brunswick: Westermann, 1949).

17 Horkheimer, 'Zum Rationalismustreit', pp. 46, 48.

18 Horkheimer and Adorno, *Dialektik der Aufklärung*, pp. 90–1, 96, 98.

19 Ibid., p. 90, English trans. *Dialectic of Englightenment*, pp. 83–4.

20 *Dialektik der Aufklärung*, pp. 91, 127.

21 Ibid., pp. 90, 98, 208–9.

22 Ibid., pp. 96, 127, 209.

23 Michel Foucault, 'Das Leben des infamen Menschen', *Tumult* 4 (1977).

24 Horkheimer and Adorno, *Dialektik der Aufklärung*, pp. 223, 247, etc.

25 Terry Eagleton, *Die Illusion der Postmoderne* (Stuttgart: Metzler, 1997).

26 Horkheimer and Adorno, *Dialektik der Aufklärung*, p. 6.

27 Ibid., p. 217; trans., p. 208.

28 Adorno, *Negative Dialektik, Ästhetische Theorie*.

29 Horkheimer and Adorno, *Dialektik der Aufklärung*, pp. 15, 62, 85, 179.

[30]   Ibid., pp. 67–9, 80.
[31]   Ibid., p. 6.
[32]   Ibid., p. 3.
[33]   Ibid., pp. 100, 196 ff, 208–9, etc.
[34]   Ibid., p. 9.
[35]   Ibid., p. 127, see p. 202.
[36]   Ibid.
[37]   Adorno, *Negative Dialektik* (Frankfurt: Suhrkamp, 1973), pp. 530–1.
[38]   Ibid., p. 530.
[39]   Horkheimer and Adorno, *Dialectic of Enlightenment*, p. 37 (see Chap. 1, s. 2 above).
[40]   Ibid., p. 78.
[41]   See H. Brunkhorst, *Theodor W. Adorno. Dialektik der Moderne* (Munich: Piper, 1990), pp. 292 ff.
[42]   Horkheimer and Adorno, *Dialektik der Aufklärung*, pp. x, 1–2, 3–4, 140, 145, etc.

3 Adorno, Heidegger and Post-Analytical Philosophy

[1]   Martin Heidegger, 'Die Zeit des Weltbilds', *Holzwege* (Frankfurt am Main: Klostermann, 1972), pp. 283–4.
[2]   See Martin Heidegger, 'Überwindung der Metaphysik', *Vorträge und Aufsätze* (Pfullingen: Neske, 1985), pp. 67–122.
[3]   Theodor W. Adorno, *Ästhetische Theorie* (Frankfurt am Main: Suhrkamp, 1973), pp. 42–3: 'Der experimentelle Gestus ... mit dem Übergang des ästhetischen Interesses von der sich mitteilenden Subjektivität an die Stimmigkeit des Objekts, ein qualitativ Anderes: daß das künstlerische Subjekt Methoden praktiziert, die es nicht absehen kann ... Dabei balanciert die experimentelle Verhaltensweise auf des Messers Schneide.'
[4]   *Ästhetische Theorie*, pp. 43–4 (Engl. trans., p. 36). With respect to the 'pain' of aesthetic truth Heidegger does not differ much from Adorno. Yet, as we will see, Adorno never would draw a line to separate the inauthentic pain of normal people from the authentic pain of extraordinary poets. More important in the quoted passage from *Aesthetic Theory* is the internal connection between the pain of aesthetic truth, avantgardist experimentalism and the collective organization of modern art in programmatic groups. Here Adorno departs definitely from Heidegger's anti-modernist track.
[5]   *Ästhetische Theorie*, p. 44 (Engl. trans., p. 37). Authentic modern art cannot be separated from art as a form of (industrial) organization or art as a functional differentiated social system. Adorno here comes

very close to sociologists like Parsons and Luhmann. Adorno therefore rejects all attempts to distance true *modernity* from inauthentic *modernism*: 'Die Abhebung des Modernismus als der Gesinnung der Mitläufer von echter Moderne ist untriftig, weil ohne die subjektive Gesinnung, die von Neuem angereizt wird, auch keine objektive Moderne sich kristallisiert. In Wahrheit ist die Unterscheidung demagogisch: Wer über Modernismus klagt, meint die Moderne . . . Kritik am Modernismus zugunsten wahrer Moderne fungiert als Vorwand, das Gemäßigte . . . als besser auszugeben denn das Radikale; in Wahrheit verhält es sich umgekehrt. Was zurück blieb, verfügt auch über die älteren Mittel nicht, derer es sich bedient' (*Äesthetische Theorie*, pp. 45–6).

6   Martin Heidegger, *Platons Lehre von der Wahrheit* (Bern and Munich: Francke, 1947), p. 46; *Identity and Difference*, tr. Joan Stambaugh (New York: Harper & Row, 1969), pp. 62–3; idem, *An Introduction to Metaphysics*, tr. Ralph Manheim (New Haven: Yale University Press, 1959), pp. 36 ff; idem, 'The Word of Nietzsche: "God Is Dead" ', *The Question Concerning Technology and Other Essays*, tr. William Lovitt (New York: Harper & Row, 1977), pp. 79–80, 90 ff.

7   'Overcoming metaphysics', *The End of Philosophy*, tr. Joan Stambaugh (London: Souvenir Press, 1975), p. 106.

8   Ibid., p. 86; 'What are poets for?', *Poetry, Language, Thought*, tr. Albert Hofstadter (New York: Harper & Row, 1971), pp. 135–6.

9   'Overcoming metaphysics', pp. 105–6.

10 'What are poets for?', p. 136; on the 'Temple of Being', p. 132.

11 'Overcoming metaphysics', p. 103.

12 Cf. Jean-François Lyotard, *The Postmodern Condition*, tr. G. Bennington and B. Massumi (Minneapolis: University of Minnesota Press, 1984).

13 R. Rorty, *Philosophy and the Mirror of Nature* (Princeton: Princeton University Press, 1979), p. 389.

14 I will come back to this point in Chap. 3, ss. 3 and 4 below.

15 Cf. K.-O. Apel, *Diskurs und Verantwortung* (Frankfurt am Main: Suhrkamp, 1989).

16 H. Putnam, 'Between new left and Judaism', in G. Boradori, *The American Philosopher* (Chicago: The University of Chicago Press, 1994), p. 63.

17 Hans Joas, *Pragmatismus und Gesellschaftstheorie* (Frankfurt am Main: Suhrkamp, 1994), pp. 96 ff., denies that, but – as we will see – it is true.

18 The first was in the 1920s, the second after the Second World War. On the second period see Jürgen Habermas, 'Martin Heidegger: the great influence', *Philosophical-Political Profiles*, tr. Frederick G. Lawrence (London: Heinemann, 1983), pp. 53–4.

19   R. Rorty, 'Heidegger wider die Pragmatisten', *Neue Hefte für Philosophie*, 3 (1984), p. 22.

20   Adorno, *Ästhetische Theorie*, p. 533; Engl. trans., pp. 491–2.

21   J.-F. Lyotard, *Der Widerstreit* (Munich: Fink, 1987) p. 263; see also pp. 9–10, 157–8, 177–8.

22   Adorno/Benjamin, *Briefwechsel*, p. 398. The letter from 1 February 1939 is part of the long debate between Benjamin and Adorno about Benjamin's 'Reproduktionsarbeit': *Das Kunstwerk im Zeitalter seiner technischen Reproduzierbarkeit* (Frankfurt am Main: Suhrkamp, 1963).

23   Adorno, *Ästhetische Theorie*, p. 523.

24   See Martin Seel, 'Sprache bei Benjamin und Heidegger', *Merkur*, 4 (1992), p. 335.

25   Heidegger, *Vorträge und Aufsätze* (Pfullingen: Neske, 1985), p. 140.

26   Heidegger, 'The Age of the World Picture', *Holzwege* (Frankfurt am Main: Klostermann, 1972), pp. 69–104.

27   Heidegger, *Vorträge*, p. 140.

28   Ibid.

29   Heidegger, 'The Age', p. 152.

30   See Heidegger, *Die Frage nach dem Ding* (Tübingen: Max Niemeyer, 1987), pp. 59 ff., 66 ff., 70–1.

31   Horkheimer and Adorno, *Dialectic of Enlightenment*, pp. 187, 190. See above, Chap. 1, s. 10.

32   See Heidegger, 'Vom Ereignis', p. 328, as well as many other passages in his works. Heidegger constantly repeats the hypothesis of the unalterable necessity of the modern subject's egocentric projections. See 'The Age' or *Die Frage nach dem Ding*, pp. 58 ff., 71 ff., and 79 ff.

33   See on this last point K. R. Popper, *Logic of Scientific Discovery* (London: Hutchinson, 1972), chap. 3.

34   See above, Chap. 1, s. 2.

35   Martin Heidegger, *Hölderlins Hymnen 'Germanien' und 'Der Rhein'* (*Gesamtausgabe*, vol. 39; Frankfurt am Main: Klostermann, 1980), pp. 176, 181–2.

36   Martin Heidegger, *Zur Sache des Denkens* (Tübingen: Max Niemeyer, 1988), p. 6.

37   Heidegger, 'The Age', p. 136.

38   Heidegger, *Hölderlins Hymnen*, pp. 181–2.

39   Heidegger, *Die Frage nach dem Ding*, p. 82.

40   Heidegger, 'The Age', pp. 137–8.

41   Cristina Lafont, *Sprache und Welterschließung: Zur linguistischen Wende der Hermenutik Heideggers* (Frankfurt am Main: Suhrkamp, 1994), p. 151. I owe a lot to this important book.

42   Heidegger, *Kant und das Problem der Metaphysik* (Frankfurt am Main: Vittorio Klostermann, 1973), p. 17.

43 Heidegger, 'Der Ursprung des Kunstwerks', *Holzwege*, p. 61.

44 Heidegger, *Die Frage nach dem Ding*, p. 31.

45 Cf. ibid., pp. 63, 67, 70.

46 Ibid., p. 69.

47 See Thomas Kuhn, *The Structure of Scientific Revolutions* (Chicago University Press, 1970).

48 See Hubert Dreyfus, 'Heidegger on the connection between nihilism, art, technology, and politics', in *The Cambridge Companion to Heidegger*, ed. Charles Gnignon (New York: Cambridge University Press, 1993), pp. 293 ff.

49 K. Popper, 'Normal science and its dangers', in I. Lakatos and A. Musgrave (eds), *Criticism and the Growth of Knowledge* (London/Cambridge: Cambridge University Press, 1970), p. 56.

50 This is the argument put forward by Cristina Lafont, following in Putnam's footsteps, in her study of Heidegger, *Sprache*, p. 151.

51 Max Weber, 'The social psychology of the world religions', *From Max Weber*, tr. H. H. Gerth and C. Wright Mills (London: Routledge & Kegan Paul, 1970), p. 272.

52 Ibid., p. 273.

53 Adorno, *Negative Dialectics*, tr. E. B. Ashton (London: Routledge & Kegan Paul, 1973), p. 203.

54 Max Horkheimer, 'Zum Rationalismusstreit in der gegenwärtigen Philosophie', *Zeitschrift für Sozialforschung (ZfS)* 3 (1934), p. 48.

55 Ibid., p. 46.

56 R. Rorty, *Objectivity, Relativism, and Truth* (Cambridge, MA: Cambridge University Press, 1991), p. 13, quote from Barry Allen, 'Critical notice on Hilary Putnam', *Canadian Journal of Philosophy*, 4 (Dec. 1994), p. 687.

57 Horkheimer, 'Zum Rationalismusstreit', *ZfS* 3 (1934), p. 46.

58 Horkheimer, 'Zum Problem der Wahrheit', *ZfS* 4 (1935), pp. 331, 334.

59 Georg Wilhelm Friedrich Hegel, *Vorlesungen über die Philosophie der Geschichte: Werke*, vol. 12 (Frankfurt am Main: Suhrkamp, 1970), p. 114.

60 Horkheimer, 'Zum Problem', p. 332; see also Adorno, *Negative Dialectic*.

61 Horkheimer, 'Materialismus und Metaphysik', *ZfS* 2 (1933), p. 29.

62 R. Rorty, *Contingency, Irony and Solidarity* (Cambridge: Cambridge University Press, 1989), p. 45.

63 Cf. R. Rorty, *Hoffnung statt Erkenntnis* (Vienna: Passagen Verlag, 1994), p. 43.

64 Horkheimer, 'Rationalismusstreit', p. 16, cf. also Adorno, 'Fortschritt', in *Stichworte* (Frankfurt am Main: Suhrkamp, 1969), p. 42: see quote above, Chap. 1, s. 7.

65 Horkheimer, 'Rationalismusstreit', pp. 1, 50; 'Traditionelle und kritische Theorie', *ZfS* 6 (1937), pp. 253, 282.

66 Horkheimer, 'Materialismus und Metaphysik', *ZfS* 2 (1933), p. 26.

67 Herrmann Cohen, 'Das soziale Ideal bei Platon und den Propheten', in H. Cohen, *Jüdische Schriften*, vol. 1 (Berlin: Schwetschke, 1924), pp. 306 ff.; Leo Strauß, 'Athen and Jerusalem', *Commentary* (June 1967); B. Uffenheimer, 'Mythos und Realität im alten Israel', in Samuel N. Eisenstadt (ed.), *Kulturen der Achsenzeit*, vol. 1 (Frankfurt am Main: Suhrkamp, 1987), pp. 192 ff.

68 Horkheimer, 'Traditionelle und kritische Theorie', pp. 261, 292.

69 Horkheimer, 'Zum Problem der Wahrheit', p. 343.

70 Willard v. Orman Quine, 'Logik und die Verdinglichung von Universalien', in Wolfgang Stegmüller (ed.), *Das Universalien-Problem* (Darmstadt: Wiss. Buchgesellschaft, 1978), pp. 133–64.

71 Adorno, 'Vernunft und Offenbarung', *Gesammelte Schriften* vol. 10 2, p. 616.

72 Isaiah 44: 10.

73 R. Rorty, 'Putnam and the Relativist Menace', *The Journal of Philosophy* 9 (1993), pp. 445, 453.

74 Isaiah 44: 14–19.

75 Jeremiah 10: 3–9.

76 R. Rorty, 'Relativist Menace', p. 453.

77 Aristotle, *The Nicomachean Ethics* (vi, 1143b).

78 Cf. for an empirical account on the connection between the experience of injustice and raising of moral conscience: Jean Piaget, *Le Jugement moral chez l'enfant* (Paris: Presses Universitaires de France, 1973), p. 311; cf. Thomas Kesselring, *Entwicklung und Widerspruch: Ein Vergleich zwischen Piagets genetischer Erkenntnistheorie und Hegels Dialektik* (Frankfurt am Main: Suhrkamp, 1981), p. 313.

79 Hilary Putnam, *The Many Faces of Realism: The Paul Carus Lectures* (La Salle, IL: Open Court, 1987), p. 44.

80 Lambert Zuidervaart, *Adorno's Aesthetic Theory: The Redemption of Illusion* (Cambridge, MA, and London: MIT Press, 1991), p. 61.

81 Herbert Marcuse, 'Über den affirmativen Charakter der Kultur', *Schriften 3. Aufsätze aus der 'Zeitschrift für Sozialforschung' 1934–1941* (Frankfurt am Main: Suhrkamp, 1979), pp. 186–226.

82 Adorno, *Negative Dialektik* (Frankfurt am Main: Suhrkamp, 1973), p. 530.

83 Adorno, *Negative Dialectics*, pp. 317–18.

84 Ibid., pp. 148–9.

85 Ibid., p. 147.

86 Ibid., pp. 298–9.

87 L. Zuidervaart, *Adorno's Aesthetic Theory*, p. 168.

88 Adorno, *Aesthetic Theory*, p. 213.

[89] Adorno, *Äesthetische Theorie*, p. 423.

[90] Ibid., p. 455.

[91] Adorno, *Negative Dialektik*, p. 202; Georg Wilhelm Friedrich Hegel, *Phänomenologie des Geistes* (Hamburg: Meiner, 1955), p. 20. See above, p. 23.

[92] Adorno, *Negative Dialektik*, p. 202.

[93] See Kesselring, *Entwicklung und Widerspruch* (Frankfurt am Main: Suhrkamp, 1979), pp. 117 ff., 141–2.

[94] Adorno, *Negative Dialektik*, p. 262.

[95] See J. Früchtl, *Mimesis, Konstellation eines Zentralbegriffs bei Adorno* (Würzburg: Königshaus und Neumann, 1986).

4 Freedom, Critique and Transgression in Adorno's Theory of Aesthetic Modernism

[1] Theodor W. Adorno's *Ästhetische Theorie* (Frankfurt am Main: Suhrkamp, 1970), p. 514.

[2] Ibid., p. 145.

[3] Ibid., p. 318: 'Daß Bewußtsein töte ist ein Ammenmärchen; tödlich ist einzig falsches Bewußtsein.'

[4] An allusion to the title of a set of Adorno's essays: *Ohne Leitbild. Parva Aesthetica* (Frankfurt am Main: Suhrkamp, 1967).

[5] Adorno, *Noten zur Literatur* (Frankfurt am Main: Suhrkamp, 1974), p. 290: 'aller Spiegelbildlichkeit lediges Spiel mit Elementen der Realität.'

[6] Adorno, *Ästhetische Theorie*, p. 416.

[7] Ibid., p. 53.

[8] Ibid., p. 45.

[9] A. Gehlen, *Zeitbilder* (Frankfurt am Main: Vittorio Klostermann, 1986), p. 64.

[10] *Als die Surrealisten noch Recht hatten* (Stuttgart: Klett, 1976), p. 28. Compare this with John Dewey: 'Dream, insanity and phantasy are natural products, as "real" as anything else in the world.' (*The Quest for Certainty*, New York: Capricorn Books, 1960, p. 243.)

[11] Adorno, *Ästhetische Theorie*, p. 442.

[12] Arnold Gehlen, *Zeit-Bilder* (Frankfurt am Main: Vittorio Klostermann, 1986), p. 64.

[13] Adorno, *Ästhetische Theorie*, pp. 380–1.

[14] Adorno, 'Versuch, das Endspiel zu verstehen', *Noten zur Literatur* (Frankfurt am Main: Suhrkamp, 1974), pp. 282, 290 ('ohne Stellung zu beziehen').

[15] Ibid., p. 290.

[16]   Adorno, *Ästhetische Theorie*, p. 285: 'Materialisation fortgeschrittensten Bewußtseins'.

[17]   Cf. Hauke Brunkhorst, *Theodor W. Adorno. Dialektik der Moderne* (Munich: Piper, 1990), pp. 15 ff., 116 ff., 125 ff., 181 ff; see also Albrecht Wellmer, 'Wahrheit, Schein, Versöhnung', in Wellmer, *Zur Dialektik von Moderne und Postmoderne* (Frankfurt am Main: Suhrkamp, 1985), pp. 43 ff. (English in Albrecht Wellmer, 'Truth, Semblance and Reconciliation', *Telos*, 62 (1984/5), pp. 89–115.)

[18]   Adorno, *Ohne Leitbild* (Frankfurt am Main: Suhrkamp, 1967), p. 58; cf. also Baden-Badener Kunstgespräche, 1959, *Wird die moderne Kunst 'gemanagt'?* (Baden-Baden and Krefeld: Agis, 1959).

[19]   Adorno, *Ästhetische Theorie*, p. 386.

[20]   'Versuch, das Endspiel zu verstehen', in *Noten zur Literatur*, p. 290.

[21]   Quotation, Elisabeth Lenk, *Kritische Phantasie* (Munich: Mathes & Seitz, 1986), p. 58.

[22]   The necessity of such a relationship between the distinct layers of meaning in Adorno's texts, which would be accessible to a 'stereoscopic reading' (Wellmer) under the unity-grounding a priori of a negative philosophy of history, is now disputed from entirely different points of departure in Adorno scholarship. Cf. e.g. Albrecht Wellmer, *Zur Dialektik von Moderne und Postmoderne*, pp. 9 ff., 48 ff., 135 ff.; Jürgen Ritsert, *Ästhetische Theorie als Gesellschaftskritik* (Frankfurt: Studientexte zur Sozialwissenschaft, n.d.); Hauke Brunkhorst, *Theodor W. Adorno. Dialektik der Moderne*; Hauke Brunkhorst, 'Die ästhetische Konstruktion der Moderne', in Leviathan, 1 (1988), pp. 77–96; Hauke Brunkhorst, 'Eine Verteidigung der "Ästhetischen Theorie" Adornos bei revisionistischer Distanzierung von seiner Geschichtsphilosophie', in Herfried Münkler and Richard Saage (eds.), *Kultur und Politik* (Opladen: Westdeutscher Verlag, 1990), pp. 89–106.

[23]   Paul Liesmann, *Ohne Mitleid* (Vienna: Passagen Verlag, 1990).

[24]   Karl-Heinz Bohrer, *Plötzlichkeit. Zum Augenblick des ästhetischen Scheins* (Frankfurt am Main: Suhrkamp, 1981); idem, *Die Ästhetik des Schreckens* (Frankfurt am Main: Ullstein, 1983).

[25]   See Christoph Menke, *Die Souveränität der Kunst? Ästhetische Erfahrung nach Adorno und Derrida* (Frankfurt am Main: Athenäum, 1988).

[26]   On the 'ontology of the false condition' see Adorno, *Negative Dialectics*, p. 22; on the Anti-Hegel: 'The whole is the false', see *Minima Moralia: Reflections from Damaged Life*, tr. E. F. N. Jephcott (London: New Left Books, 1974), p. 50.

[27]   On modernity/modernism in Adorno, see above, Chap. 1, s. 12.

[28]   On the 'expressive model', cf. Charles Taylor, *Hegel* (Cambridge: Cambridge University Press, 1975).

29   Adorno, *Beethoven. Philosophie der Musik* (Frankfurt am Main: Suhrkamp, 1993), p. 48.

30   Ibid. I am grateful to Andreas Kuhlmann for references. Cf. his review of the Beethoven book in *Die Zeit*, 'Technik und Transzendenz' (Oct. 1993).

31   Adorno, *Beethoven*, pp. 48 ff.

32   Adorno, *Minima Moralia* (Frankfurt am Main: Suhrkamp, 1964), p. 102.

33   G. W. F. Hegel, *Vorlesungen über die Ästhetik III* (Frankfurt am Main: Suhrkamp, 1971), p. 154. On Hegel and Schopenhauer vs. E.T.A. Hoffmann and Adorno cf. Andreas Kuhlmann, *Romantische Musikästhetik*, Diss. phil. Bielefeld, 1989, pp. 80 ff. (part iii: 'Musiksprache als Sprachnegation').

34   Adorno, 'Vers une musique informelle', *Gesammelte Schriften*, vol. 16 (Frankfurt am Main: Suhrkamp, 1980), pp. 495 ff.

35   G. W. F. Hegel, *Vorlesungen*, p. 190; A. Schopenhauer, *Die Welt als Wille und Vorstellung I* (Frankfurt am Main: Insel, 1991), pp. 348 ff., cit. in Kuhlmann, *Romantische Musikästhetik*, Diss.: Univ. of Bielefeld, p. 102.

36   Adorno, *Noten zur Literatur*, p. 105.

37   Adorno, *Minima Moralia*, trans., pp. 212–13.

38   R. Bubner, 'Heiter ist das Leben . . . Anmerkungen zu einem aktuellen Phänomen der Grenzüberschreitung', in Rüdiger Bubner, *Zwischenrufe* (Frankfurt am Main: Suhrkamp, 1993), p. 61. On Adorno's aesthetic reaction to his own theory, cf. the informative anecdotal observations in Gerhard R. Koch, 'Flaschenpost auf Vermittlungskurs. Gibt es ein Weiterwirken Adornos im Musikbetrieb?', in Rainer Erd, Dietrich Hoss, Otto Jacobi and Peter Noller (eds.), *Kritische Theorie und Kultur* (Frankfurt am Main: Suhrkamp, 1989), pp. 53–68.

39   Adorno, 'Die Kunst und die Künste', in Adorno, *Ohne Leitbild. Parva Aesthetica* (Frankfurt am Main: Suhrkamp, 1967), p. 159.

40   W. Benjamin, *Der Begriff der Kunstkritik* (Frankfurt am Main: Suhrkamp, 1973).

41   Adorno, 'Versuch das Endspiel zu verstehen', 359; see below, Chap. 4, s. 4.

42   Cf. Christine Eichel, *Vom Ermatten der Avantgarde zur Vernetzung der Künste. Perspektiven einer Interdiszplinären Ästhetik im Spätwerk Adornos* (Frankfurt am Main: Surhkamp, 1993). The literal translation of the German word 'Verfransung' is 'infringement' or 'fraying', but the more abstract meaning is the transgression of borders.

43   With particular regard to music, see the differentiated estimation of G. R. Koch, 'Flaschenpost auf Vermittlungskurs'.

44   Adorno, *Ästhetische Theorie*, p. 79.

45   Ibid., p. 416.

[46] For the diagnosis, see Peter Bürger, *Zur Kritik der idealistischen Ästhetik* (Frankfurt am Main: Suhrkamp, 1983), 128 ff.

[47] Gertrud Koch, 'Mimesis and Bildverbot', *Screen* 34/3 (Autumn 1993); Miriam Hansen, 'Mass culture as hieroglyphic writing: Adorno, Derrida, Kracauer', *New German Critique*, 56 (1992).

[48] See Martin Jay, 'Mimesis und Mimetologie: Adorno und die Herausforderung des Poststrukturalismus', in Gertrud Koch (ed.), *Auge und Affekt* (Frankfurt am Main: Fischer, 1995).

[49] Adorno, *Noten zur Literatur*, pp. 258–9.

[50] Ibid., p. 257.

[51] Adorno, *Prismen: Kulturkritik und Gesellschaft* (Frankfurt am Main: Suhrkamp, 1969), p. 106.

[52] Adorno, 'Aufzeichnungen zu Kafka', in *Gesammelte Schriften*, vol. 10 (Frankfurt am Main: Suhrkamp, 1977), p. 275.

[53] Ibid., p. 265.

[54] Adorno, *Ästhetische Theorie*, p. 425.

[55] E. Lenk, *Kritische Phantasie*, p. 82.

[56] Adorno, *Beethoven* (Frankfurt am Main: Suhrkamp, 1993), p. 235.

[57] See P. Liessman, *Ohne Mitleid* (Vienna: Passagen Verlag, 1992).

[58] Adorno, *Ästhetische Theorie*, p. 53.

[59] Adorno, *Negative Dialektik*, p. 46.

[60] Adorno, *Minima Moralia*, p. 157.

[61] K. Marx, *Grundrisse der Kritik der politischen Ökonomie* (Berlin: Dietz, 1953), 6.

[62] Adorno, *Einleitung zur Musiksoziologie* (Frankfurt am Main: Suhrkamp, 1962), p. 222.

[63] Adorno, *Ästhetische Theorie*, p. 143.

[64] Adorno, 'Die Kunst und die Künste', p. 181. On the dialectic of autonomy and sovereignty, cf. Christoph Menke, *Die Souveränität der Kunst* (Frankfurt am Main: Suhrkamp, 1991). A sovereignty of art broken by radical, 'hermetic' autonomy is for Adorno in 1966 the unravelling of the individual works out of an inner drive. Adorno was long on the trail of such fraying, e.g. in the 1951 essay 'Zum Verhältnis von Musik und Malerei Heute', in R. Tiedemann (ed.), *Adorno-Noten* (Berlin: Akzente-Verlag, 1984), pp. 150–63. Cp. also the following passage from the 'Aufzeichnungen zu Kafka': 'Insofar as his brittle prose spurns all musical effect, it proceeds like music. It breaks off the meanings like monuments in cemeteries of the nineteenth century.' (*Gesammelte Schriften*, vol. 10, p. 278.) The texts on Eichendorff and Rudolf Borchardt from the *Notes on Literature* are also characteristic for the anticipation of the unravelling or transgression theorem; after all, the *critic* offers here notes in the form of essays.

[65] Adorno, 'Die Kunst und die Künste', p. 160.

[66] Ibid., p. 161.

67 Ibid., p. 169. Unlike some postmodernists (see above, Chap. 3) Adorno never goes so far as to reject that there is a crucial *difference* between *what* (happened) and *how* (it is described). For Adorno not everything is 'metaphor' and 'rhetoric'.

68 Adorno, *Ästhetische Theorie*, p. 152.

69 Cf. Arnold Gehlen, *Zeit-Bilder* (Frankfurt am Main: Vittorio Klostermann, 1986), pp. 162 ff.

70 Adorno, 'Die Kunst und die Künste', p. 174.

71 Ibid.

72 Martin Heidegger, 'Der Ursprung des Kunstwerks', *Holzwege* (Frankfurt am Main: Klostermann, 1972), esp. pp. 29 ff.

73 Martin Heidegger, 'Der Ursprung des Kunstwerks', pp. 54 ff. Trans. as 'The Origin of the Work of Art', in Martin Heidegger, *Poetry, Language, Thought*, tr. Douglas Hofstadter (New York: Harper and Row, 1971), pp. 15–89.

74 Adorno, 'Die Kunst und die Künste', p. 170.

75 Adorno, *Ästhetische Theorie*, p. 15.

76 Adorno, *Aesthetic Theory*, p. 7.

77 Ibid., p. 16.

78 Adorno, *Ästhetische Theorie*, p. 15 (trans., p. 7).

79 Ibid., *Ästhetische Theorie*, p. 531 (trans., p. 490).

80 Adorno, *Minima Moralia*, tr. E. F. N. Jephcott, p. 71.

81 See Walter Benjamin, 'Der Begriff der Kunstkritik in der deutschen Romantik', in Benjamin, *Gesammelte Schriften*, vol. 1/1, *Abhandlungen* (Frankfurt am Main: Suhrkamp, 1974) pp. 7–122.

82 Adorno, *Noten zur Literatur*, p. 102.

83 Ibid., p. 313.

84 Here and in the following I take the lead of Christoph Menke's 'Der Stand des Streits. Literatur und Gesellschaft in Samuel Becketts *Endspiel*', MS, Frankfurt am Main, 1993; and his 'Literatur und Gesellschaft. Zu einigen methodischen Aspekten von Adornos Beckettinterpretation', MS, Frankfurt am Main, 1993.

85 Adorno, *Noten zur Literatur*, p. 290.

86 Ibid., p. 290.

87 Ibid., p. 306.

88 Ibid., p. 282.

89 Cf. Albrecht Wellmer, 'Wahrheit, Schein, Versöhnung', in *Adorno-Konferenz*, ed. Ludwig v. Friedeburg and Jürgen Habermas (Frankfurt am Main: Suhrkamp, 1983).

90 Adorno, *Aesthetic Theory*, p. 73.

91 Ibid.

92 Ibid.

93 Ibid.

[94] Christoph Menke, 'Der Stand des Streits'. I also adopt from Menke the following example from Beckett's *Endgame*.

[95] Adorno, *Noten zur Literatur*, p. 308.

[96] Ibid.

[97] Adorno, *Beethoven*, p. 16. (The quote is taken from Tiedemann's 'Vorrede' and stems originally from Adorno's Iphigenie essay.)

[98] On the 'mounting bleatings' see Botho Strauß, 'Bocksgesang', *Die selbstbewußte Nation* (Hamburg: Ullstein, 1994).

[99] Adorno, *Mahler, Gesammelte Schriften*, vol. 13 (Frankfurt am Main: Suhrkamp, 1971), pp. 184 ff.

[100] Adorno, 'On popular music', *ZfS* 9 (1941), p. 48.

[101] Adorno, *Ästhetische Theorie*, p. 27.

Bibliography

Works by Theodor W. Adorno

1920 'Expressionismus und künstlerische Wahrhaftigkeit. Zur Kritik neuer Dichtung', *Die Neue Schaubühne* 2/9, pp. 233–6.

1921/2 'Béla Bartók', *Neue Blätter für Kunst und Literatur*, 4/8, pp. 126–8.

1921/2 'Die Hochzeit des Faun. Grundsätzliche Bemerkungen zu Bernhard Sekles' neuer Oper', *Neue Blätter für Kunst und Literatur*, 4/3–4, pp. 61–2; 5, pp. 68–70.

1921/2 'Drei Operneinakter von Paul Hindemith: Mörder Hoffnung der Frauen, Schauspiel von Oskar Kokoschka: Sancta Susanna, 1 Akt von August Stramm; Das Nusch-Nuschi, Operette für burmanische Marionetten von Franz Blei', *Neue Blätter für Kunst und Literatur*, 4/8, pp. 121–2.

1921/2 'Kammermusik im Verein für Theater- und Musikkultur. Dritter Kammermusikabend: Arnold Schönbergs Pierrot lunaire. Vierter Kammermusikabend', *Neue Blätter für Kunst und Literatur*, 4/6, pp. 88–90.

1922/3 'Bartók-Aufführungen in Frankfurt', *Neue Blätter für Kunst und Literatur*, 5/I, pp. 5–8.

1922/3 'Zeitgenössische Kammermusik. Erster und zweiter Abend im Verein für Theater- und Musikkultur', *Neue Blätter für Kunst und Literatur*, 5/1, pp. 9–11.

1923 'Neue Musik. 7 Kammerkonzerte in Frankfurt am Main', *Zeitschrift für Musik*, 90/15–16, pp. 314–16.

1924 'Die Transzendenz des Dinglichen und Noematischen in Husserls Phänomenologie. Frankfurt am Main Phil. Diss. vom 15.12.1924. 93 pp. (under the name Theodor Wiesengrund).

1924 'Richard Strauß: Zum 60. Geburtstage: 11.6.1924', *Zeitschrift für Musik*, 91/6, pp. 289–95.

1924/6 'Volksliedersammlungen', *Die Musik*, 17/8, pp. 583–5.

1925 'Alban Berg. Zur Uraufführung des "Wozzek" ', *Musikblätter des Anbruch*, 7/12, pp. 531–7.

1925 'Béla Bartóks Tanzsuite', *Pult und Taktstock* (Vienna and New York), 2/6, pp. 105–7.

1925 'Die Serenade. Zur Aufführung von Schönbergs Serenade in Venedig', *Pult und Taktstock* (Vienna and New York), 2/7, pp. 113–18.

1925 'Strawinsky-Fest', *Musikblätter des Anbruch*, 7/10, pp. 551–3.

1925 'Über einige Werke von Béla Bartök', *Zeitschrift für Musik*, 92/7–8, pp. 428–30.

1925 'Zeitgenössische Musik in Frankfurt am Main', *Zeitschrift für Musik*, 92/4, pp. 216–18.

1925 'Zum Problem der Reproduktion. Fragmente', *Pult und Taktstock* (Vienna and New York), 2/4, pp. 51–5.

1926 'Anton Webern. Zur Aufführung der 5 Orchesterstücke in Zürich', *Musikblätter des Anbruch*, 8/6, pp. 280–2.

1926 'Drei Dirigenten', *Musikblätter des Anbruch*, 8/7, pp. 315–19 (on W. Furtwängler, H. Scherchen and A. Webern).

1926 'Metronomisierung', *Pult und Taktstock* (Vienna and New York), 37–8, pp. 130–4.

1926 'Opernprobleme. Glossiert nach Frankfurter Aufführungen', *Musikblätter des Anbruch*, 8/5, pp. 205–8.

1927 'Die Orchesterstücke op. 16', *Pult und Taktstock*, 4, pp. 36–43 (Sonderheft: Arnold Schönberg und seine Orchesterwerke).

1927 'Motive (I)', *Musikblätter des Anbruch*, 9/4, pp. 161–2.

1928 'Berliner Memorial', *Neue Musik-Zeitung*, 49/13, pp. 416–20.

1928 'Marginalien zur Sonata von Alexander Jenmitz', *Neue Musik-Zeitung*, 49/12, pp. 387–90.

1928 'Motive [II]', 'Motive [III]', *Musikblätter des Anbruch*, 10/6–7, pp. 199–202, 237–40.

1928 'Nadelkurven', *Musikblätter des Anbruch*, 10/2, pp. 47–50.

1928 'Schönbergs Bläserquintett', *Pult und Taktstock*, 5 (May/June), pp. 45–9.

1928 'Schubert', *Die Musik*, 21/1, pp. 1–12.

1928 'Situationen des Liedes', *Musikblätter des Anbruch*, 10/9–10, pp. 363–9.

1928/9 'Zur Dreigroschenoper', *Die Musik*, 6, pp. 424–8.

1929 'Alban Bergs frühe Lieder', *Anbruch*, 11/2, pp. 90–2.

1929 'Berliner Opernmemorial', *Anbruch* 11/6, pp. 261–6.

1929 'Glosse zu Richard Strauß', *Anbruch*, 11/6, pp. 250–1.

1929 'Motive [IV]: Musik von außen', *Anbruch*, 11/9–10, pp. 335–8.

1929 'Nachtmusik', *Anbruch*, 11/ l, pp. 16–23.

1929 'Schlageranalysen', *Anbruch* 11/3, pp. 108–14.

1929 'Tonales Intermezzo?', *Anbruch*, 11/5, pp. 187–93.

1929 'Zur Zwölftontechnik', *Anbruch*, 11/7–8, pp. 290–4.

1929/30 'Die Oper Wozzeck', *Der Scheinwerfer* (Blätter der Städtischen Büihnen Essen), 3/4, pp. 5–11.

1929/30 'Stilgeschichte in Schönbergs Werk', *Blätter der Staatsoper und der Städtischen Oper Berlin*, 10/32, pp. 4–9.

1930 'Bewußtsein des Konzerthörens', *Anbruch* 12/9–10, pp. 274–5.

1930 'Kierkegaard prophezeit Chaplin', *Frankfurter Zeitung* (22 May).

1930 'Kontroverse über die Heiterkeit', *Anbruch*, 12/1, pp. 19–21.

1930 'Mahagonny', *Der Scheinwerfer* (Blätter der Städtischen Büihnen Essen), 3/14, pp. 12–15.

1930 'Mahler heute', *Anbruch*, 12/3, pp. 86–92.

1930 'Motive (V): Hermeneutik', *Anbruch*, 12/7–8, pp. 235–8.

1930 'Neue Tempi', *Pult und Taktstock*, 7/1, pp. 1–7.

1930 'Ravel', *Anbruch*, 12/4–5, pp. 151–4.

1930 'Reaktion und Fortschritt', *Anbruch*, 12/6, pp. 191–5.

1930/1 'Berg and Webern – Schönberg's heirs', *Modern Music* (New York), 8/2, pp. 29–38.

1930/1 'Gegen die neue Tonalität', *Der Scheinwerfer* (Blätter der Städtischen Bühnen Essen), 4/16, pp. 4–8.

1930/1 'Widerlegungen', *Die Musik*, 23/9, pp. 647–51.

1931 'Kierkegaard', *Konstruktion des Ästetischen*. Habil.Schrift. Frankfurt am Main. Univ. 1931.

1931 'Musikstudio', *Anbruch*, 13/1, pp. 17–19.

1931 'Rede über den "Raritätenladen" von Charles Dickens', *Frankfurter Zeitung*, 285 (18 April).

1931 'Worte ohne Lieder', *Frankfurter Zeitung*, 515 (14 July).

1931/2 'Exkurse zu einem Exkurs', *Der Scheinwerfer* (Blätter der Stüdtischen Bühnen Essen), 5/9–10, pp. 15–18.

1931/2 'Warum ist die neue Kunst so schwer verständlich?', *Der Scheinwerfer* (Blätter der Städtischen Bühnen Essen), 5/2, pp. 12–16.

1931/2 'Zur Naturgeschichte des Theaters. Fragmente', *Blätter des Hessischen Landestheaters Darmstadt*, 9 and 13, pp. 101–8, 153–6.

1932 'Zur gesellschaftlichen Lage der Musik', *Zeitschrift für Sozialforschung*, 1/2–3, pp. 103–24, 356–78.

1932 'Zur Instrumentation von Alban Bergs frühen Liedern', *Schweizerische Musikzeitschrift und Sängerblatt*, 72/5–6, pp. 158–62, 196–200.

1932/3 'Das Foyer. Zur Naturgeschichte des Theaters', *Blätter des Hessischen Landestheaters Darmstadt*, 8, pp. 98–100.

1932/3 'Hoffmanns Erzählungen in Offenbachs Motiven', *Theaterwelt* (Programmschrift der Städtischen Bühnen Düsseldorf), 8/2, pp. 17–20.

1933 'Abschied vom Jazz', *Europäische Revue*, 9/5, pp. 313–16.

1933 'Mascagnis Landschaft. Zum 70. Geburtstag, 7. Dezember 1933', *Vossische Zeitung*, 552 (7 December), p. 7.

1933 'Notiz über Wagner', *Europäische Revue*, 9/7, pp. 439–42.

1933 'Vierhändig, noch einmal', *Vossische Zeitung*, 562 (19 December), pp. 5–6.

1934 'Der dialektische Komponist', *Arnold Schönberg zum 60. Geburtstag* (Vienna, 13 September 1934), pp. 18–23.

1934 'Die Form der Schallplatte', *23. Eine Wiener Musikzeitschrift*, 17/19, pp. 35–9 (under the pen-name Hektor Rottweiler).

1934 'Musikalische Diebe, unmusikalische Richter', *Stuttgarter Neues Tagblatt*, 386 (20 August), p. 2.

1935 'Ernest Krenek', *The Listener* (London, 23 October 1935), pp. 735–6 (unsigned, tr. anon.).

1935 'Zur Krisis der Musikkritik', *23. Eine Wiener Musikzeitschrift*, 20/21, pp. 5–15 (under the pen-name Hektor Rottweiler).

1935 'Zur Stilgeschichte', *Der Auftakt* (Prague) 15/5–6, pp. 65–7.

1936 'Über Jazz', *Zeitschrift für Sozialforschung*, 5/3, pp. 235–57 (under the pen-name Hektor Rottweiler).

1936 'Zur Lulu-Symphonie – Erinnerung an den Lebenden [A. Berg]', *23. Eine Wiener Musikzeitschrift*, 24/25, pp. 5–11, 19–29 (under the pen-name Hektor Rottweiler).

1937 Writings on the following works by A. Bergs, Klaviersonate op. l, Vier Lieder op. 2, Sieben frühe Lieder, Streichquartett op. 3, Vier Stücke für Klarinette und Klavier op. 5, Drei Orchesterstücke op. 6, Lyrische Suite für Streichquartett, Konzertarie 'Der Wein', in *Alban Berg*, ed. Willi Reich. Mit Bergs eigenen Schriften und Beiträgen von T.W. Adorno und Ernst Krenek. Vienna, Leipzig and Zürich: Herbert Reichner, pp. 21–43, 47–64, 91–106.

1937 'Spätstil Beethovens', *Der Auftakt* (Prague), 17/5–6, pp. 65–7.

1938 'Glosse über Sibelius', *Zeitschrift für Sozialforschung*, 7/3, pp. 460–3.

1938 Über den Fetischcharakter in der Musik und die Regression des Hörens', *Zeitschrift für Sozialforschung*, 7/3, pp. 321–56.

1939/40 'Fragmente über Wagner', *Zeitschrift für Sozialforschung*, 8/1–2, pp. 1–48.

1939/40 'On Kierkegaard's Doctrine of Love', *Studies in Philosophy and Social Science*, 8/3, pp. 413–29.

1940 'Husserl and the Problem of Idealism', *The Journal of Philosophy*, 37/1 (January), pp. 5–18.

1940 'Zu Benjamins Gedächtnis', *Aufbau. American Jewish Weekly in German and English* (18 October), p. 7.

1941 'George und Hofmannsthal. Zum Briefwechsel: 1891–1906', 'Walter Benjamin zum Gedächtnis', MS, Institut für Sozialforschung 1941.

1941 'On popular music', *Studies in Philosophy and Social Science*, 9/1, pp. 17–48 (with assistance of George Simpson).

1941 'Research Project on Anti-Semitism', *Studies in Philosophy and Social Science*, 9/1, pp. 124–43 (unsigned).

1941 (Review of) *American Jazz Music* by Wilder Hobson and *Jazz Hot and Hybrid* by Winthrop Sargeant, *Studies in Philosophy and Social Science*, 9/1, pp. 167–78 (with assistance of Enice Cooper).

1941 (Review of) *The Life of Richard Wagner, 1859–1866* by Ernest Newman, *Studies in Philosophy and Social Science*, 9/3, pp. 523–5.

1941 (Review of) *Unmittelbarkeit und Sinndeutung* by Heinrich Rickert, *Studies in Philosophy and Social Science*, 9/3, pp. 479–82.

1941 'Spengler today', *Studies in Philosophy and Social Science* (1941).
1941 'The Radio Symphony: An Experiment in Theory', in Paul Lazarsfeld and Frank Stanton (eds.), *Radio Research 1941*, New York: Duell, Sloan & Pearce, pp. 110–39.
1941 'Veblen's attack on culture', *Studies in Philosophy and Social Science*, 9/3, pp. 389–413.
1942 'A Social Critique of Radio Music', *Kenyon Review*, 7/2, pp. 208–17.
1942 'Für Ernst Bloch', *Aufbau Reconstruction* (New York), 8/48, pp. 15, 17–18.
1942 'Träume in Amerika. Drei Protokolle', *Aufbau Reconstruction* (New York), 8/40, p. 17.
1945 'Theses upon Art and Religion Today', *Kenyon Review*, 7/4 (Autumn), pp. 677–82.
1946 'Anti-Semitism and Fascist Propaganda', in Ernst Simmel (ed.), *Anti Semitism: A Social Disease*, New York: International Universities Press, pp. 125–37.
1946 'Jazz', in Dagobert D. Runes and Harry Schrickel (eds.), *Encyclopedia of the Arts*, New York: Philosophical Library, pp. 511–13.
1947 *Composing for the Films*, New York: Oxford University Press (with Hanns Eisler, not signed by Adorno).
1947 *Dialektik der Aufklärung. Philosophische Fragmente*, Amsterdam: Querido Verlag, 311 pp. (with Max Horkheimer).
1947 'Wagner, Nietzsche, and Hitler', *Kenyon Review*, 9, pp. 155–62.
1949 'Hermann Grab', *Die Neue Rundschau*, 60/4, p. 594.
1949 *Philosophie der neuen Musik*. Tübingen: Mohr (Paul Siebeck), vii, 144 pp.
1950 'Auferstehung der Kultur in Deutschland?', *Frankfurter Hefte*, 5/5, pp. 469–77.
1950 'Charakteristik Walter Benjamins', *Die Neue Rundschau*, 61/4, pp. 571–84.
1950 'Democratic Leadership and Mass Manipulation', in Alvin W. Gouldner (ed.), *Studies in Leadership*, New York: Harper & Row, pp. 418–38.
1950 'Kurt Weill – Musiker des epischen Theaters', *Frankfurter Rundschau* (15 April), p. 6.
1950 *The Authoritarian Personality*, New York: Harper & Brothers 1950, xxxiii, 990 pp. Studies in prejudice. Social studies series 3 (with Else Frenkel-Brunswik, Daniel J. Levinson, R. Nevitt Sanford and others).
1951 'Bach gegen seine Liebhaber verteidigt', *Merkur*, 5/6, pp. 535–46.
1951 'Der entzauberte Traum. Zu A. Huxleys "Brave new world" ', *Die Neue Rundschau*, 62/2, pp. 74–96.

1951 'Freudian Theory and the Pattern of Fascist Propaganda', *Psychoanalysis and the Social Sciences* (New York), 3 (1951), pp. 279 ff.

1951 'Kulturkritik und Gesellschaft', *Soziologische Forschung in unserer Zeit. Leopold von Wiese zum 75. Geburtstag*, ed. Karl Gustav Specht, Cologne: Opladen, pp. 228–40.

1951 'Lyrik und Gesellschaft', *Das literarische Deutschland*, 2/4–15, pp. 1–2, 2.

1951 *Minima Moralia. Reflexionen aus dem beschädigten Leben*, Frankfurt am Main: Suhrkamp, 488 pp.

1952 'Die revidierte Psychoanalyse', *Psyche*, 6/1, pp. 1 ff.

1952 'Die Soziogie und die Wirklichkeit. Über den Stand der Sozialforschung in Deutschland', *Frankfurter Hefte*, 7/8, pp. 585–95.

1952 *Versuch über Wagner*, Berlin und Frankfurt am Main: Suhrkamp, 204 pp.

1952 'Zum Verhältnis von Psychoanalyse und Gesellschaftstheorie', *Psyche*, 6/l, pp. 17–18.

1952/3 'Die gegängelte Musik. Bemerkungen über die' Musikpolitik der Ostblockstaaten', *Der Monat*, 5 /56, pp. 177–83.

1952/3 'Huldigung an Zerlina', *Programmheft der Städtischen Bühnen Frankfurt*, 4, p. 13.

1953 'Arnold Schönberg', *Die Neue Rundschau*, 64/1, pp. 80–104.

1953 'Aufzeichnungen zu Kafka', *Die Neue Rundschau*, 64/3, pp. 325–53.

1953 'Der Artist als Statthalter. Zu Valérys Degas-Buch', *Merkur*, 7/11, pp. 1034–45.

1953 'Fernsehen als Ideologie', *Rundfunk und Fernsehen*, 4, pp. 1–11.

1953 'Prolog zum Fernsehen', *Rundfunk und Fernsehen*, 2, pp. 1–8.

1953 'Über das gegenwärtige Verhältnis von Philosophie und Musik', *Filosofia dell' arte*. Rome and Milan, pp. 5–30. (= Archivio di filosofia, ed. E. Castelli).

1953 'Über Mannheims Wissenssoziologie', *Aufklärung*, 2/4–6, pp. 224–36.

1953 'Valéry Proust Museum', *Die Neue Rundschau*, 64/4, pp. 552–63.

1953 'Zeitlose Mode. Zum Jazz', *Merkur*, 7/6, pp. 537–48.

1953/4 'Beitrag zur Ideologienlehre', *Kölner Zeitschrift für Soziologie*, 6/3–4 (= Verhandlungen des 12. Deutschen Soziologentages), pp. 360–75.

1953/4 'Bemerkungen über Politik und Neurose', *Der Monat*, 6/65, pp. 482–5.

1954 'Form und Gehalt des zeitgenössischen Romans', *Akzente*, 1/5, pp. 410–16.

1954 'How to Look at Television', *Quarterly of Film, Radio and Television*, 8/3, pp. 213–35.

1954 'Im Schatten junger Mädchenblüte', *Dichten und Trachten. Jahresschau des Suhrkamp-Verlages* IV, Berlin and Frankfurt am Main: Suhrkamp, 1954, pp. 73–8.

1954 'Individuum und Organisation', *Darmstädter Gespřch, Individuum und Organisation,* ed. Fritz Neumark, Darmstadt: Neue Darmstädter Verlagsanstalt, pp. 21 ff.

1954 'So ergeht es dem, der heute zum ersten Male fliegt', *Frankfurter Rundschau,* (9–10 January), p. 13.

1954/5 'Das Altern der Neuen Musik', *Der Monat,* 7/80, pp. 150–8.

1954/5 'Kleiner Dank an Wien', *Kontinente* (Vienna), 8/8, pp. 31–2.

1955 'Einleitung zu Benjamins "Schriften" ', *Walter Benjamin: Schriften,* vol. 1, Frankfurt am Main: Suhrkamp, 1955, pp. ix–xxv.

1955 'Fantasia sopra Carmen', *Die Neue Rundschau,* 66/3, pp. 462–70.

1955 'Musikalische Warenanalysen', *Die Neue Rundschau,* 66/1, pp. 59–70.

1955 *Prismen. Kulturkritik und Gesellschaft,* Berlin and Frankfurt am Main: Suhrkamp, 342 pp.

1955 [Review] Benjamin's *Einbahnstraße, Texte und Zeichen,* 1, pp. 518–22.

1955 'Theater, Oper, Bürgertum', in Egon Vietta (ed.), *Theater,* Darmstadt: Neue Darmstädter Verlagsanstalt, pp. 119–34.

1955 'Wird Spengler rechtbehalten?', *Frankfurter Hefte,* 10/12, pp. 841–6.

1955 'Zum Studium der Philosophie', *Diskus. Frankfurter Studentenzeitung,* 5/2, Supplement, pp. 81–3.

1955 'Zum Verhältnis von Soziologie und Psychologie', in Adorno and Walter Dirks (eds.), *Sociologica I. Aufsätze. Max Horkheimer zum 60. Geburtstag,* Frankfurt am Main (=Frankfurter Beiträge zur Soziologie 1), pp. 11–45.

1955 'Zum Verständnis Schönbergs', *Frankfurter Hefte,* 10/6, pp. 418–29.

1956 'Alban Berg', *Merkur,* 10/7, pp. 643–51.

1956 'Ersatz für das "Studium Generale"?', *Die Zeit* (11 October), p. 4.

1956 *Dissonanzen. Musik in der verwalfeten Welt,* Göttingen: Vandenhoech & Ruprecht, 125 pp. (= Kleine Vandenhoeck-Reihe 28/29).

1956 'Musica, linguaggio e loro rapporto nelle composizioni contemporare', *Archivio di filosofia* (Roma), 2/3 (= Filosofia e simbolismo), pp. 149–62.

1956 'Rückblickend auf den Surrealismus', *Texte und Zeichen,* 2/6, pp. 620–4.

1956 'Satzzeichen. Für Gertrud von Holzhausen', *Akzente,* 3/6, pp. 569–75.

1956 *Zur Metakritik der Erkenntnistheorie. Studien über Husserl und die phänomenologischen Antinomien*, Stuttgart: Kohlhammer, 251 pp.

1956/7 'Fragen des gegenwärtigen Operntheaters', *Neue Deutsche Hefte*, 3/31, pp. 526–35.

1956/7 'Zur Partitur des "Parsifal" ', *Musik und Szene. Theaterzeitschrift der Deutschen Oper am Rhein* (Düsseldorf), 1/3, pp. 25–9.

1957 'Aberglaube aus zweiter Hand. Zur Sozialpsychologie der Zeitungshoroskope', *Jahrbuch für Amerikastudien*, 2.

1957 'Arnold Schönberg 1874–1951', *Die Großen Deutschen. Deutsche Biographie*, ed. Hermann Heimpel, Theodor Heuss and Benno Reifenberg, vol. 4, Berlin, pp. 508–23.

1957 *Aspekte der Hegelschen Philosophie*, Berlin, Frankfurt am Main: Suhrkamp, 61 pp.

1957 'Soziologie und empirische Forschung', *Wesen und Wirklichkeit des Menschen. Festschrift für Helmut Plessner*, ed. K. Ziegler, Göttingen: Vandenhoek und Ruprecht, pp. 245–60.

1957 'The Stars Down to Earth: The Los Angeles Times Astrology Column', *Jahrbuch für Amerikastudien*, Heidelberg: Carl Winter, pp. 19–88.

1957 *Vorlesungen zur Einleitung in die Erkenntnistheorie*, Frankfurt am Main: Hesa-Druck, 324 pp. (= Junius-Drucke).

1957/8 'Neue Musik, Interpretation, Publikum', *Neue Deutsche Hefte*, 4/41, pp. 822–8.

1957/8 'Zur Physiognomik Kreneks', *Musik und Szene. Theaterzeitschrift der Deutschen Oper am Rhein* (Düsseldorf), 2/13, pp. 146–51.

1958 'Die Funktion des Kontrapunktes in der neuen Musik. Berlin: Akademie der Künste August 1957', *Merkur*, 12/1, pp. 27 ff.

1958 'Die Meisterschaft des Maestro', *Merkur*, 12/10, pp. 924–37.

1958 'Gedichte von Reinhold Zickel', *Akzente*, 5/3, pp. 273–81 (with an introduction).

1958 'Im Jeu de Paume gekritzelt', *Frankfurter Allgemeine Zeitung* (20 December).

1958 'Kleine Proust-Kommentare', *Akzente*, 5/6, pp. 564–75.

1958 'Musik und Technik', *Gravesaner Blätter*, 4/11–12, pp. 36 ff.

1958 *Noten zur Literatur*, Frankfurt am Main: Suhrkamp, vol. 1/1–6, 193 pp. (= Bibliothek Suhrkamp 47); vol. 2 (1961), 236 pp. (85–71); vol. 3 (1965), 209 pp. (BS 146); vol. 4, ed. R. Tiedemann (1974), 159 pp. (BS 395).

1958 'Offenbarung oder autonome Vernunft. Thesen mit Eugen Kogon', *Frankfurter Hefte*, 13/6, pp. 397–402.

1958/9 'Erpreßte Versöhnung. Zu Georg Lukács "Wider den mißverstandenen Realismus" ', *Der Monat*, 11/122, pp. 37–49.

1958/9 'Ideen zur Musiksoziologie', *Schweizer Monatshefte*, 38/8 (Sonderheft Soziologische Probleme), pp. 679–91.

1958/9 'Klassik, Romantik, Neue Musik', *Neue Deutsche Hefte*, 5/56, pp. 1066 ff.

1958/9 'Theorie der Halbbildung', *Der Monat*, 11/32, pp. 30–43.

1958/9 'Verfremdetes Hauptwerk. Zur Missa Solemnis', *Neue Deutsche Hefte*, 5/54, pp. 886–97.

1958 'Dank an Peter Suhrkamp', *Frankfurter Allgemeine Zeitung* (9 April), p. 12.

1959 *Musikalische Schriften*, Frankfurt am Main: Suhrkamp, vol. 1, *Klangfiguren*, 366 pp.; vol. 2, *Quasi una fantasia* (1963), 440 pp.

1959 'Vorschlag zur Ungüte', *Wird die moderne Kunst 'gemanagt'?*, Baden-Baden and Krefeld: Agis (= Baden-Badener Kunstgespräche 1959. Kommentare zur Kunst der Gegenwart, 1), pp. 37–59.

1959 'Webern, der Komponist', *Merkur*, 13/3, pp. 201–14.

1959 'Wörter aus der Fremde. Funktion und Gebrauch', *Akzente*, 6/2, pp. 176–91.

1959 'Zu Schlußszene des Faust', *Akzente*, 6/6, pp. 567–75.

1960 'Kultur und Verwaltung', *Merkur*, 14/2, pp. 101–21.

1960 *Mahler. Eine musikalische Physiognomik*. Frankfurt am Main: Suhrkamp, 225 pp. (Bibliothek Suhrkamp 62).

1960 'Musik und Tradition', *Jahresring 60/61* (Beiträge zur deutschen Literatur und Kunst der Gegenwart, Stuttgart), pp. 24–38.

1960 'Rede über Alban Bergs "Lulu" ', *Frankfurter Allgemeine Zeitung* (19 January), p. 16.

1960 'Valérys Abweichungen', *Die Neue Rundschau*, 71/1, pp. 1–38.

1960 'Verbindlichkeit des Neuen', *Helos*, 27/6, pp. 167–8.

1960 'Was bedeutet: Aufarbeitung der Vergangenheit?', *Bericht über die Erzieherkonferenz in Wiesbaden, 6./7.11.1959*, ed. Deutschen Koordinierungsrat der Gesellschaften für Christlich-Jüdische Zusammenarbeit, Frankfurt am Main: Diesterweg, pp. 12–23.

1960 'Zur Frankfurter Aufführung der "Dreigroschenoper" 1928', *Bertolt Brechts Dreigroschenbuch. Texte, Materialien, Dokumente*, ed. Siegfried Unseld, Frankfurt am Main: Suhrkamp, p. 183.

1960/1 'Große Blochmusik', *Neue Deutsche Hefte*, 7/69, pp. 14–26.

1961 'Alban Berg und die Gegenwart', *Forum* (Vienna), 8, pp. 88–9, 153–5, 187–90.

1961 'Über Statik und Dynamik als soziologische Kategorien', *Neue Deutsche Hefte*, 8/81, pp. 47–68.

1961 'Voraussetzungen', *Akzente*, 8/5, pp. 463–78.

1961/2 'Bilderwelt des Freischütz', *Programm der Hamburger Staatsoper*, 5, pp. 33–8.

1961/2 'Meinung Wahn Gesellschaft', *Der Monat*, 14/159, pp. 17–26.

1962 *Einleitung in die Musiksoziologie. Zwölf theoretische Vorlesungen*, Frankfurt am Main: Suhrkamp, 225 pp.

1962 'Gedenkrede auf Wolfgang Steinecke', *Darmstädter Echo* (31 July).

1962 'Jene zwanziger Jahre', *Merkur*, 16/l, pp. 46–51.

1962 'Logik der Sozialwissenschaften', *Kölner Zeitschrift für Soziologie und Sozialpsychologie*, 14 /2, pp. 249–63.

1962 'Notiz über Geisteswissenschaften und Bildung', *4 daten. Standorte – Konsequenzen*, ed. Claus Großner and Arend Oetker, Hamburg: Lingenbrink, p. 50.

1962 [Postscript] in *Deutsche Menschen*, a series of letters selected and introduced by Walter Benjamin. 2nd edn., Frankfurt am Main: Insel-Verlag, pp. 119–28.

1962 'Titel. Paraphrasen zu Lessing. Für Marie Luise Kaschnitz', *Akzent*, 9/3, pp. 278–87.

1962 'Vers une musique informelle', *Darmstädter Beiträge zur Neuen Musik* IV, ed. Ernst Thomas, Mainz: Schott, pp. 73–102.

1962 'Zu einem Portrait Thomas Manns', *Die Neue Rundschau*, 73/2–3, pp. 320–7.

1963 [Against the Death Penalty] in *Dokumentation über die Todesstrafe*, with a comparative analysis of the problem of the death penalty by Armand Mergen, Darmstadt: Stoytscheff, pp. 13–14.

1963 'Bibliographische Grillen. Für Rudolf Hirsch', *Akzente*, 10/6, pp. 693–703.

1963 *Der getreue Korrepetitor. Lehrschriften zur musikalischen Praxis*, Frankfurt am Main: Fischer, 248 pp.

1963 *Drei Studien zu Hegel* [Aspekte. Erfahrungsgehalt. Skoteinos oder Wie zu lesen sei.], Frankfurt am Main: Suhrkamp, 173 pp.

1963 'Jargon der Eigentlichkeit', *Neue Rundschau*, 74/3, pp. 371–85.

1963 'Kann das Publikum wollen?', *Vierzehn Mutmaßungen über das Fernsehen. Beiträge zu einem aktuellen Thema*, ed. Anne Rose Katz, Munich: Deutscher Taschenbuch-Verlag (= dtv 190), pp. 55–60.

1963 *Kritische Modelle*, Frankfurt am Main: Suhrkamp, vol. 1, *Eingriffe. Neun kritische Modelle*, 1–10; vol. 2, *Stichworte* (1969), 193 pp.

1963 'Luceser Memorial', *Süddeutsche Zeitung* (9–10 November).

1963 'Sexualtabus und Recht heute', in Fritz Bauer (ed.), *Sexualität und Verbrechen. Beiträge zur Strafrechtsreform*, Frankfurt and Hamburg: Fischer (= Fischer Bücherei 518/519), pp. 299–317.

1963 'Über einige Arbeiten Arnold Schönbergs', *Forum* (Vienna), 10/ 115–17, pp. 378–81, 434–6.

1963 'Zur Bekämpfung des Antisemitismus heute', *Erziehung vorurteilsfreier Menschen. Erste Europäische Pädagogenkonferenz vom 30.10.–3.11.1962 in Wiesbaden*, ed. Deutschen Koordinierungsrat der Gesellschaften für Christlich Jüdische Zusammenarbeit, Frankfurt am Main: pp. 15–31.

1964 'Fortschritt', *Argumentationen. Festschrift für Josef König*, ed. Harald Delius und Günther Patzig, Göttingen: Vandenhoeck & Rupprecht, pp. 1–19.

1964 *Jargon der Eigentlichkeit. Zur deutschen Ideologie*, Frankfurt am Main: Suhrkamp, 139 pp. (= edition suhrkamp 91).

1964 *Moments musicaux. Neu gedruckte Aufsätze 1928–1962*, Frankfurt am Main: Suhrkamp, 185 pp.

1964 'Nachruf auf einen Pianisten. Zum Tode von Eduard Scheuermann', *Süddeutsche Zeitung* (28–9 November).

1964 'Parataxis. Zur späten Lyrik Hölderlins. Erweiterte Fassung', *Neue Rundschau*, 75/1, pp. 15–46.

1965 'Gratulator. Zu Max Horkheimers 70. Geburtstag', *Frankfurter Rundschau* (13 February), p. 3.

1965 'Henkel, Krug und frühe Erfahrung', *Ernst Bloch zu ehren. Beiträge zu seinem Werk*, ed. Siegfried Unseld, Frankfurt am Main: Suhrkamp, pp. 9–20.

1965 'Notiz über sozialwissenschaftliche Objektivität', *Kölner Zeitschrift für Soziologie und Sozialpsychologie*, 17/3, pp. 416–21.

1965 'Offener Brief an Max Horkheimer', *Die Zeit* (12 February), p. 32.

1965 [Preface] in Rolf Tiedemann, *Studien zur Philosophie Walter Benjamins*, Frankfurt am Main: Europäische Verlagsanstalt (= Frankfurter Beiträge zur Soziologie 16), vii–x.

1965 'Rede beim offiziellen Empfang im Heidelberger Schloß. Worte zum Gedenken an Theodor Heuss', *Max Weber und die Soziologie heute*, ed. Auftrag der Deutschen Gesellschaft für Soziologie von Otto Stammer, Tübingen: Mohr (= Verhandlungen des 15. Deutschen Soziologentages), pp. 99–102, 157–60.

1965 'Thesen über Tradition', *Inselalmanach auf das Jahr 1966*, Frankfurt am Main: Insel, pp. 21–33.

1965 'Über einige Relationen zwischen Musik und Malerei', *Pour Daniel-Henry Kahnweiler*, Stuttgart: Hatje, pp. 33–42.

1966 'Aus Sils Maria', *Süddeutsche Zeitung* (1–2 October).

1966 'Der mißbrauchte Barock', *Die Welt* (1 October).

1966 'Filmtransparente. Notizen zu Papas und Bubis Kino', *Die Zeit* (18 November).

1966 'Form in der Neuen Musik', *Darmstädter Beiträge zur Neuen Musik*, 10, ed. Ernst Thomas, Mainz: Schott, pp. 9–21.

1966 'Funktionalismus heute', *Neue Rundschau*, 77/4, pp. 585–600.

1966 'Gesellschaft', *Evangelisches Staatslexikon*, ed. H. Kunst and P. Grundmann, Stuttgart and Berlin: Kreuz-Verlag, pp. 636–43.

1966 [Introduction] in *Walter Benjamin: Briefe*. ed. with commentary by Gersholm Scholem and Adorno, Frankfurt am Main: Suhrkamp, pp. 14–21.

1966 *Negative Dialektik*, Frankfurt am Main: Suhrkamp, 409 pp.

1966 'Postscriptum', *Kölner Zeitschrift für Soziologie und Sozialpsychologie*, 18/1, pp. 37–42.

1967 *Die Kunst und die Künste*, Berlin: Akademie der Künste, Gebrüder Mann (= Anmerkungen zur Zeit 12), pp. 25–51.

1967 'Ist die Kunst heiter?', *Süddeutsche Zeitung*, p. 71 (supplement).

1967 *Ohne Leitbild. Parva Aesthetica*, 1–12, Frankfurt am Main: Suhrkamp, 184 pp.

1967 'Soziologische Anmerkungen zum deutschen Musikleben', *Deutscher Musikrat. Referate, Informationen*, 5 (February), pp. 2–13.

1967 'Thesen zur Kunstsoziologie', *Kölner Zeitschrift für Soziologie und Sozialpsychologie*, 19/1, pp. 87–93.

1967 'Wien, in dieser Jahreszeit', *Süddeutsche Zeitung* (10–11 June).

1967 'Zum Klassizismus von Goethes Iphigenie', *Neue Rundschau*, 78/4, pp. 586–99.

1968 'Anmerkungen zum sozialen Konflikt heute. Nach zwei Seminaren', *Gesellschaft, Recht und Politik. Wolfgang Abendroth zum 60. Geburtstag*, ed. Hans Maus Neuwied, Berlin: Luchterhand, pp. 1–19 (with Ursula Jaerisch).

1968 *Berg. Der Meister des kleinsten Übergangs*, Vienna: Lafite, 194 pp.

1968 [Contributions] in *Über Walter Benjamin*, Frankfurt am Main: Suhrkamp, 173 pp. (= edition suhrkamp 250).

1968 *Impromptus, Zweite Folge neu gedruckter musikalischer Aufsätze*, 1–8, Frankfurt am Main: Suhrkamp, 183 pp.

1968 'Interimsbescheid', *Frankfurter Rundschau* (6 March), p. 12.

1968 [Introduction] in Rudolf Borchardt, *Ausgewählte Gedichte*, Frankfurt am Main: Suhrkamp (= Bibliothek Suhrkamp 213), pp. 7–35.

1968 'Kleine musikästhetische Häresie', in *Wege und Gestalten. Texte, Dokumente, Zeichnungen*, ed. Heinz Sauereßig and Klaus Schröter, Biberbach an der Riss: Thomae.

1968 'Scientific experiences of a European scholar in America', *Perspectives in American History* (Harvard University), 2.

1969 'A l'écart de tous les courants', *Le Monde* (31 May), supplement to No. 7582.

1969 'Der Positivismusstreit in der deutschen Soziologie', *Der Positivismusstreit in der deutschen Soziologie*, Neuwied and Berlin: Luchterhand (= Soziologische Texte 58), pp. 7–79.

1969 *Komposition für den Film. Mit Notenblatt*, Munich: Rogner & Bernhard, 215, viii pp. (= Passagen) (with Hanns Eisler).

1969 'Soziologie und empirische Forschung', *Der Positivismusstreit in der deutschen Soziologie*, Neuwied and Berlin: Luchterhand (= Soziologische Texte 58), pp. 81–101.

1969 'Spätkapitalismus oder Industriegesellschaft?', in Adorno (ed.), *Spätkapitalismus oder Industriegesellschaft? Verhandlungen des 16. Deutschen Soziologentages*, Stuttgart: Enke, pp. 12–26.

1970 *Aufsätze zur Gesellschaftstheorie und Methodologie*, Frankfurt am Main: Suhrkamp, 245 pp.

1970 *Erziehung zur Mündigkeit*. Vorträge und Gespräche mit Hellmut Becker 1959–1969, ed. Gerd Kadelbach, Frankfurt am Main: Suhrkamp, 155 pp.

Gesammelte Schriften in zwanzig Bänden, ed. Rolf Tiedmann, with Gretel Adorno, Susan Buck-Morss and Klaus Schultz, Frankfurt am Main: Suhrkamp, 1970–86:

vol. l: *Philosophische Frühschriften*, ed. Rolf Tiedemann, 1973, 384 pp.

vol. 2: *Kierkegaard. Konstruktion des Ästhetischen*, ed. Rolf Tiedemann, 1979, 266 pp.

vol. 3: *Dialektik der Aufklärung. Philosophische Fragmente*, ed. Rolf Tiedemann, 1981, 336 pp.

vol. 4: *Minima Moralia. Reflexionen aus dem beschädigten Leben*, ed. Rolf Tiedemann, 1980, 300 pp.

vol. 5: *Zur Metakritik der Erkenntnistheorie. Drei Studien zu Hegel*, ed. Gretel Adorno and Rolf Tiedemann, 1971, 386 pp.

vol. 6: *Negative Dialektik. Jargon der Eigentlichkeit*, ed. Rolf Tiedemann, 1973, 531 pp.

vol. 7: *Ästhetische Theorie*, ed. Gretel Adorno and Rolf Tiedemann, 1970, 569 pp.

vol. 8: *Soziologische Schriften I*, ed. Rolf Tiedemann, 1972, 587 pp.

vol. 9: *Soziologische Schriften II*, ed. Susan Buck-Morss and Rolf Tiedemann, 1975, 924 pp.

vol. 10: *Kulturkritik und Gesellschaft. Prismen. Ohne Leitbild. Eingriffe. Stichworte. Anhang*, 2 vols., ed. Rolf Tiedemann, 1977, 843 pp.

vol. 11: *Noten zur Literatur*, ed. Rolf Tiedemann, 1974, 708 pp.

vol. 12: *Philosophie der neuen Musik*, ed. Rolf Tiedemann, 1975, 206 pp.

vol. 13: *Die musikalischen Monographien. Wagner, Mahler, Berg*, ed. Gretel Adorno and Rolf Tiedemann, 1971, 521 pp.

vol. 14: *Dissonanzen. Einleitung in die Musiksoziologie*, ed. Rolf Tiedemann, 1973, 447 pp.

vol. 15: *Komposition für den Film. Der getreue Korrepetitor*, ed. Rolf Tiedemann, 1976, 406 pp.

vol. 16: *Musikalische Schriften I-III. Klangfiguren (I). Quasi una fantasia (II). Musikalische Schriften (III)*, ed. Rolf Tiedemann, 1978, 683 pp.

vol. 17: *Musikalische Schriften IV. Moments musicaux. Impromptus*, ed. Rolf Tiedemann, 1982, 349 pp.

vol. 18: *Musikalische Schriften V*, ed. Rolf Tiedemann and Klaus Schultz, 1984, 841 pp.

vol. 19: *Musikalische Schriften VI*, ed. Rolf Tiedemann and Klaus Schultz, 1984, 665 pp.

vol. 20: *Vermischte Schriften*, 2 vols., Eine Edition des Theodor W. Adorno Archivs, 1986, 881 pp.

1970 *Über Walter Benjamin. Aufsätze, Artikel, Briefe*, ed. with annotations by Rolf Tiedemann, Frankfurt am Main: Suhrkamp, 188 pp. (= Bibliothek Suhrkamp 260). (Revised edition 1990, 184 pp.)

1971 *Eine Auswahl*, ed. Rolf Tiedemann, Frankfurt am Main: Büchergilde Gutenberg, 418 pp.

1971 *Kritik. Kleine Schriften zur Gesellschaft*, ed. and introduced by Rolf Tiedemann, Frankfurt am Main. Suhrkamp, 152 pp. (= edition suhrkamp 469).

1972 'Vorurteile und schlechte Gewohnheiten', in Karsten Witte (ed.), *Theorie des Kinos, Ideologiekritik der Traumfabrik*, Frankfurt am Main: Suhrkamp (= edition suhrkamp 557).

1973 *Philosophische Terminologie. Zur Einleitung*, ed. Rudolf zur Lippe, Frankfurt am Main: Suhrkamp, vol. 1, 224 pp. (= Suhrkamp Taschenbuch Wissenschaft 23); vol. 2, 325 pp. (= Suhrkamp Taschenbuch Wissenschaft 50).

1973 *Aufsätze zur Literatur des 20. Jahrhunderts*, vols. 1, 2, Frankfurt am Main: Suhrkamp.

1973/4 *Ästhetische Theorie*, ed. Gretel Adorno and Rolf Tiedemann, with a list of concepts, Frankfurt am Main: Suhrkamp, 571 pp. (= Suhrkamp Taschenbuch Wissenschaft 2).

1973/4 *Vorlesung zur Einleitung in die Soziologie*, Frankfurt am Main: Hesa-Druck, 160 pp. (= Junius-Drucke). Adorno and Ernst Krenek, *Briefwechsel*, ed. Wolfgang Rogge, Frankfurt am Main: Suhrkamp, 273 pp.

1975 *Gesellschaftstheorie und Kulturkritik*, Frankfurt am Main: Suhrkamp, 179 pp. (= edition suhrkamp 772).

1978 *Philosophie der neuen Musik*, Frankfurt am Main: Suhrkamp, 200 pp. (= Suhrkamp Taschenbuch Wissenschaft 239).

1979 *Der Schatz des Indianer-Joe. Singspiel nach Mark Twain*, ed. with a postscript by Rolf Tiedemann, Frankfurt am Main: Suhrkamp, 137 pp.

1979 *Soziologische Schriften*, ed. Rolf Tiedemann, Frankfurt am Main: Suhrkamp, vol. l, 588 pp. (= Suhrkamp Taschenbuch Wissenschaft 306).

1980 *Kompositionen*, ed. Heinz-Klaus Metzger and Rainer Riehn, vol. 1/2, Munich: Edition Text und Kritik (= Musik – Konzepte – Partituren).

1984 [Contribution] in *Adorno-Noten*. Mit Bildern von Manfred Schling. ed. Rolf Tiedemann, Berlin: Galerie Wewerka, 180 pp. (= Galerie Wewerka Edition 15).

1984 *Philosophie und Gesellschaft. 5 Essays*, ed. with a postscript by Rolf Tiedemann, Stuttgart: Reclam, 196 pp. (= Reclams Universalbibliothek 8005).

1986 *Die musikalischen Monographien. Wagner, Mahler, Berg*, Frankfurt am Main: Suhrkamp, 521 pp. (= Suhrkamp Taschenbuch Wissenschaft 640).

1988 'Aus einem "Scribble-In-Book". Los Angeles, 1942/43', *Perspektiven kritischer Theorie. Eine Sammlung zu Hermann Schweppenhäusers 60. Geburtstag*, ed. Christoph Türcke, Lüneburg: Dietrich zu Klampen, pp. 9–14.

1993 *Beethoven. Philosophie der Musik*, Frankfurt am Main: Suhrkamp, 388 pp.

1993 *Einleitung in die Soziologie*, Vorlesungen Bd. Frankfurt am Main: Suhrkamp, 330 pp.

1994 *Adorno/Benjamin: Briefwechsel 1928–1940*, ed. Henri Lonitz, Frankfurt am Main: Suhrkamp, vol. 1, 501 pp. vol. 2, 501 pp.

1995 *Kants 'Kritik der reinen Vernunft'*, Vorlesungen, vol. 4, Frankfurt am Main: Suhrkamp, 440 pp.

1996 *Probleme der Moralphilosophie*, Vorlesungen, vol. 10, Frankfurt am Main: Suhrkamp, 318 pp.

English Translations of Works by Theodor W. Adorno

Books

Aesthetic Theory, trans. C. Lenhardt, London: Routledge & Kegan Paul, 1984.

Against Epistemology: A Metacritique. Studies in Husserl and the Phenomenological Antinomies, trans. Willis Domingo, Oxford: Basil Blackwell, 1982; Cambridge, MA: MIT Press, 1983.

Alban Berg. Master of the Smallest Link, trans. Juliane Brand and Christopher Hailey, Cambridge: Cambridge University Press, 1991.

Aspects of Sociology. The Frankfurt Institute for Social Research, trans. John Viertel, Boston: Beacon Press, 1972.

Dialectic of Enlightenment, with Max Horkheimer, trans. John Cumming, New York: Herder and Herder, 1972.

Hegel: Three Studies, trans. Shierry Weber Nicholsen, Cambridge, MA: MIT Press, 1993.

In Search of Wagner, trans. Rodney Livingstone, London: New Left Books, 1981.

Introduction to the Sociology of Music, trans. E. B. Ashton, New York: Seabury Press, 1976.

The Jargon of Authenticity, trans. Knut Tarnowski and Frederic Will, London: Routledge & Kegan Paul, 1973.

Kierkegaard: Construction of the Aesthetic, trans., ed., and with a foreword by Robert Hullot-Kentor, Minneapolis: University of Minnesota
Press, 1989.

Mahler: A Musical Physiognomy, trans. Edmund Jephcott, Chicago: University of Chicago Press, 1988.

Minima Moralia: Reflections from Damaged Life, trans. E. F. N. Jephcott,
London: New Left Books, 1974.

Negative Dialectics, trans. E. B. Ashton, New York: Seabury Press, 1973.

Notes on Literature, vol. 1, ed. Rolf Tiedemann, trans. Shierry Weber
Nicholsen, New York: Columbia University Press, 1991.

Notes on Literature, vol. 2, ed. Rolf Tiedemann, trans. Shierry Weber
Nicholsen, New York: Columbia University Press, 1992.

Philosophy of Modern Music, trans. Anne G. Mitchell and Wesley V.
Blomster, New York: Seabury Press, 1973.

The Positivist Dispute in German Sociology, by Theodor W. Adorno et
al., trans. Glyn Adey and David Frisby, London: Heinemann, 1976.

Prisms, trans. Samuel and Shierry Weber, London: Neville Spearman,
1967; Cambridge, MA: MIT Press, 1981.

The Stars Down to Earth and Other Essays on the Irrational in Culture,
ed. Stephen Crook, New York: Routledge, 1994.

Articles

'The actuality of philosophy' (1931), *Telos*, 31 (Spring 1977), pp. 120–
33.

'The aging of the new music' (1955), *Telos*, 77 (Fall 1988), pp. 95–116.

'Alienated masterpiece: the *Missa Solemnis*' (1959), *Telos*, 28 (Summer
1976), pp. 113–24.

'Bloch's traces: the philosophy of kitsch' (1960), *New Left Review*, 121
(May–June 1980), pp. 49–62.

'Commitment' (1962), *New Left Review*, 87–8 (November–December
1974), pp. 75–90.

'Culture and administration' (1960), *Telos*, 37 (Fall 1978), pp. 93–111.

'Culture industry reconsidered' (1963), *New German Critique*, 6 (Fall
1975), pp. 12–19. Reprinted in *Critical Theory and Society*, pp. 128–
35.

'Education for autonomy' (1969), with Hellmut Becker, *Telos*, 56.

'The essay as form' (1958), *New German Critique*, 32 (Spring–Summer
1984), pp. 151–71.

'Functionalism today' (1966), *Oppositions*, 17 (Summer 1979), pp. 31–
41.

'Goldmann and Adorno: to describe, understand and explain' (1968), in
Lucien Goldmann, *Cultural Creation in Modern Society* (1971), pp.
129–45, trans. Bart Grahl, introduction by William Mayrl, Oxford:
Basil Blackwell, 1976.

'The idea of natural history' (1932), *Telos*, 60 (Summer 1984), pp. 111–24.

'Is Marx Obsolete?' (1968), *Diogenes*, 64 (Winter 1968), pp. 1–16.

'Letters to Walter Benjamin' (1930s), *New Left Review*, 81 (September–October 1973), pp. 46–80.

'Lyric poetry and society' (1951), *Telos*, 20 (Summer 1974), pp. 56–71. Reprinted in *Critical Theory and Society*, pp. 155–71.

'Metacritique of epistemology' ('Einleitung', *ME*, 1956), *Telos*, 38 (Winter 1978–9), pp. 77–103.

'Music and technique' (1958), *Telos*, 32 (Summer 1977), pp. 79–94.

'Music and the new music: in memory of Peter Suhrkamp' (1960), *Telos*, 43 (Spring 1980), pp. 124–38.

'On the historical adequacy of consciousness' (1965), with Peter von Haselberg, *Telos*, 56 (Summer 1983), pp. 97–103.

'On the question: "What is German?"' (1965), *New German Critique*, 36 (Fall 1985), pp. 121–31.

'On the social situation of music' (1932), *Telos*, 35 (Spring 1978), pp. 128–64: trans. of 'Zur gesellschaftlichen Lage der Musik', *Zeitschrift für Sozialforschung*, 1 (1932), 104–24, 356–78.

'Progress' (1964), *The Philosophical Forum*, 15 (Fall–Winter 1983–4), 55–70.

'Resignation' (1969), *Telos*, 35 (Spring 1978), pp. 165–8.

'Sociology and psychology' (1955), *New Left Review*, 46 (November–December 1967), pp. 63–80; 47 (January–February 1968), pp. 79–97.

'Theses against occultism' (1951), *Telos*, 19 (Spring 1974), pp. 7–12.

'Theses on the sociology of art' (1967), *Working Papers in Cultural Studies*, 2 (Birmingham, Spring 1972), pp. 121–8.

'Transparencies on film' (1966), *New German Critique*, 24–5 (Fall–Winter, 1981–2), pp. 199–205.

'Trying to understand *Endgame*' (1961), *New German Critique*, 26 (Spring–Summer 1982), pp. 119–50. Previously published as 'Toward an understanding of endgame', in Gale Chevigny (ed.), *Twentieth Century Interpretations of Endgame*, Englewood Cliffs, NJ: Prentice-Hall, 1969, pp. 82–114.

Bibliographies

Görtzen, René, 'Th. W. Adorno. Vorläufige Bibliographie seiner Schriften und der Sekundärliteratur', in L. von Friedeburg and J. Habermas (eds.), *Adorno-Konferenz 1983*, Frankfurt am Main: Suhrkamp, 1983, S. 402–71.

Land, Peter Christian, 'Kommentierte Auswahlbibliographie 1969–1979', in B. Lindner, and W. M. Lüdke (eds.), *Materialien zur ästhetischen Theorie Th. W. Adornos. Konstruktion der Moderne*, Frankfurt am Main: Suhrkamp, 1980, S. 509–56.

Pettazzi, Carlo, 'Kommentierte Bibliographie zu Th. W. Adorno', in H. L. Arnold (ed.), *Th. W. Adorno, Text + Kritik, Sonderband*, Munich: Verlag Text und Kritik, 1977, S. 176–91.

Schultz, Klaus, 'Vorläufige Bibliographie der Schriften Th. W. Adornos', in H. Schweppenhäuser (ed.), *Th. W. Adorno zum Gedächtnis. Eine Sammlung*, Frankfurt am Main: Suhrkamp, 1971, S. 177–239.

Zuidervaart, Lambert, 'Bibliography', in *Adorno's Aesthetic Theory. The Redemption of Illusion*, Cambridge, MA: MIT Press, pp. 351–81.

Secondary Sources on Adorno

'Adorno: Love and Cognition', *The Times Literary Supplement* (9 March 1973), pp. 253–5.

Adorno-Konferenz 1983, ed. by Ludwig von Friedeburg and Jürgen Habermas, Frankfurt: Suhrkamp, 1983.

Adorno und die Musik, ed. by Otto Kolleritsch (Studien zur Wertungsforschung, 12), Graz: Universal Edition, 1979.

Baumeister, Thomas, 'Theodor W. Adorno – nach zehn Jahren', *Philosophische Rundschau*, 28 (1981), pp. 1–26.

Baumeister, Thomas and Jens Kulenkampff, 'Geschichtsphilosophie und philosophische Ästhetik. Zu Adornos "Ästhetischer Theorie"', *Neue Hefte für Philosophie*, 5 (1973), pp. 74–104.

Beier, Christel, *Zum Verhältnis von Gesellschaftstheorie und Erkenntnistheorie. Untersuchungen in der kritischen Theorie Adornos*, Frankfurt: Suhrkamp, 1977.

Beierwaltes, Werner, 'Adornos Nicht-Identisches', in *Weltaspekte der Philosophie. Rudolf Berlinger zum 26. Oktober 1972*, ed. Werner Beierwaltes and Wiebke Schrader, Amsterdam: Rodopi, 1972, pp. 7–20. An expanded version appears in Beierwaltes, *Identität und Differenz* (Frankfurt: Vittorio Klostermann, 1980), pp. 289–314.

Benjamin, Jessica, 'The End of Internalization: Adorno's Social Psychology', *Telos*, 32 (Summer 1977), pp. 42–64.

Berman, Russell A., 'Adorno, Marxism and Art', *Telos*, 34 (Winter 1977–8), pp. 157–66.

——— 'Adorno's Radicalism: Two Interviews from the Sixties', *Telos*, 56 (Summer 1983), pp. 94–7.

Blomster, W. V., 'Sociology of Music: Adorno and Beyond', *Telos*, 28 (Summer 1976), pp. 81–112.

Böckelmann, Frank, *Über Marx und Adorno. Schwierigkeiten der spätmarxistischen Theorie*, Frankfurt: Makol, 1972.

Boehmer, Konrad, 'Adorno, Musik, Gesellschaft' (1969), reprinted in *Texte zur Musiksoziologie*, ed. Tibor Kneif, with an introduction by Carl Dahlhaus, Cologne: Arno Volk, 1975, pp. 227–38.

Bolz, Norbert, *Geschichtsphilosophie des Ästhetischen. Hermeneutische*

Rekonstruktion der 'Noten zur Literatur' Th. W. Adornos, Hildesheim: 1979.

Breuer, Stefan, 'Adornos Anthropologie', *Leviathan*, (1984/3).

Brunkhorst, Hauke, 'Die ästhetische Konstruktion der Moderne', *Leviathan* (1988/1), pp. 77–96.

—— *Theodor W. Adorno. Dialektik der Moderne*, Munich: Piper, 1990.

—— 'Eine Verteidigung der "Ästhetischen Theorie" Adornos bei revisionistischer Distanzierung von seiner Geschichtsphilosophie', in Herfried Münkler and Richard Saage (eds), *Kultur und Politik*, Opladen: Westdeutscher Verlag, 1990, pp. 89–106.

—— 'Adorno, Theodor W.', in *Die Deutsche Literatur*, Bern: Peter Lang, 1992.

—— 'Kritik statt Theorie. Adorno's experimentelles Freiheitsverständnis', in Gerhard Schweppenhäuser and Marko Wischke (eds.), *Impuls und Negativität. Ethik und Ästhetik bei Adorno*, Hamburg: Argument, 1995, pp. 117–35.

—— 'Theodor W. Adorno: aesthetic constructivism and a negative ethic of the non-forfeited life', in David M. Rasmussen (ed.), *The Handbook of Critical Theory*, Oxford: Blackwell, 1996, pp. 305–21.

—— 'Adorno', in Simon Critchley and William R. Schroeder (eds.), *A Companion to Continental Philosophy*, Oxford: Blackwell, 1998, pp. 370–81.

Buck-Morss, Susan, *The Origin of Negative Dialectics: Theodor W. Adorno, Walter Benjamin, and the Frankfurt Institute*, Hassocks, Sussex: Harvester Press, 1977.

—— 'T.W. Adorno and the dilemma of bourgeois philosophy', *Salmagundi*, 36 (Winter 1977), pp. 76–98.

Burde, Wolfgang, 'Versuch über einen Satz Theodor W. Adornos', *Neue Zeitschrift für Musik*, 132 (1971), pp. 578–83.

Cahn, Michael, 'Subversive mimesis: Theodor W. Adorno and the modern impasse of critique', in *Mimesis in Contemporary Theory: An Interdisciplinary Approach*, vol. 1, *The Literary and Philosophical Debate*, ed. Mihai Spariosu, Philadelphia: John Benjamins, 1984, pp. 27–64.

Dahlhaus, Carl, 'Adornos Begriff des musikalischen Materials', in *Zur Terminologie der Musik des 20. Jahrhunderts*, Stuttgart: Musikwissenschaftliche Verlags-Gesellschaft, 1974, pp. 9–21.

—— 'Soziologische Dechiffrierung von Musik. Zu Theodor W. Adornos Wagner-Kritik', *The International Review of the Aesthetics and Sociology of Music*, 1 (1979), 137–47.

Dawydov, Juri, *Die sich selbst negierende Dialektik. Kritik der Musiktheorie Theodor Adornos*, Frankfurt: Verlag Marxistische Blätter, 1971.

Düver, Lothar, *Theodor W. Adorno. Der Wissenschaftsbegriff der Kritischen Theorie in seinem Werk*, Bonn: Bouvier, 1978.

Eichel, Christine, *Vom Ermatten der Avantgarde zur Vernetzung der*

Künste. Perspektiven einer interdisziplinären Ästhetik im Spätwerk Theodor W. Adornos, Frankfurt: Suhrkamp, 1993.

Fehér, Ference, 'Rationalized Music and its Vicissitudes (Adorno's Philosophy of Music)', *Philosophy and Social Criticism*, 9/1 (Spring 1982), pp. 41–65.

Figal, Günter, *Theodor W. Adorno. Das Naturschöne als spekulative Gedankenfigur. Zur Interpretation der 'Ästhetischen Theorie' im Kontext philosophischer Ästhetik*, Bonn: Bouvier Verlag Herbert Grundmann, 1977.

Focht, Ivan, 'Adornos gnoseologistische Einstellung zur Musik', *International Review of the Aesthetics and Sociology of Music*, 5 (1974), pp. 265–76.

Frow, John, 'Mediation and Metaphor: Adorno and the Sociology of Art', *Clio*, 12/1 (Fall 1982), 57–65.

Frücht, Josef, *Mimesis. Konstellation eines Zentralbegriffs bei Adorno*, Würzburg: Meisenhain, 1986.

Geyer, Carl-Friedrich, *Kritische Theorie: Max Horkheimer and Theodor W. Adorno*, Freiburg: Karl Alber, 1982.

Grenz, Friedemann, *Adornos Philosophie in Grundbegriffen. Auflösung einiger Deutungsprobleme*, Frankfurt: Suhrkamp, 1974.

Gripp, Helga, *Theodor W. Adorno*, Paderborn: UTB, 1986.

Hohendahl, Peter U., 'Autonomy of art: looking back at Adorno's *Ästhetische Theorie*', *German Quarterly*, 54 (March 1981), pp. 133–48.

Hrachovec, Herbert, 'Was läßt sich von Erlösung Denken? Gedanken von und über Th. W. Adornos Philosophie', *Philosophisches Jahrbuch*, 83 (1976), pp. 357–70.

Huhn, Thomas, 'Adorno's aesthetics of illusion', *Journal of Aesthetics and Art Criticism*, 44 (Winter 1985), pp. 181–9.

Hullot-Kentor, Robert, 'Popular music and Adorno's "The Aging of the New Music"', *Telos*, 77 (Fall 1988), pp. 79–94.

—— 'Back to Adorno', *Telos*, 81 (Fall 1989), pp. 5–29.

Huyssen, Andreas, 'Adorno in Reverse: From Hollywood to Richard Wagner', *New German Critique*, 29 (Spring–Summer 1983), pp. 8–38.

Jay, Martin, 'The concept of totality in Lucács and Adorno', *Telos*, 32 (Summer 1977), pp. 117–37.

—— *Adorno*, Cambridge, MA: Harvard University Press, 1984.

—— 'Adorno in America', *New German Critique*, 31 (Winter 1984), pp. 157–82.

Jimenez, Marc, *Theodor W. Adorno: Art, idéologie et théorie de l'art*, Paris: Union Général, 1973.

Kaiser, Gerhard, *Benjamin. Adorno. Zwei Studien*, Frankfurt: Athenäum Fischer Taschenbuch, 1974.

Kerkhoff, Manfred, 'Die Rettung des Nichtidentischen. Zur Philosophie

Th. W. Adornos', *Philosophische Rundschau*, 20 (1974), 150–78, and 21 (1975), 56–74.

Knapp, Gerhard, *Theodor W. Adorno*, Berlin: Colloquium, 1980.

Koch, Gertrud, 'Mimesis and Bilderverbot', *Screen*, 34 (1993), p. 3.

Koch, Traugott, Klaus-Michael Kodalle and Hermann Schweppenhäuser, *Negative Dialektik und die Idee der Versöhnung. Eine Kontroverse über Theodor W. Adorno*, Stuttgart: W. Kohlhammer, 1973.

Kofler, Leo, 'Weder "Wiederspiegelung" noch Abstraktion: Lukács oder Adorno?', in *Zur Theorie der modernen Literatur: Der Avantgardismus in soziologischer Sicht*, 2nd edn., Düsseldorf: Bertelsmann Universitätsverlag, 1974, pp. 160–87.

Krahl, Hans-Jürgen, 'The Political Contradictions in Adorno's Critical Theory', *Telos*, 21 (Fall 1974), pp. 164–7.

Künzli, Arnold, *Aufklärung und Dialektik. Politische Philosophie von Hobbes bis Adorno*, Freiburg: Rombach, 1971.

Kuspit, Donald B., 'Critical notes on Adorno's sociology of music and art', *Journal of Aesthetics and Art Criticism*, 33 (Spring 1975), pp. 321–7.

Lang, Peter Christian, *Hermeneutik, Ideologiekritik, Ästhetik: Über Dadamer und Adorno sowie Fragen einer aktuellen Ästhetik*, Königstein/ Ts.: Forum Academicum, 1981.

Levandowski, Joseph D., 'Adorno on jazz and society', *Philosophy and Social Criticism*, vol. 22/5 (1996), pp. 103–21.

Lüdke, W. Martin, *Anmerkungen zu einer 'Logik des Zerfalls': Adorno-Beckett*, Frankfurt: Suhrkamp, 1981.

Lyotard, Jean-François, 'Adorno as the Devil', *Telos*, 19 (Spring 1974), pp. 127–37.

Materialien zur ästhetischen Theorie Theodor W. Adornos. Konstruktion der Moderne, ed. by Burkhardt Lindner and W. Martin Küdke, Frankfurt: Suhrkamp, 1979.

Menke, Christoph, *Die Souveränität der Kunst: Ästhetische Erfahrung nach Adorno und Derrida*, Frankfurt am Main: Athenäum, 1988.

Mörchen, Hermann, *Macht und Herrschaft im Denken von Heidegger und Adorno*, Stuttgart: Klett-Cotta, 1980.

Müller, Harro, 'Gesellschaftliche Funktion und ästhetische Autonomie: Benjamin, Adorno, Habermas', *Literaturwissenschaft: Grundkurs*, 2, ed. Helmut Brackert and Jörn Stückrath, Reinbeck bei Hamburg: Rowohlt, 1981, pp. 329–40.

Müller-Doohm, Stefan, *Die Soziologie Theodor W. Adornos*, Frankfurt: Campus, 1996.

Müller-Strömsdörfer, Ilse, 'Die "helfende Kraft bestimmter Negation". Zum Werke Th. W. Adornos', *Philosophische Rundschau*, 8 (1960), pp. 81–105.

Naeher, Jürgen (ed.), *Die Negative Dialektik Adornos – Dialog*, Stuttgart: Klett, 1984.

Narskii, I. S., 'Adorno's Negative Philosophy', *Soviet Studies in Philosophy*, 24 (Summer 1985), pp. 3–45.

Nebuloni, Roberto, *Dialettica estoria in Theodor W. Adorno*, Milan: Vita & Pensiero, 1978.

Oppens, Kurt, et al., *Über Theodor W. Adorno*, Frankfurt am Main: Suhrkamp, 1978.

Paetzhold, Heinz, *Neomarxistische Ästhetik*, part 2, *Adorno, Marcuse*, Düsseldorf: Pädagogischer Verlag Schwann, 1974.

Pettazzi, Carlo, Th. *Wiesengrund Adorno: Linee die origine e di sviluppo del pensiero (1903–1949)*, Florence: La Nuova Italia, 1979.

Plessner, Helmuth, 'Zum Verständnis der ästhetischen Theorie Adornos', *Philosophische Perspektiven*, 4 (1972), pp. 126–36.

Puder, Martin, 'Zur Ästhetischen Theorie Adornos', *Neue Rundschau*, 82 (1971), pp. 465–77.

―― 'Adornos Philosophie und die gegenwärtige Erfahrung', *Neue Deutsche Hefte*, 23 (1976), pp. 3–21.

Rehfus, Wulff, *Theodor W. Adornos. Die Rekonstruktion der Wahrheit aus der Ästhetik'*, Cologne: Universität zu Köln, Inaugural-Dissertation, 1976.

Reijen, Willem van, *Adorno zur Einführung*, Hanover: SOAK, 1980.

Revue d'esthétique, special issue on Adorno, NS 8 (Toulouse, 1985).

Ries, Wiebrecht, ' "Die Rettung des Hoffnungslosen". Zur "theologia occulta" in der Spätphilosophie Horkheimers und Adornos', *Zeitschrift für philosophische Forschung*, 30 (1976), pp. 69–81.

Ritsert, Jürgen, *Ästhetische Theorie als Gesellschaftskritik*, Frankfurt: Campus, Studientexte Sozialwissenschaft, n.d.

Rose, Gillian, *The Melancholy Science: An Introduction to the Thought of Theodor W. Adorno*, London: Macmillan Press, 1978.

Sauerland, Karol, *Einführung in die Ästhetik Adornos*, Berlin: Walter de Gruyter, 1979.

Scheible, Hartmut, *Theodor W. Adorno*, Reinbek: Ruwohlt, 1989.

Schweppenhäuser, Gerhard, *Ethik nach Auschwitz. Adornos negative Moralphilosophie*, Hamburg: Argument, 1993.

Schweppenhäuser, Gerhard and Mirko Wische (eds.), *Impuls und Negativität. Ethik und Ästhetik bei Adorno*, Hamburg: Argument, 1995.

Schmucker, Joseph F., *Adorno – Logik des Zerfalls*, Stuttgart: Frommann-Holzboog, 1977.

Schoeller, Wilfried F. (ed.), *Die neue Linke nach Adorno*, Munich: Kindler, 1969.

Siebert, Rudolf J., 'Adorno's theory of religion', *Telos*, 58 (Winter 1983–4), pp. 108–14.

Specht, Silvia, *Erinnerung als Veränderung. Über den Zusammenhang von Kunst und Politik bei Theodor W. Adorno*, Mittenwald: Mäander Kunstverlag, 1981.

Steinert, Heinz, *Adorno in Wien*, Vienna: Passagen, 1989.

Studia Philosophica Gandensia, 9 (Adorno-Heft) (Meppel, 1971).

Subotnik, Rose Rosengard, 'Adorno's diagnosis of Beethoven's late style: early symptom of a fatal conditon', *Journal of the American Musicological Society*, 29 (1976), pp. 242–75.

—— 'Why is Adorno's music criticism the way it is? Some reflections on twentieth-century criticism of nineteenth-century music', *Musical Newsletter*, 7/4 (Fall 1977), pp. 3–12.

Sziborsky, Lucia, *Adornos Musikphilosophie. Genese – Konstitution – Pädagogische Perspektiven*, Munich: Wilhelm Fink, 1979.

Theodor W. Adorno (1977), ed. Heinz Ludwig Arnold, 2nd enlarged edn., Munich: Edition Text + Kritik, 1983.

Theodor W. Adorno zum Gedächtnis. Eine Sammlung, ed. Hermann Schweppenhäuser, Frankfurt: Suhrkamp, 1971.

Tichy, Matthias, *Theodor W. Adorno. Das Verhältnis von Allgemeinem und Besonderm in seiner Philosophie*, Bonn: Bouvier Verlag Herbert Grundmann, 1977.

Über Theodor W. Adorno, with contributions by Kurt Oppens et al., Frankfurt: Suhrkamp, 1968.

Waldmann, Diane, 'Critical Theory and Film: Adorno and "The Culture Industry" Revisited', *New German Critique*, 12 (Fall 1977), pp. 39–60.

Weitzman, R., 'An introduction to Adorno's music and social criticism', *Music and Letters*, 52 (1971), pp. 287–98.

Wellmer, Albrecht, *Zur Dialektik von Moderne und Postmoderne. Vernunftkritik nach Adorno*, Frankfurt am Main: Suhrkamp, 1985.

Werkmeister, O. K., 'Das Kunstwerk als Negation. Zur geschichtlichen Bestimmung der Kunsttheorie Theodor W. Adornos', in his *Ende der Ästhetik*, Frankfurt: S. Fischer, 1971, pp. 7–32.

Wiggershaus, Rolf, *Theodor W. Adorno*, Munich: Beck, 1987.

Wohlfahrt, Irving, 'Hibernation: on the tenth anniversary of Adorno's death', *Modern Language Notes*, 94 (December 1979), pp. 956–87.

Wolin, Richard, 'The de-aestheticization of art: on Adorno's *Aesthetische Theorie*', *Telos*, 41 (Fall 1979), pp. 105–27.

Zeitschrift für Musiktheorie, 4 (Adorno-Heft, 1973), 1.

Zenck, Martin, *Kunst als begriffslose Erkenntis. Zum Kunstbegriff der ästhetischen Theorie Theodor W. Adornos*, Munich: Wilhelm Fink, 1977.

—— 'Auswirkungen einer "musique informelle" auf die neue Musik: Zu Theodor W. Adornos Formvorstellung', *International Review of the Aesthetics and Sociology of Music*, 10/2 (1979), pp. 137–65.

Zuidervaart, Lambert, *Adorno's Aesthetic Theory. The Redemption of Illusion*, Cambridge, MA: MIT Press, 1995.

Index